PERFORMANCE ENG. COE
PG&E

Related Books of Interest

Implementing ITIL Configuration Management, 2nd Edition

By Larry Klosterboer

ISBN: 0-13-138565-8

Practical, Real-World ITIL Configuration Management—From Start to Finish

Now, there's a practical, start-to-finish guide to ITIL configuration management for every IT leader, manager, and practitioner. ITIL-certified architect and solutions provider Larry Klosterboer helps you establish a clear roadmap for success, customize standard processes to your unique needs, and avoid the pitfalls that stand in your way.

You'll learn how to plan your implementation, deploy tools and processes, administer ongoing configuration management tasks, refine ITIL information, and leverage it for competitive advantage. Throughout, Klosterboer demystifies ITIL's jargon, illuminates each technique with real-world advice and examples, and helps you focus on the specific techniques that offer maximum business value in your environment.

The New Era of Enterprise Business Intelligence, 1st Edition

Using Analytics to Achieve a Global Competitive Advantage

By Mike Biere

ISBN: 0-13-707542-1

A Complete Blueprint for Maximizing the Value of Business Intelligence in the Enterprise

The typical enterprise recognizes the immense potential of business intelligence (BI) and its impact upon many facets within the organization—but it's not easy to transform BI's potential into real business value. In *The New Era of Enterprise Business Intelligence*, top BI expert Mike Biere presents a complete blueprint for creating winning BI strategies and infrastructure, and systematically maximizing the value of information throughout the enterprise.

This product-independent guide brings together start-to-finish guidance and practical checklists for every senior IT executive, planner, strategist, implementer, and the actual business users themselves. Drawing on thousands of hours working with enterprise customers, Biere helps decision-makers choose from today's unprecedented spectrum of options, including the latest BI platform suites and appliances. He offers practical, "in-the-trenches" insights on a wide spectrum of planning and implementation issues, from segmenting and supporting users to working with unstructured data.

Listen to the author's podcast at:
ibmpressbooks.com/podcasts

Sign up for the monthly IBM Press newsletter at
ibmpressbooks/newsletters

Related Books of Interest

The Art of Enterprise Information Architecture

A Systems-Based Approach for Unlocking Business Insight

By Mario Godinez, Eberhard Hechler, Klaus Koenig, Steve Lockwood, Martin Oberhofer, and Michael Schroeck

ISBN: 0-13-703571-3

Architecture for the Intelligent Enterprise: Powerful New Ways to Maximize the Real-time Value of Information

In this book, a team of IBM's leading information management experts guide you on a journey that will take you from where you are today toward becoming an "Intelligent Enterprise."

Drawing on their extensive experience working with enterprise clients, the authors present a new, information-centric approach to architecture and powerful new models that will benefit any organization. Using these strategies and models, companies can systematically unlock the business value of information by delivering actionable, real-time information in context to enable better decision-making throughout the enterprise–from the "shop floor" to the "top floor."

Enterprise Master Data Management

An SOA Approach to Managing Core Information

By Allen Dreibelbis, Eberhard Hechler, Ivan Milman, Martin Oberhofer, Paul Van Run, and Dan Wolfson

ISBN: 0-13-236625-8

The Only Complete Technical Primer for MDM Planners, Architects, and Implementers

Enterprise Master Data Management provides an authoritative, vendor-independent MDM technical reference for practitioners: architects, technical analysts, consultants, solution designers, and senior IT decision makers. Written by the IBM® data management innovators who are pioneering MDM, this book systematically introduces MDM's key concepts and technical themes, explains its business case, and illuminates how it interrelates with and enables SOA.

Drawing on their experience with cutting-edge projects, the authors introduce MDM patterns, blueprints, solutions, and best practices published nowhere else—everything you need to establish a consistent, manageable set of master data, and use it for competitive advantage.

On Podcasts — Listen to the author's podcast at: ibmpressbooks.com/podcasts

Sign up for the monthly IBM Press newsletter at ibmpressbooks/newsletters

ITIL Capacity Management

ITIL Capacity Management

Larry Klosterboer

IBM Press
Pearson plc

Upper Saddle River, NJ • Boston • Indianapolis • San Francisco
New York • Toronto • Montreal • London • Munich • Paris • Madrid
Cape Town • Sydney • Tokyo • Singapore • Mexico City

ibmpressbooks.com

IBM Press Program Managers: Steven M. Stansel, Ellice Uffer
Cover Design: IBM Corporation

Associate Publisher: Dave Dusthimer
Marketing Manager: Stephane Nakib
Acquisitions Editor: Mary Beth Ray
Publicist: Heather Fox
Development Editor: Susan Brown Zahn
Technical Editors: Charles Betz, Brian Hopper
Managing Editor: Kristy Hart
Editorial Assistant: Vanessa Evans
Cover Designer: Alan Clements
Project Editor: Anne Goebel
Copy Editor: Cheri Clark
Indexer: WordWise Publishing Services, LLC
Compositor: Nonie Ratcliff
Proofreader: Linda Seifert
Manufacturing Buyer: Dan Uhrig

Published by Pearson plc
Publishing as IBM Press

IBM Press offers excellent discounts on this book when ordered in quantity for bulk purchases or special sales, which may include electronic versions and/or custom covers and content particular to your business, training goals, marketing focus, and branding interests. For more information, please contact

U. S. Corporate and Government Sales
1-800-382-3419
corpsales@pearsontechgroup.com

For sales outside the U. S., please contact

International Sales
international@pearson.com

Library of Congress Cataloging-in-Publication Data is on file.

Pearson Education, Inc.
Rights and Contracts Department
501 Boylston Street, Suite 900
Boston, MA 02116
Fax (617) 671 3447

ISBN-13: 978-0-13-706592-9
ISBN-10: 0-13-706592-2

Text printed in the United States on recycled paper at Courier in Westford, Massachusetts.
First printing February 2011

This book is for Brittiany.
As you continue to grow in wisdom and strength,
may you always keep your childlike joy.

Contents

Preface

Every IT organization is already managing its capacity. Unfortunately, many organizations manage capacity poorly because they have not recognized the importance or value of a capacity management program. Others recognize the importance of managing capacity but lack essential knowledge and organized systems to maintain capacity information. Still other organizations manage capacity effectively in one or two areas, but need consistency and a stronger team to effectively manage all IT capacity. If you recognize yourself in any of these categories, this book is for you. You will learn the essential skills and understand the fundamental concepts that will help you to manage the IT capacity your organization uses much more effectively than you do today.

This book is much more than the opinion of one author. It is based on a set of best practices that have been consciously and conscientiously gathered over decades by literally thousands of IT organizations. Every one of those organizations struggled with the same issues that your organization struggles with. Every one of them learned lessons the hard way. But they didn't stop there! They also reached out to share those lessons they have learned and to help others understand what techniques and tools work. The British Office of Government Commerce took the time and put forth the effort to gather all of this wisdom in one place called the Information Technology Infrastructure Library® (ITIL®), and now you can benefit from it.

This book is firmly based on the concepts gathered and published in the ITIL core library. It will expand on the roughly 20 pages you'll find describing capacity management in the *ITIL Service Design* volume. This deeper coverage allows for a more remedial approach and I hope makes the book more accessible. The only assumption I'll make on your current skill level is that you're an IT person who is interested and responsible for helping your organization manage IT capacity better than it does today.

Organization of This Book

This book is organized around three separate parts serving three related purposes. Part I, "Concepts in Managing Capacity," focuses on the core concepts of capacity management. As with any new endeavor, it is important that you understand the vocabulary and general ideas before you can effectively apply the knowledge you will gain. This first section provides the necessary background for those who are relatively new to the capacity management terms used in ITIL.

Chapter 1, "Introduction to Capacity Management," starts at the very beginning with a bit of background on the ITIL library and the place of capacity management in the library. It helps you to understand both the pros and the cons of capacity management, and prepares you for the risks you might run into.

An extended metaphor runs throughout Chapter 2, "The Geography of Managing Capacity." This important material describes capacity management as the stewardship of a set of pools and streams. The pools represent homogenous capacity groupings that are managed via component capacity management, and the streams represent heterogeneous IT groupings that are managed via IT service capacity management. This chapter is referenced frequently throughout the book, as these concepts are critical to the best practices found in ITIL.

Chapter 2 describes the primary objects used in capacity management, which are capacity pools and capacity streams. Chapter 3, "Understanding Capacity Demand," demonstrates the primary action of capacity management, which is tracking capacity utilization and predicting what future utilization will look like. This is the heart of the capacity management process. The mature capacity management program will excel at the techniques described in Chapter 3.

Part I closes with some details about how capacity grows in an environment. Much of the material in Chapter 3 will seem obvious, but if you don't consider all the possible sources of growth you will be forever trapped with less than accurate forecasts. The techniques for understanding growth presented in Chapter 4, "Dimensions of Capacity Growth," complement the techniques for predicting utilization in Chapter 3 to complete your understanding of how capacity is managed.

Part II, "Best Practices in Capacity Management," focuses on the actual deployment of an effective capacity management program. By *program* we don't mean a specific piece of computer software or any specific tool. Instead, the capacity management program is an effective process managed and executed by trained staff and automated with appropriate tools to produce useful and accurate data. All four components (process, people, tools, and data) are essential, and the goal of Part II is to provide balanced treatment of all four of these components.

We begin Part II with data. In Chapter 5, "Establish the Capacity Management Information System," you'll learn about the Capacity Management Information System (CMIS), which is the database used to store all capacity management data. This database is a fundamental component of an effective capacity management program, and since most organizations I've encountered don't have a working CMIS, I go into significant detail on what it should include and how it should be organized.

The data theme continues in Chapter 6, "Define and Manage Capacity Plans," with a deeper look at a particular kind of entry in the Capacity Management Information System, the Capacity Plan. The chapter includes in-depth descriptions on how to create capacity plans, what they should include, and how to maintain them so that they can be useful documents for your organization. There is a section on how to store capacity plans so that they can be an integral part of your CMIS.

Chapter 7, "Staff the Capacity Management Team," puts the focus squarely on the people who will be involved in your capacity management program. You will need one set of people to implement capacity management and most likely a separate set of people to manage capacity after the program has been set in motion. Separate roles are described for these two teams, along with some general observations about the skills required for each role. The information in Chapter 7 will enable you to determine whether the same people are involved with both teams.

When you understand the data you need and have people to implement the program, you are ready to deploy the process. The *ITIL Service Design* book provides a great understanding of what the fundamental building blocks of a capacity management process should be. Rather than restating that material, Chapter 8, "Implement the Capacity Management Process," gives you practical advice on how to set that process in motion. I assume you have no process or procedures today and describe how to get them implemented and start the road to maturity.

In Chapter 9, "Relate Capacity and Performance," we extend the process discussion to investigate the relationship between capacity management and performance management. I make the case that performance management is a necessary subset of the entire capacity management process, and provide some ideas of how to implement a performance management subprocess while focusing on capacity management.

Chapter 10, "Choose Capacity Management Tools," and Chapter 11, "Produce Capacity Reports," focus on the tools and outputs of your capacity management program. In Chapter 10 we focus specifically on what parts of the process are typically automated. You won't find any specific tool recommendations, but instead you will find a wealth of detail on the tools marketplace and characteristics you should consider when shopping for capacity management tools. Even if you already own tools that provide some functions, Chapter 11 will help you understand other areas you might be able to automate in the future.

In Chapter 11, I continue the tools discussion with a specific focus on reports. You will find specific ideas for reports that you might want to use, along with a rationale for why those reports have been important to other organizations. You'll learn that there are reports about capacity and also reports that describe the health of your capacity management program. Both kinds are important, and Chapter 11 will help you get the right reports to the correct audience.

Part III, "Common Issues in Capacity Management," delves into some specific issues that arise around managing capacity. This section might appear to be a hodgepodge, but I've tried to cover topics that have caused difficulty for many of my colleagues and many of the customers I work with. The theme throughout Part III is integration and making the capacity management program part of a fully functioning IT organization.

The first topic, presented in Chapter 12, is "Business Capacity Planning." ITIL insists that a full capacity management program also plans to meet the needs of the business. But it is sometimes very difficult to get the business units outside of IT to describe what those needs are. This chapter will help you bridge the gap between IT and the business and gives you some hints on what to do when the business doesn't cooperate so well.

Chapter 13, "Smoothing the Order Cycle," explores the relationship between capacity management and IT procurement. Much of the cost benefit of capacity management comes from avoiding IT spending, so this chapter focuses on how to use the techniques of capacity management to avoid spending as long as possible while not running out of capacity. The important concept of a "reorder level" is applied to capacity management in Chapter 13.

Another important area of integration is between the capacity management team and various IT project teams. Since all new projects require capacity and many of them add capacity, there is a natural affiliation between project management and capacity management. This relationship is explored in Chapter 14, "Capacity Management in a Project Context."

The final chapter takes a wider view to explore the relationship between capacity management and other IT disciplines described by ITIL. In Chapter 15, "Integrating Capacity Planning with IT Processes," you'll learn how to integrate capacity management with several other process areas. The integrations described here will help whether or not those other process areas are already mature, or you will implement them for the first time several years from now. The common theme is that capacity management is made stronger as it is integrated with other parts of your IT operations.

Acknowledgments

The creation of a book is a long, slow marathon. Without the help and encouragement of the other runners, there is no way to get to the finish line. I want to thank my team of very dedicated technical reviewers—Brian and Charles—for the many hours of reading my opinions and turning them into facts that the reader can rely on.

The IBM® Press team has again proved both their professionalism and their passion for helping authors succeed. My heartfelt thanks go to the team for helping me through the process as I juggled my writing with my regular job.

Of course, my biggest thanks are saved for those who once again have allowed me to turn their businesses into laboratories. My customers and I have learned this material together, and not without some mistakes along the way! I sincerely appreciate the patience and support of the customers I've worked with, especially those in Minneapolis, Camden, Amsterdam, and Detroit. You know who you are.

About the Author

Larry Klosterboer is a professional IT architect specializing in service management. He works for IBM Global Technology Services as the lead architect for large, complex outsourcing customers. Larry has more than 20 years of experience in IT operations and service delivery, spanning technologies from mainframe to networking to desktop computing. Much of his career has been spent in helping organizations implement service management processes and tools, which is to say undoing the mistakes that he and others have made in this area!

PART I

Concepts in Managing Capacity

Capacity management can be almost anything your organization chooses to make it. Among practicing capacity managers, certain concepts and vocabulary are used to enable sharing of best practices. These first four chapters bring you into the dialog by sharing the concepts and vocabulary of capacity management.

CHAPTER 1

Introduction to Capacity Management

As an information technology (IT) manager, you must balance many forces to accomplish your mission. You need to hire and retain highly skilled employees without going over your personnel budget. You must be sure your security precautions protect against a wide variety of attacks without restricting legitimate users from accomplishing useful work. You need to balance the risk of new technologies against the features and functions your user community demands. Making trade-offs is the daily routine of every IT manager.

This book is fundamentally about another trade-off that every IT manager must face: how to deploy enough hardware and software to run the business without deploying so much that you are incurring unnecessary cost. The discipline of understanding and achieving balance between "too little" and "too much" is called capacity management, and whether you have a formal process with automated tools or you simply act on instinct, every IT manager is by definition a capacity manager.

Although capacity management has been an organized part of mainframe operations for many years, only recently have people been actively trying to manage capacity in the distributed server and workstation arenas. Many of the techniques learned in the mainframe data center still apply, but some important new concepts are required as well. In recent years, the community of people thinking critically about capacity management has begun to share best practices with one another, and those best practices have found their way into the set of all IT operational best practices, known as the IT Infrastructure Library or ITIL. The goal of this book is provide you with practical guidance in implementing those best practices for your organization.

The ITIL Life Cycle

Although this book focuses on capacity management, it is difficult to understand that discipline without at least some background in ITIL. This section is not intended as a substitute for the actual books of the library, but it helps remind you of the salient points about ITIL.

The Overall Library

The IT Infrastructure Library is now in its third version. You can find information about the latest version from the British Office of Government and Commerce. This group provides central administration of the library and offers the latest information about ITIL on its website, www.best-management-practice.com.

Currently the library consists of six books. The first book is an introduction to the entire area of IT service management, and the other five books form the core of the best-practice recommendations. Ultimately that is what ITIL is—a set of recommendations based on thousands of examples and the combined centuries of experience of its many contributors. Because of all that experience and the heavy scrutiny the recommendations have received, none should be taken lightly. On the other hand, it is quite likely that none of those experienced contributors has worked in your exact situation, so they couldn't possibly foresee every nuance and challenge that you will face in implementing capacity management or any other ITIL discipline.

Unfortunately, you can't simply take ITIL "out of the box" and implement it. You must adopt it and tailor it to fit your situation and to optimize exactly the services you want to provide to your IT consumers. That is the goal of this book. This book isn't a substitute for the books of the ITIL library, but it is a supplement that provides a concrete set of steps that help you tailor the recommendations of ITIL to your needs.

The Service Management Life Cycle

Setting aside the introductory volume, the five core books of the ITIL Version 3 library describe a circle of activities that describe almost all IT projects. The circle, called the service management life cycle, is composed of five segments. The titles of the core books of ITIL describe the segments:

- *Service Strategy*
- *Service Design*
- *Service Transition*
- *Service Operation*
- *Continuous Service Improvement*

The service strategy volume focuses on establishing organizational policies and strategies that will undergird your entire service management effort. As you would expect, this volume helps you to define requirements for capacity management and make some key decisions about high-level capacity management policies. It is also extremely valuable in understanding the vocabulary that is used throughout the other volumes in the library.

The service design volume specifically defines the capacity management process. This is natural because capacity management is a key process for designing every IT service. The question of "how big" or "how many" is a fundamental one in designing any kind of service, and those questions are answered by capacity management. The service design volume also describes the other key elements that are part of designing an IT service, such as service-level management and information security management.

The service transition book focuses on disciplines that introduce or retire IT services. Change management and release management fall into this volume, but capacity management is not ignored here. A key element of introducing a service is to validate the capacity assumptions that were made during design time. In retiring a service, capacity management must document any resources that are freed up for use in the next service, and sometimes makes suggestions on how to use those assets in the future. These concepts are described in various ways by the service transition volume.

The service operation book primarily deals with the day-to-day management of services that are in operation. Processes such as incident management and problem management are covered in detail in the service operation book, but again capacity management is not ignored. Failures of capacity management eventually become incidents, and insufficient capacity management is often cited as a contributing factor or even a root cause of an IT problem.

Finally, the ITIL volume on continuous-service improvement describes an overall approach to ensuring the quality of the services delivered. Metrics and reporting on services play an important role and are described in this book. This volume has the least to say directly about capacity management because its recommendations for continual improvement of the processes relate equally to all processes, so no one process is singled out.

These five volumes together describe the service life cycle, which is the major innovation found in the third ITIL version (see Figure 1.1). It is important to be somewhat familiar with this cycle in order to understand the place of change and release management in relation to the other ITIL processes.

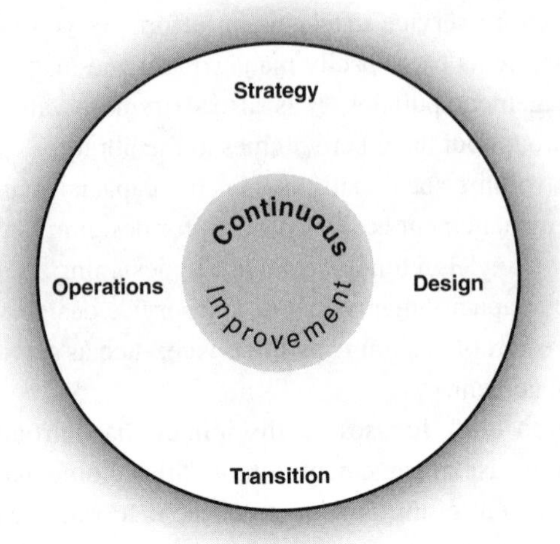

Figure 1.1 The IT Infrastructure Library defines a service life cycle.

The Purpose and Goals of Capacity Management

You probably would not have picked up this book without some idea of the purpose and goals of capacity management. You may already have a very detailed idea of what capacity management can do for your organization. It is still helpful, however, to review what the experts have defined for us in the ITIL documentation. This section describes the overall goals of capacity management and gives you some ideas on how to refine these general goals into a specific set of requirements for your implementation.

The Major Purpose

The major purpose of capacity management is to avoid waste. Wasting money in the form of time, computer resources, or human resources is generally to be avoided, but capacity management specifically has the goal of ensuring that all IT resources are not wasted. An effective capacity management program helps your organization make the most of the hardware and software you already own and purchase just the right amount of new hardware and software as it is needed.

Recently, IT people have become much more conscious of the impact of computing on the environment. Every new piece of hardware requires one set of resources to produce it, another set of resources to ship it to the data center, and energy for power and cooling while it is in the data center. After the useful life of that hardware is over, many of the materials are not able to be recycled, so the environment is impacted yet again by the disposal. One of the emerging themes of capacity management is to minimize the impact of this cycle on the environment, a part of making IT more sustainable.

You'll see throughout this book that waste can take several forms, and capacity management seeks to avoid all of them. Certainly, having servers sitting idle or at very low utilization is wasteful, and a strong capacity management process produces recommendations to avoid this situation. But having unexpected business events drive utilization so high that a business application fails is also wasting resources by having systems down and people working on repairs rather than more proactive work. The purpose of capacity management is to avoid wasted resources of any kind.

Other Purposes

While avoiding waste can save money for your organization and is a terrific purpose of capacity management, there are other compelling reasons for implementing capacity management. An effective capacity management discipline smooths the implementation of new IT services by ensuring that adequate resources are available at launch time. Another purpose of capacity management is to provide resource forecasts for budget and planning activities. The financial community will appreciate an IT team that creates accurate forecasts.

General Goals for Capacity Management

The goals for capacity management spring directly from its purpose. There are a set of general goals that almost every organization wants to achieve. These high-level goals are summarized here in order to prepare you to define specific, measurable goals for your own implementation. The next section builds on these general goals by describing how to create your own goals.

A fundamental goal of managing capacity is to *avoid purchasing additional capacity.* Proper management of IT capacity includes reclaiming unused resources, and these reclaimed resources can then be assigned to a new project. In a poorly managed environment, each project begins with the purchase of new hardware and software which will be used by that project alone. This approach is wasteful because each project uses only a portion of the capacity it purchases, and techniques like virtualization and consolidation can help avoid purchasing new equipment for at least some projects.

An organization that is a bit more mature in managing capacity encounters the second goal quite quickly. The second goal for capacity management is to *avoid running out of resources.* Imagine that your organization has decided to put all new databases on a single database server. That achieves the goal of not purchasing additional hardware, but eventually you will find that there simply isn't enough room for the next new database that must be added. A well-managed environment enables you to see that day coming far enough in advance that a new server can be acquired and installed just before it is needed.

The third goal of capacity management is thus to *smooth out the acquisition cycle.* In an unplanned model, capacity is added when you notice that your existing capacity is exhausted. This leads to delays in projects because those projects need to wait through the acquisition cycle before they can continue. When capacity management is in effect, you can predict in advance where new capacity will be needed and ensure that it is available when new projects are ready to take advantage of it.

A fourth goal for capacity management is to *predict future capacity needs.* Chapter 3, "Understanding Capacity Demand," describes this prediction process in great detail. It is not sufficient to simply observe historical growth patterns because there may be business events that alter those patterns. Nor is it practical to assume that your user or project teams will be able to tell you how much capacity they will need in the future. A combination of techniques, along with the maturity driven over time, will yield accurate predictions of future capacity.

Defining Specific Goals for Your Organization

Implementing ITIL capacity management is complex and expensive. Your organization will naturally want to have well-defined goals before embarking on this journey. The goals previously defined provide a good high-level outline, but they are certainly not specific enough to explain the return on investment you are likely to get from your own implementation. For that, you need to define very specific and measurable goals for your organization.

Such goals are also called requirements and are defined iteratively. Begin with the high-level goals provided earlier, and think about ways to make them more specific. For example, you might decide that one of your goals is to smooth out the acquisition cycle for your virtual desktop infrastructure. You regularly add users to that infrastructure, but sometimes you find that you need to add more capacity instead of simply adding a few more users. So you can define a goal that has specific reorder points based on the number of users who can be added.

During the next round of definition, you think about the process of adding a user to the virtual desktop infrastructure and realize that several resources are involved. The user must have a "thin client" terminal to use, software licenses must be available, server capacity must support additional users, and storage must be available to store the users' data. You can then define even more detailed requirements such that your implementation helps you manage the capacity of each of these individual components, achieving your higher-level goal of not slowing down VDI deployment.

Continue to break down general requirements into more specific requirements to generate a solid picture of all the things your implementation project should accomplish. Eventually you should find that you have requirements that revolve around the capacity management process, tools, reporting, and data. If you use those requirements to form a detailed project scope, you should be off to a very successful start.

Interfaces to and Dependencies on Other ITIL Processes

No process in the ITIL library can stand alone. Each process is dependent on others for some of its inputs, and each process sends some of its outputs to other processes. These dependencies and interfaces are important because they help put context around your implementation of capacity management. You explore them thoroughly in Chapter 15, "Integrating Capacity Planning with IT Processes." However, a brief preview is offered here.

Capacity Management and Service Continuity

Service continuity management provides ways for the important IT services to continue through unusual circumstances such as terrorist incidents, natural disasters, or significant labor disputes. One key aspect of service continuity involves providing an alternative IT infrastructure in the event that the primary infrastructure is not available. Capacity management defines the amount of alternative infrastructure that must be available. Like most other IT situations, having too little capacity stops necessary business operations, while having too much capacity wastes money. Capacity management is needed to determine the right mix of components to have on hand when a disaster strikes.

Capacity Management and Configuration Management

Configuration management describes the complete IT environment in terms of individual configuration items and the relationships between them. As you learn in Chapter 2, "The Geography of Managing Capacity," understanding configurations enables you to manage the capacity of IT services. Without the knowledge provided by configuration management, it would be extremely difficult to understand capacity bottlenecks or to determine the best way to add capacity to support an overall business system or application. Thus, capacity management is dependent on configuration management.

Capacity Management and Release Management

Release management is the ITIL discipline that plans for deployment of new technologies and capabilities into the organization. A release consists of a group of interrelated components that together provide some useful function to the business. A key function of release management is to provide testing to be sure that the release provides the functions and performance defined in the requirements for that release. This is where capacity management comes into play. The capacity management team must validate each release to ensure two things. First, there must be sufficient capacity available to actually deploy the release as defined. Second, the release must have enough capacity to ensure that it can meet its objectives. So release management is strongly dependent on capacity management.

Other Interfaces

We could literally address every process discipline in ITIL and show that it is related to capacity management. Financial management requires capacity management to know when additional investments are needed. Incident management is invoked when capacity management fails and systems are threatened by lack of capacity. Change management must be invoked by capacity management in order to increase capacity anywhere. Many of these dependencies are explored throughout this book. It is important to remember that capacity management, like every other ITIL discipline, is an interconnected part of the whole and is not a separate process.

The Business Case for Capacity Management

There are no organizations that can implement process discipline simply because it helps make people feel better. Significant costs are involved, and there is no reason to incur those costs if the organization won't gain financial benefits to outweigh those costs. This is especially true with theoretical frameworks like ITIL.

The good news is that many organizations have already demonstrated the business value of ITIL-based process discipline. In this section, you learn the major points that should go into your business justification. We talk about the significant business advantages and touch on some of the important costs that must go into an implementation project. Using this information, you should be able to build a solid business case for why capacity management should be implemented in your organization.

Cost Avoidance

The major reason to implement a strong capacity management program is to avoid unnecessary purchases. Study after study has shown that IT infrastructure is dramatically underutilized. At home you wouldn't start a new box of cereal after you'd eaten only half of it, but in the office we frequently purchase new servers even though existing servers are less than 30% utilized.

The reason we don't push utilization rates higher is that we don't have confidence in our capacity management capability. Growth might occur from some unexpected quarter, and the tools in place might not catch it, so we leave "breathing room" on each server, each storage device, and each network to allow for this unexpected growth. The net result is that even small businesses are spending thousands more than they absolutely have to.

There is also a notion that having more hardware and software somehow makes computing resources more highly available. Although it is often true that high-availability systems include redundancy, we should never confuse having spare capacity with being highly available. Creating a highly available system is about intelligent engineering techniques and requires a stronger degree of capacity management and configuration management than creating a system with ordinary availability. It isn't possible to achieve high availability by simply "throwing more hardware at the problem."

To build a business case for capacity management, consider the benefit of increasing the utilization of each of your servers by 20%. If you have 5 servers, you can avoid the cost of number 6. If you have 50 servers, you can avoid buying the next 10, and if you are a very large organization with more than 5,000 servers, you have probably already identified enough cost savings to justify the implementation of capacity management and several other ITIL disciplines!

The good news is that cost avoidance is not simply a hardware issue. Each server you save represents software licenses that can be avoided as well. Avoiding extra equipment also keeps your labor costs lower or reduces the charges in an outsourced environment. Reducing the complexity of the environment also reduces the costs of related disciplines like configuration and change management. Overall, reducing the number of IT devices reduces the cost of IT in dozens of ways.

But what happens to your cost case if you aren't growing enough to need more servers anyway? You can't avoid costs that you wouldn't normally have to spend. For slow-growing (or shrinking) environments, you need to introduce consolidation as a cost-saving strategy. Instead of thinking about infrastructure you won't have to purchase, determine how much infrastructure you can retire with effective capacity management.

When you take hardware and software out of the environment, you can either save by terminating leases early or make a bit of money back by selling purchased equipment on the used marketplace. When you retire equipment, you also save on hardware and software maintenance agreements, on future version upgrade costs, and on the labor needed to support the retired equipment.

Business Agility

While cost containment is important, it is hardly a strategy for growing the business. To grow and expand, every organization needs a healthy revenue stream. Sound capacity management practices can help in this area as well.

By understanding your available capacity and managing it well, you can quickly move into new market opportunities while your competitors are struggling to build out the necessary infrastructure. Combined with good configuration management, capacity management even enables you to reallocate resources quickly to ramp up to unforeseen levels. Only organizations that understand all of the pieces of their infrastructure can quickly rearrange those pieces to optimize around any business opportunity.

Capacity management helps drive business in another way as well. If you are closely controlling your costs through sound capacity management practices, you can convince your executive team to funnel some of those savings toward new growth opportunities. Any time you can instantiate a new IT project without increasing the overall IT budget, you are putting your organization in a better position to win in the marketplace.

Business agility may be difficult to calculate in a business case, so you may have to use examples of previous projects that were delayed or perhaps not started at all. If you have missed an opportunity in the past, try to calculate the value of that missed opportunity and project it forward to opportunities that will arise in the future.

A Great Start for Financial Management

Another strong business reason to implement capacity management is that it provides a solid base upon which you can build an IT financial management process. When the world economy was much stronger, many IT organizations could get away with calling themselves a "cost center" and ignoring finance for the most part. Today IT organizations are under increasing pressure to understand their costs and allocate those costs fairly back to the business users who are gaining the benefit.

Capacity management provides the critical piece for IT chargeback. Specifically, it is through careful management of your capacity that you will understand the utilization of IT resources. Breaking down that utilization enables you to provide detailed reports regarding which users are taking the most advantage of which resources and how the costs of those resources should be allocated back to the business.

Important Risks to Consider

Capacity management is certainly worth implementing, but it is not without risks and difficulties. This section discusses several things that can derail your implementation of capacity management. These are certainly not the only risks, but they are important because they tend to pop up in almost every new implementation.

Missing Business Capacity Data

Ideally, service capacity management flows from business capacity management, and component capacity management flows from business capacity management. You can work from the bottom and begin your efforts by managing individual components, but you run a risk of managing the wrong things. Ultimately, the people in the C-suite offices don't care how many IT gizmos and gadgets you can build—they want to know how much business the IT organization can support.

Unfortunately, not many organizations have thought deeply about the capacity of their business. It isn't unusual to discover that there are no defined measures of business capacity. It is even less likely that your organization has already linked IT services to those business capacity measurements in a meaningful way.

It would be ideal if you could hold off on IT capacity management until some experts could work with your organization to create an enterprise model and define useful capacity measurements. Then you could link those capacity measurements to specific IT services and define very useful service capacity management metrics that reliably link to the business goals.

Of course, we don't live in an ideal world. You will most likely have to make some guesses as to what your organization feels is important. Fortunately, you can often lean on industry norms and your experience within the organization to make some assumptions about what the key elements of business capacity are. In a manufacturing organization, for example, the keys are likely engineering, manufacturing, and distribution. Any IT services that support those will be key to helping the business achieve maximum capacity.

If you are in a situation where you simply don't understand which capacity measures might be important to the organization, find colleagues at other organizations in the same industry and lean on their understanding.

Inconsistent Component Capacity Data

A second obstacle that stands in the way of many implementations is a lack of consistent data from each of the components you want to manage. Maintaining accurate utilization data is absolutely vital, and without it you will not be able to predict when capacity will run low or know when you might need to add capacity.

The first challenge in getting consistent data is to instrument all the components that you want to manage. For smaller organizations, the price of monitoring tools can often be prohibitive, leaving you to work with open-source tools or limited versions of tools that are bundled with the hardware. In larger organizations the problem is often getting enterprise tools rolled out to all corners of the operational world. Either way, if you can't get tools to consistently report data on how much capacity is being used, you end up without the ability to manage component capacity.

The other challenge that can sometimes happen is incompatibility between multiple tool sets. One client I worked with, for example, had storage area network (SAN) equipment from two different vendors in the same data center. Each SAN vendor offered a different tool to help manage their own equipment, and each tool reported different measurements. The client had to create a spreadsheet to manually combine data from the different tools in order to manage disk capacity, which they considered as a single capacity pool.

Of course, the problem of consistent data is exacerbated by the sheer volume of data that must sometimes be kept. For very large organizations, the sheer numbers sometimes make tracking component capacity data quite difficult. Automated tools can help but only if they can be implemented consistently across every component. The real key to resolving this problem is to have a strong configuration management program that provides line-of-sight mapping from the component level up through IT services and into the business services your organization provides. This is another key reason why capacity management must work within the overall ITIL framework to be completely effective.

Lack of Analysis Skill and Tools

While lack of data is certainly a hindrance, inability to analyze and make good use of data is a more insidious problem. Many organizations believe that if they just had good capacity data, all issues would be solved. Unfortunately, it takes a very highly skilled individual to turn data into a workable plan.

Component capacity analysis is highly specific to the component being analyzed. The thresholds for action are very dependent on both the technology and the way it has been implemented. Having less than 5% left of the capacity of a very large tape library may be perfectly normal, while having less than 5% of the space remaining on the local disk drive of a server might be catastrophic. It is critical to have people with the skill to know when to take measured action and when to simply keep watching the situation.

Service capacity management requires even more skill to successfully analyze. The chains of individual components that make up a complete IT service can span many different technologies. To fully define a capacity plan for the whole IT service requires a good understanding of each of those technologies and a solid sense of how they contribute to the overall service.

If your organization has the skills to do complex capacity analyses, consider yourself fortunate. For the rest of us, you may want to include training or even recruiting into your plans to deploy the capacity management process.

Summary and Next Steps

This chapter provided an introduction to the world of ITIL capacity management. It began with a brief introduction to ITIL and explained that every IT service is part of the five-step life cycle: strategy, design, transition, operation, and continuous improvement. The ITIL library provides a separate volume for each phase of this life cycle. Although capacity management is important throughout the life of every service, the process description itself is found in the ITIL volume on service design, reflecting the idea that capacity considerations should be designed into every service.

In the second section you learned why your organization should invest the money to build and mature your capacity management program. More than any other IT process, capacity management helps manage the costs of your IT infrastructure. Unless you already have very effective capacity management practices, you will get a great return on any investment you make in this process area. You saw that main goals of capacity management are to avoid overspending on resources and to avoid running out of resources when your critical business processes need them. This theme of balance between spending and IT shortages is a continuing theme.

You began to explore the place of capacity management among your other IT processes. One of the central tenets of ITIL is integration between process areas. Capacity management is highly dependent on configuration management and is a key enabler of service continuity management and release management. This topic of interplay between processes is so important that a whole chapter is devoted to it later in the book.

You looked at the business case for capacity management in some detail. You learned that cost avoidance is the biggest part of that case, because most organizations have already purchased enough hardware to last them for the next year or so if they will only manage their capacity more carefully. Consolidation and virtualization are strategies that enable you to free up space for future projects without spending more on hardware, and in some cases software. Good capacity management can also improve the ability of your organization to respond to new business conditions, and provide a great foundation for better management of your IT finances.

Finally, you took a quick tour of some of the risks associated with capacity management programs. Getting good projections from your business units on how much capacity they need can be problematic because many times the business is not accustomed to describing their needs in capacity management terms. The wide variety of components in the typical IT shop can lead to inconsistent measurements and metrics, making it hard to effectively manage the capacity of IT services that use many different components. Finally, the tools and skills needed to manage capacity effectively are not always available. Hopefully this book can provide a good start on the skills challenge, and an entire chapter is devoted to finding the right tools to help you. Being aware of these risks will help you to avoid them or at least mitigate their impact as you move forward.

Chapter 2 defines the terms and explains the concepts involved in managing IT capacity. As with any new discipline, there is a certain vocabulary you'll need to acquire. Fortunately, it is neither complex nor obscure. By the end of Chapter 2, you'll be able to speak fluent capacity management!

C H A P T E R 2

The Geography of Managing Capacity

One great way to think about IT capacity is in geographic terms. This chapter describes capacity as a series of pools and streams that can each be managed individually. Taken together, all the pools and streams in your organization describe the total of your IT capacity. Good management of all the pools and streams results in all the benefits of capacity management described in Chapter 1.

Capacity Pools and Component Capacity Management

In ITIL, capacity management falls under three related topics. At the top level is business capacity management, which deals with an overall organization's ability to make full use of its resources to further the enterprise. In classical manufacturing terms, business capacity management deals with attempts to maximize how many widgets move to the end of the assembly line. Business capacity management is much more complex than IT capacity management; it is dealt with in Chapter 12, "Business Capacity Planning."

ITIL defines service capacity management as the way IT applies resources to provide the services it has promised to the business. It frequently requires many different parts to provide a complete service, so service capacity management involves blending the resources from several technologies and understanding how a shortage of resources in one area might impact the entire service. Service capacity management is defined in much greater detail later in this chapter.

The final layer of capacity management defined by ITIL is component capacity management. This is the most elemental layer, where individual pieces of technology exist. Managing the capacity of a single server or a single network switch ensures that these resources can be used in the fulfillment of IT services.

Defining Capacity Pools

A capacity pool is a group of like components that are essentially managed in the same way. The set of Solaris servers in a particular data center would form a capacity pool, while the set of Linux servers in that data center might form a different pool. The key to forming a single pool is that any element within the pool must be interchangeable with any other. If you have a group of blade servers that support only the payroll function while a different group supports engineering functions, then the two sets are not part of the same pool even if they consist of the same model of blade server and even if they exist in the same rack.

There are many technical and organizational reasons to divide resources into pools. In one case a set of servers might be managed differently and with different service levels than another, so they would be considered a different pool. In another case, resources from two different pools might be identical in all respects except in how they are paid for, so the two pools must remain separate since the resources are not interchangeable. Strong engineering standards and clear organizational ownership of resources helps reduce the number of capacity pools and make the pools larger, which is in everyone's best interest.

Capacity management tracks three key measurements for each capacity pool. The first measurement is the quantity of available resources in the pool. If you have a pool of laptop computers that are to be used as replacements, it is critical to know at any time how many are in the pool. This seems easy to track, but it isn't always so. Consider the pool of licenses of Microsoft® Office, for example. You might have to go to several purchase orders and perhaps even interpret differing terms and conditions statements to understand the total number of licenses that are really available in the pool.

A second key measurement for every capacity pool is the quantity already used. In a fairly simple pool like mobile phones, this might be very simple to count. In a complex pool such as software licensed for concurrent use, sophisticated tools might be required to count the actual usage of resources in the pool, and the number may change rapidly. For many hardware resources like memory and processing power, the quantity used can be very difficult because it changes very frequently. For those cases we tend to measure average quantity used and peak quantity used and track these as two separate measurements for the capacity pool.

The final key measurement is derived from the first two, but it is most important to capacity managers. This is the number still available in the capacity pool. If you know the total number of resources and the number being used, you will understand the quantity that can still be used.

Boundaries of Capacity Pools

Like pools of water, capacity pools have defined, albeit changeable, boundaries. These boundaries are interesting because they determine how and when you add more capacity to each pool. When the preceding section described capacity pools as groups of like resources, it failed to take into account that you may have many resources of the same type that cannot be managed together. You might, for example, have multiple data centers, each of which has its own storage area network (SAN). Free disk space in the first data center cannot be used by servers in the second, so in effect there are two separate pools of SAN disk space.

Of course, there may also be network attached storage (NAS) in each of the data centers, which results in four separate pools of capacity to be managed—two for SAN and two for NAS. Each of these pools has a boundary determined by the use (SAN and NAS are used differently) and the location. The important point is that each pool must be managed separately because excess resources in one area cannot be used by another pool.

This notion of separately managed pools is at the heart of component capacity management. The foundation for effectively managing the IT capacity across your organization is the understanding and management of each of the separate capacity pools. If you wish to manage the capacity of some component, you need to define it as a pool first.

Location and common use are only two ways to define the boundaries of capacity pools. It is possible to have different groups managing resources of the same type at the same location. This can happen, for example, in an outsourcing agreement. The outsourcing provider may manage all the workstations for the organization, while the retained organization manages the executive suite workstations to provide a higher level of service. In this case, the same resource type in the same location is split into two pools based on who manages them. The outsourcing agreement may support the same pool of spare equipment or separate pools, but there are essentially two separate capacity pools.

Capacity pools can also be divided by how they are funded. If a specific line of business or department maintains their own departmental servers, they will be a different capacity pool than the servers of other departments or those shared across a larger organization. If the boundary isn't strictly observed, there may be significant delays when it comes time to fund the next server as business units argue about who should pay for the next resource based on who caused the capacity shortage. One strong goal of capacity management should be to uncover these funding issues and help the organization see that they are detrimental to effectively managing capacity. Larger capacity pools are more effective because they maximize the ability to use any unused capacity within the pool.

Specify the technology type, the purpose, and the boundary of every capacity pool that you want to actively manage. Without this information, operational questions will arise and need to be settled before effective capacity management can happen. Capacity managers depend on the ability to watch the utilization of resources, predict when a shortage will happen, and acquire new capacity just before that shortage actually occurs. If logistics, politics, or funding get in the way of that acquisition, Murphy's Law says that resources will run out on the most critical project or application. Having strong definitions along with clear responsibilities for each capacity pool will help keep Murphy at bay.

Granularity of Capacity Pools

It is time to define the nebulous term "like components." Thinking deeply about IT components quickly results in the understanding that every component in IT can be broken down into smaller pieces. For example, a workstation is really a composite of one or more hard disks; a motherboard with lots of individual chips on it; some memory cards, each with multiple chips; some external parts like a keyboard, a mouse, a display; and so forth. This raises the question of how fine-grained our capacity pools really need to be.

For a storage area network, it may make sense to break down several different capacity pools rather than managing it as a single large pool of disk space. System administrators provision a logical unit of storage but also connect servers to physical ports in the SAN switches. Most capacity managers find it convenient to manage disk space and switch space separately within the SAN.

Considering granularity normally leads to thoughts about how capacity grows. In a modern IT shop, most hardware resources can be expanded in two ways, internally and externally. Internal expansion means that you add more memory, processing power, disk space, or capability to interface with the outside world. For example, if you have a router that currently connects two wide area network links to three separately routed local area networks, you may be able to grow that router to support more network connections by adding another card to it. Similarly, workstations, servers, and a whole host of other equipment can get more capacity by adding resources within the frame.

External expansion is often possible as well. Rather than adding more memory to a server, you might choose to add a second server and balance the workload between the two machines. External expansion is normally an architectural choice made due to the benefits of having parallel devices accomplishing a single purpose. Internal and external capacity growth are examined in much more detail in Chapter 4, "Dimensions of Capacity Growth."

The question of granularity ultimately rests with your unit of purchase and your unit of deployment for any given resource. I've worked with clients who believed that memory modules were expensive, so they would routinely swap memory from one server to another in an attempt to get the optimum performance from each server without purchasing more resources. Clearly their capacity pool was memory modules and not servers. More recently, however, organizations have recognized that the total cost of owning a server goes up dramatically when the server is opened and hardware is added or removed. They manage servers as a capacity pool, and favor adding another server rather than more memory because this helps them maintain standards and provides for load balancing and other advantages that are not possible with adding more resources to a single server. As the capacity manager, you should help your organization understand that the best practice in capacity management is to purchase servers with a standard configuration and then manage the servers as resource units rather than individual components of the servers.

Most organizations today have embraced virtualization to some extent. The capability to carve one piece of hardware into multiple logical units enables the overall hardware to reach higher levels of utilization but adds a layer of complexity to managing capacity. Now the capacity manager needs to be concerned with how many logical partitions or guest operating systems to host on a single server. The capacity pool is defined by the physical boundaries of the hardware, with memory, CPU power, and input/output capability becoming resources to be allocated to the individual operating systems within the pool. New technologies with names such as V-Motion and Live Partition Mobility enable these guest operating systems to be moved seamlessly between physical hosts, creating an even more complex environment for the capacity manager. The impact of virtualization on capacity management is explored more fully later in this chapter.

Managing Capacity Pools

Capacity pools are managed using basic inventory management techniques. Each pool should be viewed as a single inventory item and should be tracked separately in your capacity management database. It is important to know basic information about each pool such as how many items are available in the pool, how long it takes to order new items, and how many should be ordered at a time. When the inventory on hand gets low, a new order should be placed to replenish your supply.

For a simple capacity pool such as hand-held devices, the management of the capacity pool is quite simple. Most organizations allocate a secured area to store devices before they are sent out, and tracking the quantity on hand is as simple as counting the units in that area. You might choose a model in which you buy a new unit only after someone has requested it, in which case your reorder number is effectively zero, or you might choose to have some number of units in inventory to reduce the time the requester needs to wait. If you choose to have inventory, you will quickly learn how many to reorder and how quickly to reorder so you never quite run out of stock, but you also don't have units sitting idle very long.

Great skill is required to manage a more complex capacity pool, however. IBM Websphere® Application Server (WAS) licenses, for example, are very difficult to track if your organization has entered into a subcapacity license agreement. Under this agreement, the number of "value units" of software in use (and thus the number remaining) changes depending on which server the software is installed on. If a server is upgraded to enable more processors, the number of value units of WAS licenses increases. If your WAS environment is very dynamic, with servers being added and removed frequently, it can be a great challenge to know when the license pool is getting low and it is time to reorder. Fortunately, one of the conditions for entering into a subcapacity agreement is installation of a tool to help you track the utilization of the IBM software.

Capacity Streams and Service Capacity Management

The concept of capacity pools makes component capacity management much easier to understand, but it doesn't cover the more complex case of service capacity management. ITIL tells us that most IT services are made up of a sequence of components, so managing the capacity of an IT service involves combining the capacities of each of the components within that service.

Defining Capacity Streams

A capacity stream consists of all the individual components required to implement a complete IT service. Streams typically cut across at least two, and sometimes dozens of, capacity pools. The process of defining capacity streams relies heavily on another ITIL discipline: configuration management. If you don't understand the configuration of your environment, it will be extremely difficult to identify and manage capacity streams.

As an example of a typical capacity stream, consider a payroll application. This particular payroll application runs with an Oracle database, two load-balanced web servers, and two load-balanced application servers, all of which is accessed by users with a web browser across the company network. This capacity stream crosses capacity pools for Oracle licenses, database servers, load-balancing appliances, web servers, application servers, LAN bandwidth, and perhaps WAN bandwidth. To understand whether we can push more payroll transactions requires understanding the capacity available within each of these pools.

Ideally, capacity streams should be measured by the same criteria as capacity pools—total capacity, used capacity, and remaining capacity. Unfortunately, it is extremely difficult to determine the total available capacity of a capacity stream. Consider the payroll application described earlier. Is there an upper limit to the number of paychecks that can be run? Is it possible to reach a point where you cannot add one more user to the system or where you cannot support payroll for one more employee? Those limits are very difficult to define exactly.

Part of the difficulty lies in understanding the capacity of a capacity stream. Whereas capacity pools could be defined in terms of technical limits and numbers, the units of measurement in a capacity stream must be defined in terms of business units. ITIL describes service capacity management as measuring the ability of IT to provide services out to the business it serves, so the capacity metrics used should be expressed in terms the business can understand. This is a difficult leap for hard-core IT people who are accustomed to thinking of everything in technical terms. Let's return to the payroll application. Some potential capacity measurements are described above—logged-in users, people being paid, paychecks being processed. Others might include specific transactions such as number of tax updates or number of employee address changes. In most cases, capacity streams have a group of measurements that work together to describe the capacity of the stream.

Understanding how large a capacity stream can potentially be normally involves creating an artificial test variously called a "performance test" or "load test." A variety of representative transactions are defined and then executed repeatedly on the system to simulate various loads on the system. Through the use of a testing tool, the workload can be ratcheted up little by little until the system becomes so slow as to be unusable, or some hidden parameter in the software causes the system to fail. This kind of test determines the breaking point or highest potential for executing the transactions specified in the test. From this the savvy capacity analyst can make some predictions about the maximum size of the capacity stream.

Confluences and Shared Capacity

Just as a single lake can be fed by several streams, so too can several capacity streams use the same capacity pool. Such a confluence of streams happens most frequently when infrastructure is shared between business applications or IT services. For example, many organizations build database servers and then host databases for many different applications on one server. This leads to a confluence of capacity streams where each business application represents a specific stream and the database server is shared among all of them.

Shared resources are becoming increasingly important in the struggle to manage capacity and contain costs. In the storage arena, for example, having a shared pool of many different disk drives in an array is dramatically more efficient than having individual disks associated with each server. With individual disks, each server has to maintain a buffer space of several gigabytes to allow for temporary files and data growth. In a large shared array, all servers can share those few gigabytes, enabling much more of the overall disk space to be utilized and much less to be left idle.

This same approach can be applied to servers, and even middleware platforms like databases and application servers. The more ways you share a resource, the less idle capacity is needed. Of course, this must be balanced with the operational risk of having many different IT services counting on a shared resource pool. This kind of trade-off between risk and reward is at the heart of effective capacity management.

Virtualization adds another kind of shared capacity for each capacity stream to consider. If any component within the stream is part of a virtual capacity pool, it must be treated the same as any other shared capacity pool because virtualization always implies shared resources. Again, virtualization is covered in depth later in this chapter.

The Value of Capacity Streams

Capacity streams are complex and difficult to measure well, so the natural question is why they are so important. Capacity streams are at the intersection between ITIL capacity management and capacity management without ITIL. Many organizations get along by managing only their capacity pools. They have become adept at not running out of resources for the key components in their infrastructure, and they have even developed an intuitive feel for which of those components are the most important, although they might be hard-pressed to define why they are important.

This is why ITIL introduces the concept of IT services. Rather than thinking of our information technology as a series of related parts, ITIL chooses to define IT in terms of the services it provides to the larger organization that supports it. This concept is so important that the entire set of ITIL disciplines is called *service* management. ITIL deals with services, and you cannot understand the capacity of a service without understanding the entire capacity stream used to provide that service.

The difficulty in measuring capacity streams really stems from the chief difficulty in implementing ITIL. It requires a change of thought process for most organizations. Instead of thinking of individual components and how to mix them into systems or applications, service management suggests that you think of services first and consider components as mere building blocks for services. This mode of thinking is necessary for establishing service levels, defining configurations, ensuring service availability, and many other aspects of IT operations using the ITIL framework. So don't think of defining and measuring capacity streams as difficult— think of it as necessary foundation work for implementing other ITIL processes.

Managing Capacity Streams

Managing capacity streams takes more effort than managing capacity pools. Rather than using time-tested inventory techniques, you need to develop some new capabilities to help you deal with the complexity of capacity streams. Fortunately, others have managed capacity streams before, and you can learn from their success.

The beginning of effective management is the definition of measurements. For each capacity stream, you should determine the measure of capacity you will use. The measure should be some unit that is relatively easy to calculate, yet has distinct value to the business that will consume your IT service. For a business application, this is frequently the number of users supported or perhaps the number of certain kinds of transactions that can be executed.

After determining the overall measure to be used, you need to break down that measurement into its various components. Determine the number of resources needed from every capacity pool touched by this capacity stream. For example, if your measurement is the number of business users that can be supported, you need to determine what percentage of a server (CPU, memory, and disk space) that user requires, consider the software license requirements to support one user, calculate the network bandwidth required for a user, and throw in the workstation equipment and software licenses required for that use to access the business application. Each of these component parts should be part of a capacity pool that you can manage as described earlier in this chapter.

By breaking down your capacity stream into components, you may discover some capacity pools that you hadn't thought of before. Determine whether they are important enough to manage separately, and if so add them to your capacity management plans.

After you have defined the capacity stream in terms of its component parts, you can effectively manage the stream through the demands placed by the business. When you see the number of transactions growing, you can reflect that growth across the various capacity pools and determine whether you need to add capacity to the pools to support growth of the stream. When you begin to get accurate capacity forecasts as described in Chapter 3, "Understanding Capacity Demand," you will be able to understand which pools are short on capacity and which have enough to satisfy the projected needs.

While managing capacity streams is harder than simply managing a series of disconnected pools, it provides a much higher value to your organization. You will find that only IT people ask questions that can be answered through managing capacity pools alone. The really important questions come from executives and business units, and their answers are available only if you're closely managing your capacity streams.

How Virtualization Affects Capacity Management

Virtualization is a hot topic in IT. The promise is that you can take a single piece of hardware and divide it into smaller parts, each of which can operate independently. The net result is that you can run lots of individual workloads on a single physical server and thus use most of the resources that the server has to offer. Depending on the virtualization engine chosen and the hardware capabilities, the separate virtual servers might be able to dynamically share resources with one another to even out spikes in utilization between servers.

Virtualization Creates Subpools

Virtualization creates smaller, more granular capacity pools within the single physical resource that is being virtualized. For example, an IBM pSeries® server might be broken into ten logical partitions, or LPARs. Using a technology called micro-partitioning, each LPAR starts with some share of the total physical processors and memory that are allocated to the server. But as those LPARs run software that needs more or less resources, the hypervisor manages both CPUs and memory within the limits set by the system administrators. An LPAR that isn't busy might lose some of its memory, whereas one that is very busy might be granted more memory and CPU cycles by the hypervisor.

Fortunately, modern virtualization engines like Microsoft Hyper-V™, VM Ware's vSphere, and IBM's Hypervisor take care of these lower-level details and the moment-by-moment management of resources. As a capacity planner, your concerns will be with setting the boundaries and parameters that the virtualization engine uses in making its decisions.

Managing Virtual Capacity Pools

To manage these virtual capacity pools, you must have a reasonable understanding of how the virtualization engine makes resource decisions. Typically, you can set a starting parameter for each kind of virtual resource (memory, CPU power, disk space, access to input/output devices, etc.). You normally can also set a parameter describing the upper limit that the virtual server is allowed to consume. This is important because you don't want a runaway process to make a server look exceptionally busy and thus rob other virtual servers of resources they might need. You may also be able to set a minimum level, indicating that the virtual server will never give up resources below that level. Be very careful of minimums because setting them too high directly reduces the value of virtualization.

In defining the starting points, maximums, and minimums, you are essentially determining how many virtual servers can run in any given hardware configuration. Clearly, if you specify a minimum CPU amount of one-half for every server, you cannot run more than 16 virtual servers in a physical server that has eight real CPUs. If your minimum sizes are mixed, you need to determine the number of virtual servers based on the sizes you want those servers to be.

In addition to the purely mathematical calculation of adding up all the minimum sizes, it is critical to consider peak loads for each virtual server and understand what might happen if all the virtual servers in a single physical server hit their peak loads at the same time. Most virtualization engines enable you to set the maximum sizes such that not all virtual servers could possibly use their maximums at the same time. This is where you, as a capacity planner, must understand how the business will use the servers in order to determine which physical host should accommodate each virtual server as you built them.

Sharing Virtual Resource Pools Between Streams

Choosing which physical server will host each virtual server is the added layer of complexity that virtualization brings to capacity management. Without virtualization, each new IT instance uses a single component from the capacity pool, but when you choose to create virtual servers, each physical server becomes its own capacity pool, and you must determine which pool to use for each new instance.

In most cases a physical server that is virtualized has virtual servers from multiple different capacity streams. In other words, the same physical server is shared between multiple streams. But it is also possible to share a virtual server between streams. For example, you might choose to build a single virtual web server and host multiple business applications on that single server. In this case you've shared a virtual server between IT services.

As you can imagine, the complexity grows enormously when you start to deal with virtualization. Don't let the extra complexity be a reason to ignore the benefits of virtualization, however. Throughout this book you will find insights for managing complexity while keeping your sanity!

Over-Subscription and Risks of Virtualization

You will quickly learn that it is possible in a virtual environment to assign more resources than actually exist. As mentioned earlier, many capacity planners choose to set up virtualization so that the sum of all maximum resource levels is greater than the amount of physical resources that are actually on the host server. This situation, in which there are more virtual resources allocated than physical resources present, is called over-subscription.

When handled carefully, over-subscription is desirable. It allows the virtualization engine to do its job by actively managing resources and balancing work load across the virtual servers. When abused, however, over-subscription can lead to performance problems that are difficult to resolve. If you choose to over-subscribe your physical resources, make sure that you have good tools in place to monitor the performance of the virtual servers so that you can better understand when issues might arise.

In addition to the dangers of over-subscription, virtualization can lead to some other risks. The virtualization engine requires resources to perform its functions. If you have a single physical resource split into many parts, the overhead associated with virtualization can grow quite high. If you need one entire CPU just to track and execute the management of the virtual servers, the cost of virtualization might start exceeding its benefits. Unfortunately, it can also be difficult to track the virtualization engine separately since many tools work only within the virtual servers and do not see the overhead associated with managing the virtualization.

The rapid adoption of virtualization by the IT industry shows that these limitations and risks can be overcome, but the wise capacity manager must at least be aware that they exist.

Summary and Next Steps

This chapter has described some of the basic terms involved in capacity management. You were first introduced to the idea of capacity pools, which enable the concept that ITIL calls component capacity management. You learned that capacity pools are groups of IT resources that are designed and managed in the same way. The boundaries of capacity pools can be defined by geography or organizational politics, but you learned that the broader the pool, the more effective you will be in managing it.

Capacity pools can be defined at a very granular level, but it is normally better to define your pools at a higher level to avoid the overhead involved in managing thousands of changes to the pools. You learned that managing capacity pools is a lot like managing the inventory for a manufacturing organization—you want to have resources available just in time and minimize the number of resources that are idle at any point.

The second section of the chapter introduced the concept of capacity streams. Whereas pools are groups of like resources, streams are groups of heterogeneous resources that work together to provide a common IT service. Capacity streams form the basis of what ITIL calls service capacity management. By looking at these streams, you can begin to understand how much capacity you need to provide an end-to-end service to your IT consumers.

You saw that capacity streams frequently intersect with one another because similar infrastructure resources are often shared between different IT services. When these streams form a confluence, capacity management should be especially careful to clearly identify the implications of shared capacity. Managing capacity streams, or managing service capacity as ITIL calls it, is more complex than managing simple pools of resources, but it is much more valuable. The difficult business questions are normally resolved by careful management of capacity streams rather than by management of capacity pools.

Because virtualization is so prevalent in today's IT environments, this chapter included a section on how virtualization affects capacity management. You learned that virtualization creates more pools of resources to manage, but that modern hypervisor programs manage those resources effectively in most cases. The values that virtualization brings to an environment greatly outweigh the overhead costs of managing the virtualization engine.

In the next chapter, you expand on your growing knowledge of capacity management by looking at how organizations predict how much capacity they will need in the future. Accurately predicting the future needs of your organization will make you a much more effective capacity manager and allow you to take a much more active role in helping your organization reduce the cost of IT.

CHAPTER 3

Understanding Capacity Demand

Chapter 2 looked at how to measure the capacity of existing components and services. This chapter approaches ITIL capacity management from the opposite direction by examining the ways to predict how much capacity will be needed. Every dynamic organization goes through periods of greater and lesser need for IT services, and these cycles determine the demand for IT capacity.

Predicting the future needs of the organization will never be an exact science. In this chapter, you look at several methods for formulating an estimate, and hopefully some combination of these will be effective for your organization.

Trend-Based Forecasts

Perhaps the most obvious way to forecast future need is to look at historical trends. If you know the rate at which your organization has consumed IT resources over the past two or three years, you can predict the amount of resources that will be needed in the coming year. Yours would be a rare organization if your consumption isn't growing over time, so it is important to consider more than one period in the past so you can see the rate of growth. Whether your growth is seasonal, consistent, or wildly variable, this section describes how to forecast future needs based on historical trends.

Component-Based Trends

If you are following the recommendations in Chapter 2, "The Geography of Managing Capacity," establishing component-based trends is relatively easy. Using the component pools that you've defined for tracking, you simply need to get historical numbers showing the rate of utilization in each pool. Let's say that you were tracking overall CPU usage on a VMware ESX host server as a pool. In March the tools recorded that the average utilization was 18% and the peak utilization was 72%. In April the numbers went up slightly, to 19% and 75%, and in May they went to 21% and 74%. Using a simple trend graph, you can plot a line predicting the average and peak utilization for future months, as demonstrated in Figure 3.1. Extending the line beyond the simple data points enables you to predict when the virtual machines on this particular host will not have enough CPU to meet their peak needs. This may result in slower application performance or other issues with service, so it is important to know when it may happen.

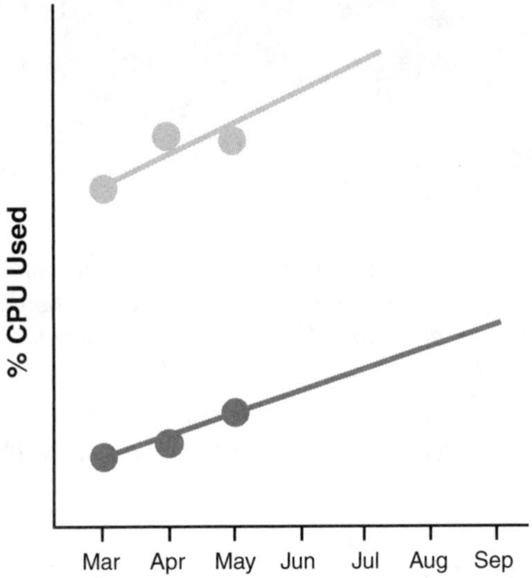

Figure 3.1 Future demand can be predicted by past consumption.

Of course, the farther back into history you go, the more accurate your trend line will be. Any good statistician will tell you that using just three months allows a very wide margin for error. But if you don't happen to have three or four years of data handy, don't despair! Start recording utilization now so that in two or three years you will have the ability to forecast very accurately.

The same general technique can be used to provide summary reports across similar pools. If you manage dozens of individual ESX host servers, you could create a composite graph showing the average and peak utilization across all these servers and plot a single graph. That might show, for example, that you could move virtual machines between ESX hosts rather than having to acquire another server. This kind of aggregate reporting begins to show the value of capacity management across environments.

Aggregate reporting can also be very helpful across different but related capacity pools, especially at different granularities. For example, if you track the CPU utilization of an AIX® logical partition but also track the utilization of the entire server, you may see a trend that says with just a little more CPU power you could build five new partitions on a server. Capacity analysis can almost always be improved with additional data.

Service-Based Trends

Trend-based forecasting can also be used to determine the need for more capacity in a service. The technique again depends on having a sound way to measure the capacity of the service in the first place. If you know how many users were served, or how many transactions were processed for the past several periods, you can create a trend graph to predict the needs of the service into the future.

You should find a general correlation between the service capacity trend and the component capacity trends for that same service. If the number of transactions is going down while the need for memory, processors, and disk space is going up, you have a strong indication that something is wrong with the way the service is being provided or measured. Perhaps in setting up your measurement you misunderstood the actual components that make up the service. It is also possible that the components used in the service are shared with other services, in which case you would need to look to those other services for correlation with the component demand trend. Of course, trends of this type are only an indication because the correlation is very general. Correlating trends can provide data points, but don't mistake any correlation you see for absolute fact.

Aggregation of service trends is much more difficult than aggregation of component trends. It is usually difficult to find services that are similar enough to aggregate together into a single trend graph that makes sense. If you want to explore the possibility, the best way to start is to examine services that work together to achieve a single business process. For example, you might find that you have IT services defined for printing paychecks, processing 401K deductions, and supporting payroll users. A single graph showing trends for all three of these services as three separate lines might indicate something significant about the way your IT organization is supporting the payroll business process. Of course, you will want to mature your ability to make and use component trends before moving on to the much more difficult art of IT service trending.

Business-Based Trends

While the data that business capacity trends provide is somewhat less clear to the IT group, they are worth watching for the IT capacity manager. Every organization creates executive reports that highlight the growth (or shrinkage) of the organization. Whether units sold, deposits collected, viewers tuned in, or new products developed, all these statistics relate in some way to the amount of IT that is needed to support the trend. When the trend is up and the organization is flourishing, IT should expect to see increased demand. If the trend is down and the business is struggling, IT should start looking for ways to cut costs by reducing capacity. Of course, as an IT capacity manager, you should be ready to defend and explain the trends in IT service usage and IT component usage in light of the business capacity reports. It can be a very difficult conversation to ask for funding for a new storage area network when the business capacity reports are showing an overall shrinking revenue stream!

You learn more about business capacity management and how to link these business trends into the IT trends in Chapter 12, "Business Capacity Planning." You may not be able to make a direct correlation between the business trends and your IT capacity, but you should at least look at whatever your organization publishes and see how it compares to your component and service trends.

Portfolio-Based Forecasts

The problem with trend-based forecasts is that they assume you will continue to do what you've always done. Simply projecting a trend forward does not account for significant innovations or major new projects that fundamentally shift the way IT works. In a dynamic, rapidly changing organization you should also make forecasts based on the portfolio of IT projects. Every organization goes through some sort of budget cycle each year, and during that cycle the IT group is always asked to predict what projects they will deploy into the environment. This project data can help you to shape the forecast by introducing additional data beyond simple trending.

For most organizations, you can more accurately predict future capacity demand by forecasting IT needs during the coming cycle. The set of projects, whether scientifically determined or simply guessed at, makes up the IT portfolio. You can forecast the amount of capacity needed by estimating the needs of each of the projects within the portfolio. In other words, your total forecast should include those projects that you know will consume capacity.

Business-Driven or "Top Down" Portfolio

In some organizations the IT portfolio begins with a set of business priorities. It might be gaining a larger market share, reducing operational expenses, or improving your compliance with industry and financial regulations. The executives communicate these goals to the CIO, who in turns hands them down to the IT management team with a request to define the role IT can play in achieving the goals.

The IT team then takes the business goals and imagines projects that might help to achieve those goals in some way. They estimate the resources required to complete each of the projects and put these together into a portfolio. Some prioritization is assigned, and the executive team then decides which efforts will be funded and thus executed during the year.

If this cycle is familiar, you are already doing some portfolio-based capacity forecasting. The funded projects compose the IT portfolio and determine the IT demand for the planning period. After the demand is forecasted this way, there is a clear set of steps leading back to the business. Specific IT projects are defined based on the ideas submitted and the resource estimates given at the time. These projects begin execution and provide regular status reports, including the amount of the budget they have spent and the IT resources consumed. Eventually these projects get completed, and the investment board receives a final status on the business results achieved.

Capacity planning can help in this planning process by looking for opportunities across the portfolio to reuse or retire equipment. Often a wider view across the known set of projects helps you see such opportunities. For example, if one of the projects is retiring a web server, another project might be able to use that web server. In addition to getting forecasting data from the portfolio planning process, the capacity manager can provide this kind of insight back to the project teams.

Figure 3.2 illustrates the complete cycle.

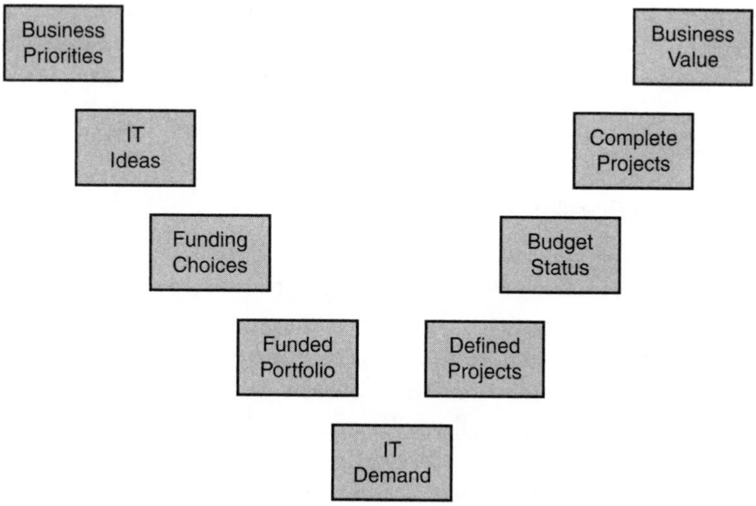

Figure 3.2 A complete portfolio cycle includes an estimate of the IT demand.

IT-Driven Portfolio

Many times the portfolio of IT projects includes those that are not directly linked to business priorities. The IT team often creates projects to refresh hardware that is out-of-date, to move to a new version of supporting IT tools, or to implement new business functions. These projects also create IT demand, but they tend to get left out in demand planning because they are not as visible as the business-driven portfolio projects. In some cases IT projects get funded out of the IT budget directly and thus do not necessarily get reported outside of IT.

The IT team should plan just as the business does. The executive over IT needs to define the priorities for the year, and the rest of IT needs to generate project proposals to meet those priorities. If the business doesn't define or announce priorities, the IT priorities might have a strong business flavor, including cost reduction, enhancing the organization's compliance, and revenue generation. The priorities might be defined in broad strokes, such as "upgrade all software to current releases," or they may be very specific, such as "implement a new incident management tool by third quarter." In either event the priorities must be clearly stated to facilitate idea generation by the IT team.

The ideas that get generated will be prioritized, and eventually someone will make the difficult decisions about what is being funded. Those funding decisions will then indicate the demand for IT resources for the specified planning period.

If your organization doesn't go through a planning exercise similar to the ones described previously, you may find it difficult to forecast IT demand. Perhaps IT team members propose projects as they think of them or uncover something that needs to be done. The management team evaluates the proposal against their sense of what is important and decides whether the IT budget can sustain the project. If they decide that the project can be funded, it begins execution immediately. Such an ad hoc planning process significantly reduces your ability to forecast future demand, thus undermining the effectiveness of your capacity management program. You should advocate a change to a more forward-looking plan.

Innovation-Driven Portfolio

Although a regular, formal planning process is the most effective way to predict future IT demand, you should always allow room for innovation outside of the planning cycle. Innovations can be very small, such as eliminating a printer cover page to save paper and toner, or very large, such as implementing virtual desktops to eliminate separate hardware for each business user. Innovative ideas generally don't follow anyone's schedule, so you need to factor in some estimate of capacity demand for the innovations that will come in during the year.

Any knowledge of future projects you can gain, from whatever source, is helpful in predicting the need for IT capacity. Whether your organization follows a formal planning cycle based on direction from the business or you simply start up projects as they are imagined, you should use whatever lead time you have available to project the demands that these projects will put on your IT capacity.

Business Event Forecasts

Portfolio-based capacity forecasts provide a better way to understand the real capacity growth of your organization than simple trend-line forecasts.. Unfortunately, they focus only on the significant new additions to the environment, and don't take into consideration the growth that might need to occur within the resources that are already deployed. Applications without an archive feature require more storage each year. Increased use of systems drive the need for more memory and CPU cycles. Adding locations or increasing the number of users in existing locations might create a need for more network bandwidth. All these examples show that understanding and predicting business events provide another way to forecast the IT capacity needed.

Business events come in many forms and are driven by many forces. Some organizations have a very predictable cycle that increases the need for resources at the end of every month, quarter, or business year. Sometimes increased demand comes seasonally with the holiday retail season, the influenza season, the tax season, or even the academic year. Often business events are driven by significant marketing activity, such as the launch of a new product or the opening of new functionality on an external web page. The savvy capacity manager monitors these business events and projects how they will influence the need for more IT capacity.

Of course, some business events are unpredictable. Product launches are sometimes held very closely to avoid speculation in the marketplace. An audit might be announced suddenly and drive a need for additional resources. As these unpredictable events take place, the capacity management team must be in a position to respond quickly and state clearly how the increased demands will be satisfied. If resources need to be reallocated, the capacity team should be involved to determine how many resources are needed. Although it is generally good to not leave too much unused capacity in your environment, these unpredictable business events dictate that there must be at least some spare capacity at any point in time.

Skill is required to predict IT demand based on business events because it is often difficult to predict exactly what the response to a particular event will be. When IBM first considered supporting the Olympic games in 1996, they had no idea of the number of people who would be interested in reading about the games on a website. It turned out to be quite a lot of people, and the system didn't initially have the capacity it needed. By the time the Sydney games rolled around in 2000, IBM had a much better capacity plan.

To predict the impact of any event on your organization, use historical data (trend-based forecasting), project data from any projects that are part of the event (portfolio-based planning), and your own experience with similar events. Combining these three sources enables you to form a capacity estimate for nearly any predictable business event.

The Blended Capacity Forecast

Now that you have seen the various tools you can use to make a forecast, it is time to consider how to blend these together to greatly improve the accuracy of your forecast. While each individual technique is helpful, most capacity managers find that they need to use some combination of all the techniques to get the best picture of the capacity demands they face.

A very common blended forecast consists of a blend between trend data and portfolio data. The assumption is that the trend data predict future growth accurately while the portfolio information determines significant new use of resources. This is a reasonable assumption to make, and history shows that a blended forecast with trend and portfolio data is typically better than 90% accurate, which is a great improvement over not having a forecast at all, or using just one of the techniques.

To create a blended forecast, follow the steps described earlier to create a trend-based forecast. Starting with a trend-based forecast enables you to see a timeline onto which you can allocate the resource needs of the portfolio-based projects. For example, assume that you are managing capacity for a large data center with 15 Oracle database servers. You want to create a forecast that indicates when it is time to order and install the 16th server.

Your first stop should be the historical records of growth for your Oracle servers. You might measure these in terms of CPU and memory utilization on the servers, or perhaps by server input/output operations or similar technical details. Whichever metric you have selected, make a simple line graph showing the usage over the past 9 to 12 months. Using statistical analysis, you can now extend the graph to project future use of the existing Oracle servers and even to make a guess as to when a new server will be required. You should extend the graph by the number of months in your planning cycle for which you have portfolio data. For example, if you have just received the annual budget showing which projects have been funded for the next 12 months, extend your trend graph by 12 more months. The resulting graph will look something like what's shown in Figure 3.3.

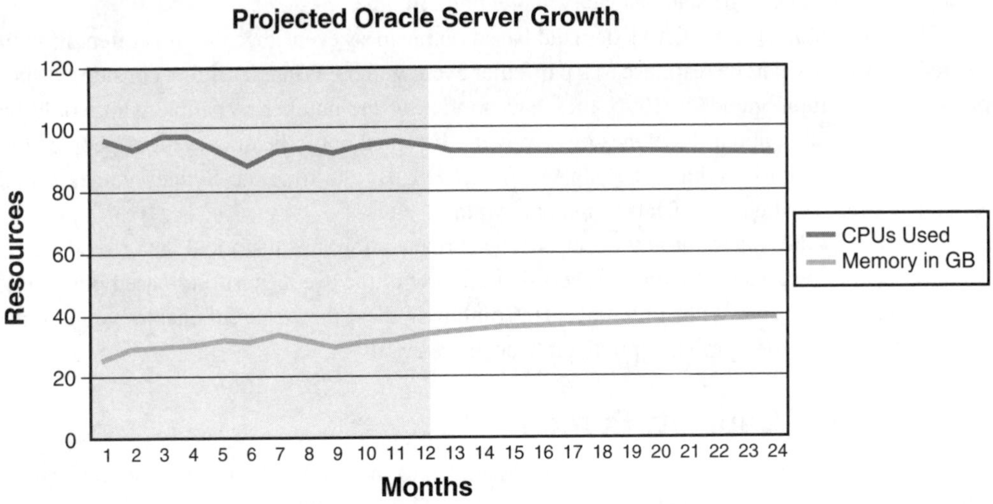

Figure 3.3 A trend line can forecast future capacity needs.

After you have projected growth, you can start to allocate each project. For each project that requires new Oracle databases, you need to estimate the resources that will be used. I typically just sort projects into large, medium, and small sizes, and then use the same estimate for each project of the same size. Add those estimated values to the projected trend line for the appropriate months, and you will end up with a capacity forecast that shows a smooth upward curve with stair-step increments for each new project.

For capacity forecasting with even more accuracy, you can blend the trend, portfolio, and business event forecasts in much the same way. After the project estimates are in place, estimate each known business event, and plot those on the same graph as additional stair steps. The result shows the complete picture that can be forecasted.

After the blended demand graph is in place, you need to manage it regularly. The slope of the trend forecast line may shift slightly as new data is gathered each month. The portfolio might become more clear as projects hit (and miss) their scheduled dates. New business events might become known. All these will impact your capacity forecast in predictable ways, and should drive you to update the capacity forecast.

If you build and maintain a capacity forecast as described here, you will find people coming to ask "what if"-type questions. By managing the forecast regularly, you can predict the impact of a proposed business event or IT project. You will gain a good feel for when new capacity needs to be acquired and which capacity pools are being drained too quickly. In short, you will be actively managing capacity rather than simply observing!

Of course, simple linear scaling is a bit simple for many environments. There are times when IT demand tends to arrive in clusters rather than in a linear fashion. If you start with these simple linear forecasting techniques, however, you will soon have the skills and maturity needed to adopt the forecasting mechanism to your industry and organization.

Using the Forecast for Cost Management

To make the forecasting exercise more real, this section provides an extended example of how an accurate capacity forecast can help manage IT costs.

Cost Avoidance Through Increased Utilization

An accurate forecast helps you increase the utilization of your existing resources. This works much like packing the car for a trip. If you bring the entire luggage set out to the car and know exactly what needs to fit, you have a much better chance of getting everything in. If you work piecemeal and just grab things one at a time, you may be struggling to fit the final pieces in.

Capacity planning works much this same way. Organizations that operate without adequate capacity forecasts tend to leave "headroom" in all their environments. People who have underestimated the need once tend to overestimate in the future. This leads to situations where hardware and software resources get significantly underutilized, resulting in purchases that aren't strictly necessary.

When an organization has a solid capacity forecast, however, they can see the difference between what they have and what they need. If that gap grows too small, an informed purchase decision can be made at the right time to augment capacity only when it is truly needed. The more accurate and more forward-looking your capacity forecast becomes, the more easily you can justify new acquisitions when they are truly necessary. Delaying purchases until then will save your organization money.

Cost Reduction Through Decommissioning and Recovery

Thus far we've put a very positive spin on capacity planning. The examples have talked about capacity growth and new purchases. But what if your trend is downward? An accurate capacity forecast is as important to a shrinking environment as it is to a growing one.

When you see a significant trend toward less utilization of your existing capacity, it might be time to institute a consolidation program. If you have four servers, but three could do the work, you can remove one server, saving on hardware maintenance, software maintenance, power, cooling, floor space, and server administration. Of course, these savings are offset by the costs of executing the consolidation, so you want to have an accurate capacity forecast so you know that you won't be consolidating now only to expand again later.

Each piece of IT capacity has an ongoing cost of ownership, and those costs can be reduced if the capacity is never needed. Larger organizations seem to have a more difficult time achieving these cost reductions. Most of the outsourcing customers I work with still purchase new software licenses for each new project they deploy. This is a horrendous waste of money because servers are being decommissioned as older applications are retired. Normally a software license remains usable as long as maintenance is paid on it. This means that the next project that requires DB2® can use the license recovered from the application that was sunset last month. Recovery of software licenses in this way requires the administrative tracking overhead, but it has saved over $40 million in one very large organization I've worked with!

Projecting and Tracking Cost Avoidance and Cost Reduction

If you've followed the advice earlier in this chapter, you will have a capacity forecast that looks like a timeline. The basic trend of utilization will be overlaid with project activities and business events to show when more (or less) capacity is needed.

This timeline can be turned into a budgeting forecast by translating the capacity needs into the money that must be spent to meet those needs or the money that can be saved by avoiding those needs. In other words, for each time that you have to acquire or discard capacity, you can make a cost estimate of that capacity and map it into the timeline of your forecast. The result will be a fairly accurate picture of the nonlabor cash flow through IT. That should definitely make your finance people happy. Good forecasting techniques allow you to not only identify what costs might be coming, but also allocate them to the appropriate organizational groups.

Summary and Next Steps

In this chapter you examined three separate techniques to forecast the amount of IT resources your organization will need in the future. The first technique simply relies on observing how many resources you've used in the past and assuming that your rate of consumption will stay rather steady. This can be surprisingly effective and generally requires very little extra effort on the part of the capacity management team. You learned that you can track component utilization, IT service utilization, and even business utilization using this simple trend-line approach.

A second way to predict future utilization is to look at the activities that your IT organization is planning for the future. These could be very large and visible projects such as implementation of a major new business application. On the other hand, you can also predict future utilization by looking at the day-to-day projects involved in upgrading operating systems, refreshing hardware, and maintaining your environment. Predictions based on planned IT activities have the advantage of being based in real anticipated work rather than an assumption that you will continue to do what you've always done.

Finally, you looked at business events as a way to predict future IT needs. While not nearly as specific as planned IT activities, it is quite often possible to predict growth in IT resource utilization by looking at the activities your whole organization will undertake.

You learned that the most accurate forecast will come from blending the various techniques. Using everything you know about what you've done before plus anything you can learn about IT and business projects, you should be able to assemble a very complete and accurate projection of your IT capacity needs. After you have this accurate forecast, there are a number of ways to use it to manage your upcoming IT costs.

The next chapter details how capacity grows within an organization and some of the ways you can manage this growth as the capacity planner.

CHAPTER 4

Dimensions of Capacity Growth

Thus far you have learned about capacity management in general (Chapter 1), the terminology used in managing capacity (Chapter 2), and the way to predict capacity needs (Chapter 3). In this chapter we turn to a deeper understanding of how capacity is consumed.

It might seem obvious that as the organization wants to do more, it requires more IT capacity. But that simple understanding isn't nearly enough to be an effective manager of capacity. We must think more deeply about the dimensions of growth to really understand how to manage that growth in an effective way. This chapter guides you in that thinking.

Grow the Base

A computer system fills up much more slowly than you might believe. The CPU might be 100% busy, or the memory might need to be swapped out to cache, but the system gladly keeps trying to execute instructions and even launch new programs. Those instructions and programs may take longer and longer to run, but the computer will still keep trying to accomplish more work.

This simple observation extends to other parts of the IT infrastructure as well. A router slows down, but it will not stop accepting network traffic because of its workload. A software application may be built to disallow extra users if the license count is exceeded, but if this protection isn't built in, it continues to let more users log on regardless of how busy it is.

Because of this characteristic of much of the IT infrastructure, capacity management is made more difficult. The base usage of the IT infrastructure can grow and the capacity manager must often track the growth without knowing what the absolute upper limit is. You must make informed decisions about how much workload each piece of the IT environment can handle. Those decisions should be based on the service-level agreements you have made with your user community.

This kind of growth that comes from incrementally adding more users, data, and transactions to the existing environment is known as base growth. The base of your computing environment is growing, and a significant piece of capacity management deals with managing this base growth.

Growth by Demand

Much of the base growth happens by increasing demands against the various capacity pools. More users, more transactions, more data, or some combination of these generally create a condition in which the infrastructure has to handle more work. This extra work might impact an entire IT service with multiple components, but it always manifests itself in one component at a time.

Consider an example in which an application runs in a data center in Minneapolis but serves users in Portsmouth in the U.K. As the organization grows, more users are added to the overall system, and the existing users exercise the functions of the application more frequently. This added work needs to be carried over the data network, so the LAN switches, WAN circuits, and routers that connect them all need to do more work. At the same time the servers supporting the application in the data center need to process more transactions and store more data than they did before. Those are the obvious dimensions of growth by demand.

But the growth is not normally detected at the level of a switch, router, or server. Instead, the tools detect the amount of free memory on the server, or the number of bytes flowing over the interface of a router. Even a simple statement that the server is busier needs to be broken down and analyzed in more detail. Is the server using more processing cycles? Perhaps it is using more memory. Maybe the server needs additional software licenses or extra storage space. These are all parts of the growth of just one component in the overall IT service that is the application.

Understanding an IT service, and even the components we track, at this level of detail is difficult work. You learn more about how to keep track when we consider the capacity management information system (Chapter 5, "Establish the Capacity Management Information System") and capacity plans (Chapter 6, "Define and Manage Capacity Plans"). Essentially, you need to bridge the gap between the level of detail collected by the tools you use and the level of detail that is useful in describing capacity to your management team. Tools tend to describe capacity in bits, milliseconds, and hertz, whereas managers like to think of capacity as people, computers, and money, and it is up to you as a capacity manager to bridge these differing levels of detail. Figure 4.1 illustrates this gap, which leads many people to believe that capacity management is more art than science.

Growth by Refresh

Although growth by increasing demand is the first area most people think of, there is another way that the base environment grows. This is by refreshing individual components.

Anyone who has been involved with IT for a while has come to realize that each new version of a software product requires more resources than the previous version. Although not always considered, a decision to move to the latest version of the web server or transaction processing software is a decision to use more resources on the servers. New features and new functions are compelling, and moving to the latest versions of software typically keeps support costs lower, but the capacity manager must be aware that additional resources will probably be required.

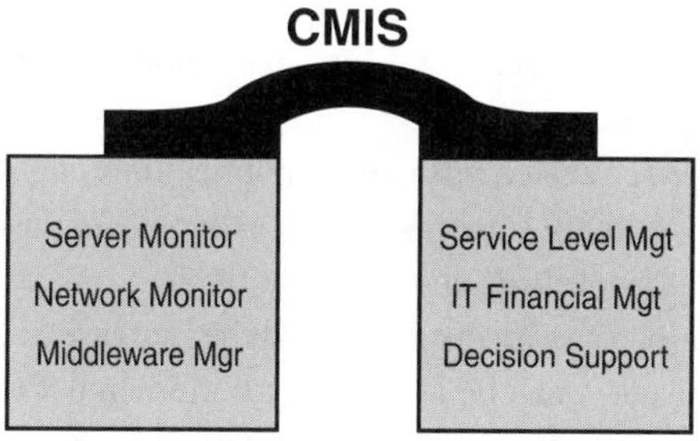

Figure 4.1 Tools cannot normally measure growth of components directly.

Interestingly, refresh of hardware does exactly the opposite. Because of Moore's Law, new hardware adds capacity to the overall environment in almost every case. It is very difficult to find an exact technical match for a server you are retiring, so most people substitute a server with a much greater ability to process information even if they are intending to do a one-for-one replacement. This juxtaposition of new software that requires additional resources and new hardware that provides more resources often makes the net outcome of a refresh project more difficult to predict.

Planning for a software refresh is particularly difficult because you cannot really measure how much additional capacity is necessary until the software is installed. Hopefully you have a test environment and process in which new software is hosted before being put into production, but even then you may have to work hard to get a scheduled time when you can really measure the resource usage on the server to compare to the usage before the new software was installed. In many organizations performance testing of new software is simply considered too expensive or too time-consuming and not performed. This leaves the capacity manager to rely on the software publisher's defined resource requirements and hope that the new package doesn't noticeably impact the production environment.

Often multiple components are refreshed as part of a release. Imagine a software application going to a new major version. The new version most likely has prerequisites such as upgrading the application server component and the database management system. In this case you have three new pieces of software that all increase the demand on computing resources. As a capacity manager, you should insist that performance testing be part of the overall release testing strategy. Whether that testing is done in-house, by the software vendor, or even by a third party, you should insist on having some performance numbers for every new software release.

Of course, capacity is also affected by hardware refresh. We make the assumption that obsolete hardware is always replaced with hardware that is faster, bigger, and better. What this really means is that the new component normally has a larger capacity than the one being replaced. From the perspective of a capacity manager, this greater capacity needs to be tracked because all the assumptions you might have been making about the capacity of an IT service using this component could now be false.

While a hardware refresh project might introduce more capacity in one part of an IT service, it does not necessarily increase the overall capacity of the entire service. Consider an IT service to provide an enterprise service bus that all applications can use to interoperate with one another. Refreshing the server that transmits messages would seem like a logical way to allow more messages to flow, thus increasing the capacity of the services. This would only be true, however, if the network bandwidth already supported the increase in message traffic through the server. Many very costly mistakes can be avoided if you remember to analyze the complete service before ordering hardware or software to add capacity where you think it might do the most good.

Grow the Business

Capacity management would be much easier if growth happened only in your existing base set of components and services. But we know that IT is a dynamic environment where new services are added, old services are retired, and existing services often add or lose components. We call this dimension "business growth" because it is largely determined by the business needs and priorities that your IT team is working with. This section describes how to track and manage IT capacity as you grow the business.

Project-Based Growth

Most IT organizations think growth happens as a result of projects. As the business identifies new needs, those needs get translated to IT project requests. When the projects are approved and implemented, they inevitably result in more IT demand. Some projects add capacity to meet their own demand, while others use existing capacity. Either way, the capacity manager must track the new capacity and the new demand.

Let's first consider a traditional project that implements a new business application. If this is a standard commercial application and not custom developed, the software publisher provides a description of the environment that should be deployed. Normally this includes a specific operating system type, the amount of CPU, memory and disk space required, and often the prerequisite versions of supporting software. The project team acquires exactly that configuration for production use and sometimes acquires a matching configuration for other uses such as test, training, and preproduction staging.

Assume that the application requires a Java™-based application server, a database, and a web server. The project team knows that this application will be heavily used, so they specify that each of these functions should be on a separate server. In an environment without adequate capacity management, each function of the application is placed on its own physical server with just the middleware that supports that function—the Java environment with the application on one server, the web pages and configuration files with the web server on a second machine, and the database with a database management system on a third machine. When you move to a second similar application, you need six separate servers, as shown in Figure 4.2.

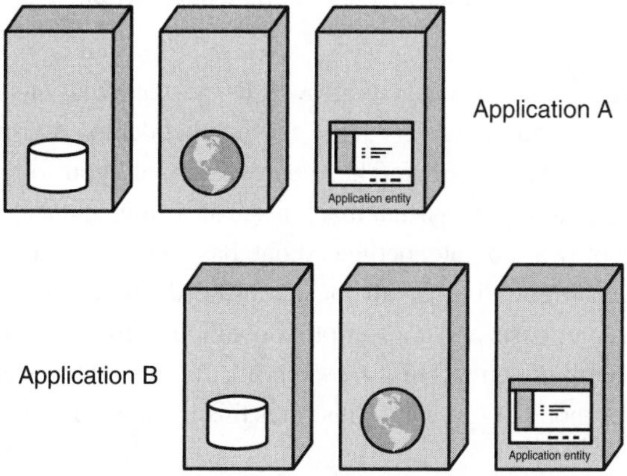

Figure 4.2 Traditional application deployment uses many servers.

If you see nothing wrong with this deployment method, capacity management will save your organization lots of money. With adequate capacity management you should quickly recognize that a single server can hold one licensed copy of the database management system and support dozens or even hundreds of individual databases that might be used by many different applications. Instead of using a separate database server for every application that requires one, you create a database server capacity pool that many applications can share. Of course, you'll want more memory and CPU power in your server than you would have assigned for a dedicated server, but even with more expensive hardware you will still save money over separate hardware and separate DBMS software for each application.

Of course, this same theory holds true for web servers and Java application servers. You can create and manage a single pool of capacity and then share that capacity with new applications as they are built. This is a much more cost-effective solution, but it depends on your ability to manage these capacity pools instead of relying on the vendors' advice for server sizes. If your organization hasn't already taken advantage of shared servers in this way, this alone can be a huge win for your capacity management program. Figure 4.3 shows how you can save three servers by sharing two different applications on the same set of database, web, and application servers.

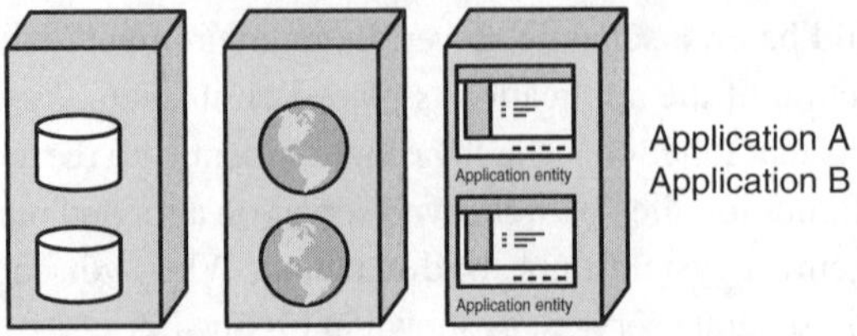

Figure 4.3 Shared deployment treats each server as a capacity pool.

An alternative way to provide capacity growth for new applications is by deploying virtual servers. In this scheme, you purchase very large servers and deploy a virtualization engine such as Microsoft Hyper-V or VMware ESX. These engines enable you to host dozens of separate operating system images, known as "virtual machines," on a single physical server. Using virtualization, you can still deploy a separate, dedicated database, web, and application server for each new application. The difference is that all these can be deployed on one piece of hardware, greatly reducing data center costs and consumption over either the dedicated server or the shared server approach and enabling you to build new servers dramatically faster than if you were following a physical server model. Figure 4.4 illustrates this approach for two applications.

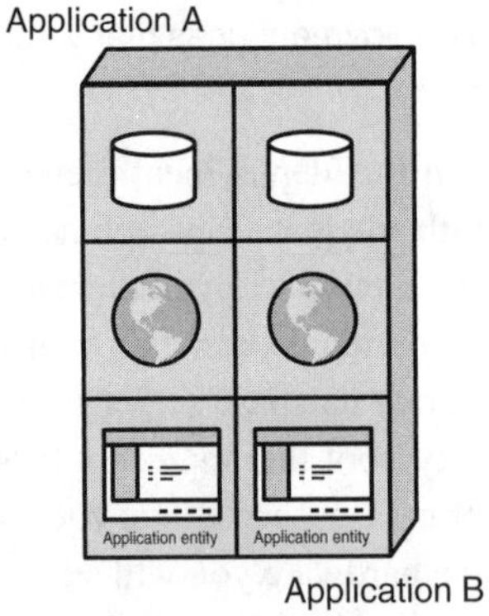

Figure 4.4 Virtualization greatly reduces the number of servers needed.

Virtualization gives you, as a capacity manager, a completely different set of capacity pools to manage. Each physical server becomes a pool of CPU and a pool of memory, and you allocate resources from these pools each time a new virtual machine is needed. When all the physical CPU and memory on the server reaches a high utilization rate, another server is added and the capacity pools have more space in them.

Service-Based Growth

When your organization gets more mature in its journey toward IT service management, you will begin to realize that growth happens in the context of services. New services are introduced that require completely new infrastructure components or place additional demands on existing components. A service change such as increasing the availability may dictate that new components are added to the mix. Even a service retirement might generate a temporary need for more capacity as data is archived or transition activities take place. As a service-oriented IT organization, you must plan for the capacity changes that service transitions produce.

You will understand and document the growth of a service only if you have a complete understanding of the components that make up the service. As discussed in Chapter 2, "The Geography of Managing Capacity," this is the base for all service capacity management. Assuming that you do have this understanding, tracking service growth is a simple matter of following the same formula you use for calculating service capacity utilization in the first place.

Service growth is more difficult to project into the future as services become more complex. Additional components that make up the service become additional variables that might change the growth projections. This doesn't mean you shouldn't try, however. When you first begin to track service capacity and use trends to project service growth, you may not be very accurate, but you will be acquiring important skills. As your capacity management maturity and skill increase, your forecasts will include trends and known future changes to the service and will become more accurate.

Over time you will observe the ways that your services grow. When you record these observations, you will be able to develop better procedures for tracking service capacity.

Summary and Next Steps

This chapter takes the optimistic view that your organization is growing, and describes how to measure and manage the corresponding growth of your IT environment. In many cases your IT environment may be growing even if the overall organization is not. Tracking and managing IT growth is an important role for the capacity manager.

You first learned about base growth—the natural growth that happens as your IT systems are used and as they evolve to newer versions. You learned that the capacity manager is responsible for setting the upper limit for system growth because in many cases the computer systems and software don't do that for themselves. You also learned that there is a gap between the way that tools report this growth and the way it should be displayed for management consumption. It is up to the capacity manager to bridge that gap.

You next looked at how business growth can impact IT capacity growth. You saw that the business can be expanding in one of two ways. It can provide new goods or services to its customers, which will generally grow revenue and probably expenses as well. When this growth occurs, there is almost always a resulting growth in IT utilization, which may involve growing the infrastructure. The other way that business can grow is by implementing internal projects to cut costs, enhance security, optimize compliance with industry regulations, or make the business more sound in other ways. These projects may or may not increase the demand on IT, and consolidation projects often reduce the IT demand. The savvy capacity manager needs to understand how the business is growing and be ready to respond with the best possible information to help the business make decisions.

The first four chapters have introduced you to the key concepts of capacity management. We've set the context of capacity management against the ITIL framework, and you've learned how capacity management must interact with other ITIL process disciplines to be successful. You looked at capacity pools and capacity streams as a metaphor for what ITIL calls "component" capacity management and "service" capacity management. You've learned how to make predictions about future IT demand, and in this chapter you've begun to think about the ways that growth impacts your capacity management program. Now that you have a firm foundation, you can explore the best practices in capacity management as defined by the ITIL process.

In the next chapter you look at the first of those best practices—the capacity management information system (CMIS). You'll learn why you need a CMIS and how to manage it. You will explore the CMIS in a way that doesn't depend on any single tool or implementation approach, and then we circle back around to the best tools in Chapter 10, "Choose Capacity Management Tools."

PART II

Best Practices in Capacity Management

In Part I, you learned the general concepts about managing IT capacity. In this second part of the book, you learn the specific details needed to begin actively managing capacity for your organization. The chapters in this part delve into the details that are mentioned as best practices in the ITIL documents. By pulling from these best practices, you should have a solid base to implement your very own capacity management program.

CHAPTER 5

Establish the Capacity Management Information System

Effective capacity management depends on accurate capacity information. The ITIL library recognizes the importance of a specific system to deal with capacity information and calls that system the capacity management information system (CMIS). Although the name isn't very imaginative, the concept itself is quite an innovation for most organizations. The idea of storing disparate capacity management data in a single system seems obvious, but it isn't an easy one to implement. This chapter describes the CMIS and teaches you how to implement one for your organization.

Purpose of the Capacity Management Information System

Before launching any new IT application, you should define a solid set of requirements. If the need is not obvious from the requirements, don't build the system. For a capacity management information system, the need is very compelling. In this section, we investigate some of the more common requirements for the CMIS. Most likely you will add some of your own to the list presented here to establish a firm base for your implementation project. Figure 5.1 depicts the three key reasons to implement the CMIS as they are described in this section.

Repository of Capacity Information

Fundamentally, the CMIS is a place to store capacity information. Although this fact is obvious, it is also very important. Most IT organizations today have multiple places to store capacity information, and no single place to look for data when it is needed. As a single repository, the CMIS provides a single source that can satisfy all the capacity questions that are likely to be asked. Having a single source makes it far more likely that capacity questions will be answered quickly and correctly.

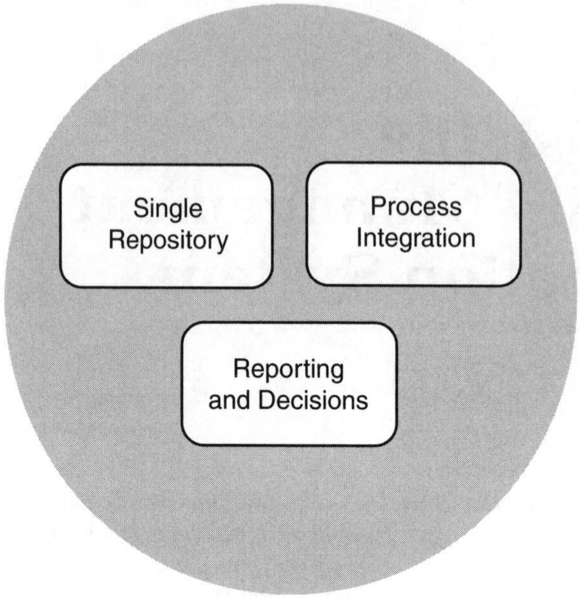

Figure 5.1 There are three primary reasons to implement the capacity management information system.

The capacity management information system is much like the configuration management system (CMS). Both are likely to be federated out of a mixture of various data sources. Although configuration management makes use of inventory systems, source code control systems, and even personnel systems, the capacity management information system is likely to be made up of data from a wide variety of capacity and performance monitoring tools along with data that is entered directly by capacity analysts. In both cases, the system pulls together data that would otherwise be scattered and difficult to locate.

The capacity management information system and the configuration management system are both vital to an effective service management program, and will be most effective if the two work together to provide a complete picture. The CMS stores the information about what elements make up the IT environment, where they are located, and how they work together both physically and logically. The CMIS adds an understanding of how heavily those elements are utilized and how they are performing. When they're used together, your organization can make a very wide range of decisions using the information from the CMS and the CMIS.

Interface to Integrated Service Management

A capacity management information system makes integrated service management much more feasible. Organizations with multiple sources for capacity data find it difficult and expensive to build and maintain integrations between each of them and a common incident management system or configuration management system. With a single CMIS, only one interface needs to be created and maintained, leading to a much less expensive integrated tool set for all of your ITIL-based process disciplines.

Tool integration is important, but even more important is information integration. If your organization is trying to maintain capacity management information in multiple separate systems, you will undoubtedly have different schemas for each of those systems. It might be that one system tracks the disk usage of Unix® systems as available bytes, another system tracks the usage of mainframe disks as the number of total blocks free, and a third system tracks disk usage of Windows servers using a percentage of the disk that is full. This is just one example. As you look at the various ways you measure capacity in your environment, you will find dozens of different units of measurement that need to be reconciled.

Even if the units are measured the same way, there is often a need to reconcile the meaning of those units. For example, saying that a Windows server with a dual core processor is running at 18% CPU utilization is not the same as saying that a mainframe with a 64 core CPU is running at 18%. Two tools that report the same unit of measure (CPU %) may confuse people who use the data. Without a CMIS, every time you need to create a report using data from multiple systems, you will face a huge integration task. It makes much more sense to integrate the data from these systems one time when defining a single CMIS.

In addition to integrating capacity management data, the CMIS should be able to interface with other key service management tools. An integrated capacity management information system should use configuration identifiers from the configuration management system so that each piece of hardware is identified uniquely and consistently. The CMIS should be integrated with the change management tool so that it can be understood when an implemented change impacts capacity or utilization in the environment. Incident management should also be integrated with the CMIS so that any service disruptions due to capacity shortages can automatically be linked to the correct capacity plans in the CMIS. All these integrations help you to mature not only your capacity management service but your other service management disciplines as well.

With service management, the whole really is greater than the sum of its parts. As you implement a strong, centralized capacity management information system, you will find many other ways it helps other process areas. Financial management becomes much easier because you can use the CMIS to predict the need for future spending. Service-level management is enhanced because you can use capacity information to avoid long-term service disruptions. Even service continuity is enhanced with a high-quality capacity management information system because you can clearly define how much capacity you will need and where it will be available in any kind of disaster-recovery scenario. Some of these benefits may not be apparent immediately, especially if you have not fully implemented these related process disciplines. Over time, you will find that the capacity management information system will become an essential link in your integrated service management tool set.

Reporting and Decision Making

As an information system, the CMIS is useful for making informed decisions. You will undoubtedly want to define a full set of reports that get produced regularly. In addition, you need the capability to query capacity information as needed to answer questions from your business units, project teams, and IT managers. The capacity management information system should be built with these demands in mind.

The most fundamental capacity reports highlight areas where demand soon exceeds available capacity. Typically, this is an exception report that shows only components and services that are in danger of running short of capacity. The report should be reviewed regularly by IT management and action taken to ensure that capacity does not run out. The thousands of components or hundreds of services that have spare capacity are not shown on this standard report.

Another common report is the trending report, which shows components or services that are experiencing significant changes in their utilization. This report helps to highlight areas that need to be watched for the future. For example, if the average bandwidth consumed on a wide area network line has been around 10% for months, it may jump to 15% one month and 30% the next month. Even though it is not running out of capacity yet, such an unusual increase would bear watching. Typically, the capacity management team would use this report to investigate the anomaly in the trend data and raise any issues found to IT management.

Your goal in implementing reporting from the CMIS is to anticipate the decisions that need to be made and provide information that makes those decisions easier. Chapter 11, "Produce Capacity Reports," describes capacity management reporting in much more detail, and gives you a solid base from which to derive your own reporting needs.

Contents of the Capacity Management Information System

As you begin to implement capacity management within your organization, there will probably be very high expectations for the capacity management information system. To meet these expectations, you need to populate the CMIS with data that meet the needs of all of your stakeholders. Although the *ITIL Service Design* book describes the CMIS at a very high level, there has been very little detail about what a capacity management information system should contain. This section seeks to close that gap by defining the details of a typical CMIS in such a way that you can evaluate tools and implement the system for your organization.

Much of what you can implement in your CMIS depends on the tools you choose. This section focuses on the concepts to be included in the CMIS, and Chapter 10, "Choose Capacity Management Tools," describes how to choose the best tools to implement these concepts.

Utilization Data

The bulk of data in the capacity management information system tracks the utilization of various components and services. Normally, each component in the environment has some tool that tracks its utilization regularly. These tools capture data periodically, and often average it before putting it into the CMIS. For example, you might be using Microsoft System Center Operations Manager (SCOM) to monitor CPU utilization on a set of Windows servers. SCOM can be configured to gather data every seven minutes for each server. That data can be directly stored in the CMIS, or SCOM can average the data to provide an hourly average that can be stored.

The granularity of the data you choose to store in the CMIS depends on your reporting needs. If you want to spot long-term trends and use the CMIS to make decisions about when to acquire more capacity, you will most likely want high-level averages. If you want to understand the daily cycle of usage of your resources, you will want to keep detailed data for at least a few days. Many organizations find that detailed data is best stored in the data collection tools themselves (SCOM in our example) while longer-term averages are stored in the CMIS. This allows for both kinds of reporting when it is needed.

If you have a lot of virtual servers in your environment, the amount of data stored in the CMIS might become very large. You will want to store information about the physical server resources as well as each virtual server that shares the physical resources. In the past many tools had difficulty working at both the physical and the virtual layers within the same environment, but today most capacity tracking tools are able to understand the workings of the virtualization engines to provide both kinds of data.

One of the challenges in storing utilization data is the wide variety of units that are used. Network devices might report in bits per second, packets per minute, or frames per second. Memory might be reported as bytes used or percentage of available memory. Disk space can be reported in blocks or bytes. Even similar systems such as HP/UX servers and Linux® servers might report very similar metrics using different units. You should let your reporting needs be your guide once again. If you need a summarized report of all network devices, you have no choice but to reconcile the units to create the report. If you never need to report them together, however, you can store the different units separately and not worry about the differences.

Another great challenge in building and maintaining the capacity management information system is information overload. Even in a moderately complex organization, you can easily accumulate hundreds of thousands of data points very quickly. Storing just average utilization data can help to some extent, but there will still be many entries. The best approach to handling data overload is to make sure you have a tool set that is capable of handling the expected volumes. If reports take too long to generate or new data uploads are too complex, the overall value of the CMIS is diminished. You learn more about capacity management tools in Chapter 10.

Although there are many excellent tools for capturing and storing utilization data for IT components, there are almost none that accomplish the job for IT services. As described in Chapter 2, "The Geography of Managing Capacity," the capacity of a service is an aggregate of the capacity of the various components used by the service. If you can define a mathematical formula to support this aggregating of component data, you can have the CMIS directly calculate utilization data for your IT services. Where there isn't a mathematical formula, however, you will most likely need to have the capacity management team enter utilization data for services from whatever sources they have available. This can be a very time-consuming and expensive operation.

Over time, you should try to define formulas to calculate the utilization for all the IT services you want to track.

As an example of a service capacity formula, consider a simple web hosting service. To host a departmental website, IT uses a disk storage component (*d*), and a web server component that is made up of memory utilization (*m*) and CPU utilization (*c*). Because each distinct website is a separate directory on a web server, it is easy to calculate how many websites are being hosted at any time. Call this number *w*. So each website uses *d/w* disk space, *m/w* memory, and *c/w* of the processing unit. To define the total utilization of the website hosting service, we can use *d, m,* and *c* directly (assuming that no other services use this set of web servers). This enables us to understand the utilization of the web hosting service, and as new websites are proposed we can determine whether they "fit" or whether we need to add more servers to increase the capacity of the service.

Capacity Data

Although the majority of the data in the CMIS is utilization data, that data will not be very useful if we don't also store capacity data. Remember that it is the difference between the capacity and the current utilization that determines whether we need to add more resources. So if you have utilization data but no capacity indicator, you will not be able to make very many decisions.

Capacity data is typically stored as the maximum capacity that a component or service can support. This may be expressed in absolute units such as gigabytes or frames per second, or it may be expressed as a percentage. Typically, percentages are used in situations in which there may not be an absolute maximum capacity. The percentage indicates the maximum theoretical limit up to which your organization believes that the resource can be used. For example, you might establish a policy which says that any network circuit that is over 75% utilization for more than ten minutes is out of capacity. Seventy-five percent is then your capacity maximum, even though the circuit could run at 80% or even 100% utilization for short bursts. Many times you can get these theoretical limits from the manufacturer or provider of the IT component, so you don't need to make the estimate yourself.

Along with capacity amounts, the CMIS should also store thresholds for each capacity pool. These thresholds provide warning levels that can be used to alert your operations team when utilization is getting close to the maximums. Most organizations use two thresholds for each capacity pool. The first threshold indicates that an investigation should take place to determine whether the situation will become permanent or is a temporary condition. This will typically raise a yellow or moderate-level alert, and a capacity manager will be assigned to investigate the situation. The second threshold indicates that immediate action is required to avoid a situation in which capacity shortfalls might cause a service disruption. This second threshold should be linked to an automated notification mechanism so that action can take place quickly when it is breached. Some organizations choose a third threshold between these two so that they can do a more urgent investigation and avoid reaching the panic stage.

Whatever set of thresholds you choose to establish should be stored in the capacity management information system because they provide yet another data point to help people make sound capacity decisions. Another reason to store thresholds is to allow your CMIS to support dashboards or other reports that indicate the thresholds.

Table 5.1 shows a sample from a typical capacity management information system. This example shows all the information described thus far for each of the components and services listed in the table. The example gives you a very simplified idea of the volume of data that is likely to be needed in the CMIS. There are multiple rows for each significant piece of the IT infrastructure, and multiple rows for each IT service being tracked. Of course, the threshold values and capacity values will not change for every utilization sample and would not necessarily need to be repeated with each row of data.

Table 5.1 Sample Data from a Capacity Management Information System

Capacity Pool	Date/Time	Units	Utilization	Yellow	Red	Capacity
appsrv1 CPU	04/21/2010 07:30:15	%	18	75	90	100
appsrv1 RAM	04/21/2010 07:30:15	MB	3122	7700	8000	8192
appsrv1 Disk	04/21/2010 07:30:15	MB	57422	65000	78000	80000
appsrv1 CPU	04/21/2010 07:30:30	%	14	75	90	100
appsrv1 RAM	04/21/2010 07:30:30	MB	3148	7700	8000	8192
appsrv1 Disk	04/21/2010 07:30:30	MB	57423	65000	78000	80000
appsrv2 CPU	04/21/2010 07:30:15	%	18	75	90	100
appsrv2 RAM	04/21/2010 07:30:15	MB	3122	7700	8000	8192
appsrv2 Disk	04/21/2010 07:30:15	MB	57422	65000	78000	80000
appsrv2 CPU	04/21/2010 07:30:30	%	14	75	90	100
appsrv2 RAM	04/21/2010 07:30:30	MB	3148	7700	8000	8192
appsrv2 Disk	04/21/2010 07:30:30	MB	57423	65000	78000	80000

Capturing service capacity is every bit as difficult as capturing service utilization. You will normally need to define the total capacity of a service by policy rather than by having any physical maximum that a service can sustain. Consider, for example, the problem management service that IT performs. There is probably no real maximum number of problems that can be worked simultaneously, although trying to work too many at the same time degrades the quality of work on each of them. Most IT services have no maximum capacity, so you need to determine a capacity that you want to define as the maximum for your organization. Typically, this is done with the assistance of your application architects or enterprise architecture team.

Now is as a good time for a brief discussion of the linkage between the capacity management information system and the configuration management system. You'll note in Table 5.1 that the capacity pools look suspiciously like server names. You will probably also have rows for things like SAN arrays, network switches, application software, and WAN circuits. In fact, many of the things that you track as configuration items in the CMS become capacity pools in the CMIS. The configuration management service is responsible for identifying and tracking each of these things, so the capacity management information system should simply use the same identifiers that are already present in your CMS. This will help you avoid duplicate or conflicting naming schemes, and will help your organization understand which components are being discussed as you present capacity data.

Your data architect plays a very important role in this regard. She or he should have a good understanding of the data in both the CMIS and the CMS and should be able to suggest specific ways to link these data elements together.

Of course, there may be times when a capacity pool consists of a group of individual CIs, such as all the servers in a VMware cluster. It really doesn't matter which particular host a new virtual machine is located on, so the entire cluster can be treated as a single pool of capacity for hosting virtual machines. If you haven't already identified the whole cluster as a composite configuration item, I would urge you to consider it. This enables you to treat it as a single entity across your entire integrated service management process set. Many organizations shy away from creating composite configuration items because they believe that they are difficult to track, but experience shows that failing to identify composite CIs simply wastes effort in other process areas. So if you find a capacity pool that doesn't correspond to an existing configuration item, consider creating the configuration item rather than having capacity pools that don't link to your CMS.

Capacity Plans

The final pieces of content for the configuration management information system are the capacity plans. You learn all about capacity plans in Chapter 6, "Define and Manage Capacity Plans," but for now you simply need to know that they are unstructured text documents. They do not fit neatly into rows and columns like utilization data and capacity data, but your capacity management information system should still find some way to store them because they provide valuable information about your strategy for adding capacity and for dealing with unexpected capacity shortages. Linking the capacity plans to the capacity management information system ensures that everyone in your organization can locate them when they are needed the most.

You will not typically be able to report on the contents of capacity plans directly from the CMIS, but having them available as you work on capacity issues is invaluable.

First Steps to Implementation

Now that you understand the contents of the CMIS, it is time to consider how to actually put those contents in place. The steps are straightforward and follow the pattern used to implement many IT initiatives. This section briefly describes the steps needed to get your capacity management information system off the ground.

I have seen many attempts at implementing a Capacity Management Information System. The attempts that have failed generally start out with the notion that capacity management is an operational problem so the operations team should find some spare time to implement a CMIS along with the many other things they do. If you have that opinion, read this section carefully. It would be a rare operations team that has the time to properly take all the steps described here. The message is that you should treat implementation of the CMIS as an IT project with a full life cycle and not as a spare bit of work for operations.

Define Requirements

As with most IT efforts, it is important to understand requirements before you begin to implement. Although the general requirements for the capacity management information system are similar for every organization, you should clarify the needs of your organization before you begin to populate the CMIS.

The requirement list normally begins with reporting in mind. If you survey the various stakeholders who want to make decisions using CMIS data, you can form a list of reports that are needed. Break this list into specific data elements, and then determine how best to capture each of the needed pieces of data. Working through this exercise provides a solid list of data requirements for the CMIS.

The second-most-common way to derive CMIS requirements is by thinking through the various groups that have to use the system. Talk to the capacity managers and document what they need the system to do. Work with the people who do your IT purchasing to understand how the CMIS can make their jobs easier. Interview the IT managers who will use the system only occasionally, and understand how to make it easy for them to get the data they need. All this information can go into your requirements list.

After you have gathered the requirements, you should review them with a wide audience. Help everyone catch a vision of what the CMIS will be, and you will have much broader sponsorship for the implementation effort. Prioritize the requirements into those that must be met, those that would be nice to meet, and those that are strictly optional, and get concurrence on those priorities. When everyone has a clear understanding of the desired finished product, there should be fewer missed expectations at the end.

Because implementation of the CMIS is a complex project, you will most likely want to group your requirements into a set of distinct project phases. Normally, projects that attempt to accomplish all requirements at the same time lack direction and stretch out far too long. Instead, implement the CMIS in short phases so the outcome of each phase represents real value to the business. It is better to have a very solid grasp of the capacity of your mainframe after 3 months of effort than to wait 18 months and hope that you can get a firm grasp on all capacity pools at the same time.

Select Tools

After the requirements are well understood, the next order of business is to select the tools you will use as the foundation of the capacity management information system. Tool selection should be based on the requirements rather than the quality of the marketing materials you see. It is easy to be impressed with professional tool demonstrations and the long lists of features and functions that marketing people can produce, but the real measure of value is the degree to which those functions will be used in your organization.

Chapter 10 describes the various capabilities you are likely to find in the marketplace, but as a quick preview, here are some key aspects to consider as you select a base CMIS tool:

- Extensible database schema
- Prebuilt integration with your existing tools
- Good differentiation of roles for users
- Works with your standard operating systems, databases, and middleware

Choose the tool set that has the best combination of these functions, and you are off to a solid start in building the CMIS.

Gather Data

After you have solidified your requirements and selected the tool you'll use to maintain capacity information, it is time to start gathering that information. The difficult part is not finding information but organizing it. Use the concepts of capacity pools and capacity streams from Chapter 2 to define the sources of data. For each capacity pool, you should determine how frequently you will measure utilization, what thresholds you will use for alerting, and what the maximum capacity of that pool will be. Likewise for each capacity stream, or IT service; define the same things.

Most organizations already have a variety of tools in place for gathering capacity information. These tools are often part of operating systems or included with hardware purchases. They typically have names related to monitoring or performance management. Whatever these tools are in your organization, you should understand what data they are capable of collecting and how they store that data. For each tool that is gathering important utilization data, you should plan an interface to automatically pull that data into your capacity management information system.

Gathering utilization data from automated systems is the fundamental part of every CMIS, but as you learned earlier, utilization data alone is not sufficient. You need to understand how threshold information and capacity information will be gathered for each of your components and services. In many cases, threshold and capacity data is gathered manually using a spreadsheet or similar tool, and then entered by hand into the CMIS. If this is your situation, be sure that the spreadsheet template is complete before the data is gathered so that you won't have to go through the exercise a second time to make up any gaps.

For most organizations the most difficult part of gathering data is collecting or creating capacity plans. If you already have capacity plans in place, you should certainly gather them into the CMIS. If you don't have capacity plans created yet, you can start the CMIS without them and simply add them as they get defined and documented.

Implement Processes

Data that is gathered without good process discipline quickly grows stale. At the same time that you are gathering data, you should begin to implement the capacity management processes, which ensures that the data stays accurate. Chapter 8, "Implement the Capacity Management Process," is dedicated to capacity management processes, so this section just provides a quick overview.

The key process areas for capacity management involve gathering accurate data and then using that data to make decisions. For each capacity pool and capacity stream, you should define the threshold values, and you should have a good process for reviewing those thresholds frequently. As your ability to create capacity plans matures, you will refine the threshold values to be more precise, so you need a procedure to update these values.

Another important decision that should be assisted by your capacity management process work is the acquisition of new capacity. Most organizations determine a specific difference between available capacity and used capacity at which they will choose to start the purchasing cycle to add more capacity. Of course, that point may change based on the financial position of your organization, but you should at least have a process in place that ensures you will make an informed decision before capacity runs out.

Process measurements are an important part of the overall process implementation. You should define and implement measurements that help you assess the health of the capacity management service. Sample measurements are provided in Chapter 8.

Train Staff

Regardless of how clear your requirements, how solid your tools, how accurate your data, and how detailed your process, the capacity management information system will not be successful without trained people to manage it. This is where many organizations mistakenly decide to cut corners. The training plan should include all roles involved in capacity management, including those who are gathering data, those who are making capacity plans, those who are analyzing data, and those who are responsible for generating measurements.

Training should be based on the processes and procedures that have been defined and should include training on how to execute those processes using the tool that has been implemented. Training on the tool alone will be too detailed and leave people with an idea of features and functions but unable to actually perform the needed work. Training on the process alone will help people know how to do their jobs but will leave them frustrated and lacking support. The best training combines the process and the tools.

Using the Capacity Management Information System

At this point you should have a good understanding of how to implement a capacity management information system. But after you've implemented, how do you make sure to get the best value out of the system? In this section, we dig a bit deeper into the various ways your organization can use the CMIS to achieve your capacity management goals.

Forecasting Capacity Needs

The primary use of the CMIS is prediction. Because the system holds the possible capacity and the used capacity for each component and service, you can see the trends and determine with reasonable accuracy when you run out of capacity. This technique is described in Chapter 3, "Understanding Capacity Demand."

Beyond individual components and services, however, you can use the capacity management information system to predict overall capacity needs. This is especially useful in managing an annual budgeting process. If you know, for example, that your organization typically grows by seven or eight servers per year, you have a very strong justification to put those servers into the annual budget. If you don't have the historical data to back up your growth rate, the accuracy of your budget forecast is likely to be much lower.

Making Capacity Decisions

The capacity management information system is useful even when you have plenty of capacity. In fact, the most important reason to manage your IT capacity closely is so you won't purchase more than you need. Although thresholds that warn you when capacity is running out are important, those thresholds that tell you when resources are significantly underutilized will provide more benefit. You should regularly use the CMIS to find and address situations where you have much more capacity than you need.

Reducing the overall footprint of IT makes you very popular. Virtualization and consolidation projects provide a very good return on the money spent, and almost always get funded. They also reduce the demand for energy and physical space in your data center, and require fewer resources that eventually land in a scrap heap. With an accurate CMIS available you will be able to identify and launch these projects with good assurance that the consolidation of today won't hamper the business expansion of tomorrow.

Integrating Service Management

Finally, you can use the capacity management information system to tie together other ITIL process disciplines. We've explored the links between capacity management and configuration management already, but the CMIS enables other links as well. Consider linking your release management tools to the CMIS so that you can better predict the capacity that will be consumed as new releases are deployed. You might want to relate your CMIS to your service continuity plans to enable "spare" capacity to be used in the event of a disaster. You can certainly link the CMIS to your IT financial management systems to help track the cost and timing of major new capacity acquisitions.

As your knowledge of ITIL grows and your comfort with the reliability of the capacity management information system grows as well, you will find dozens of ways you can use this single source of all capacity knowledge to link the various processes. We explore some of these ways in Chapter 15, "Integrating Capacity Planning with IT Processes."

Summary and Next Steps

The capacity management information system is a vital tool for understanding how much IT capacity is available to your organization and where you may need more. Inexplicably, many organizations do not yet have such a system implemented. In this chapter you learned not only what a CMIS can be, but also how to implement one.

At the beginning of the chapter, you learned that the purpose of the CMIS is to store all capacity-related data in one repository so that it can be integrated with other service management disciplines and so that you can produce capacity-related reports from an authoritative source. Next you learned that the CMIS stores data on the utilization and capacity of your IT components and services, but that it also stores your capacity plans.

The middle part of the chapter described how to implement a capacity management information system using a very typical IT project development life cycle. You learned that the CMIS must be treated as a high-priority IT project and not just as staff work assigned to the operations team to handle.

This chapter concluded with some of the more obvious uses for the CMIS. Over time, you will find more uses, but initially you will use the CMIS to forecast capacity needs, make capacity decisions, and integrate capacity management with your other ITIL processes.

It is almost impossible to discuss the capacity management information system without touching on capacity plans. This chapter introduced the basic idea, but the next chapter dives into the details of what makes an effective capacity plan and how you can build capacity plans for your organization.

CHAPTER 6

Define and Manage Capacity Plans

One of the key pieces of information that should be stored in your capacity management information system is the capacity plan. The ITIL Service Design *book offers a great high-level look at the contents of a capacity plan. It assumes, however, that you will create a colossal document that includes all the capacity details for all your services and components. Then the book goes on to say you should take the time to create an executive summary because the main document will be so large that very few will actually read it!*

This chapter goes beyond the ITIL documentation to describe a working formula for capacity plans. It suggests that you create more customized plans for those areas that really need detailed plans and keep them current through a repeatable process. You will learn the details of what goes into a capacity plan and how and when to create your plans.

Scope of a Capacity Plan

As the name implies, a capacity plan is a plan for how to manage the capacity of a specific IT service. Although you could attempt to create a single plan that defines the current and future capacity needs for every IT service you manage, it would soon break down into a series of individual chapters by service. So why not create an individually managed plan for each service from the outset? The scope of each plan is thus the service that is defined in that particular plan document.

Service Capacity Plans

Throughout the preceding chapters, we've been using the geography analogy from Chapter 2, "The Geography of Managing Capacity," to describe the two types of resources for which you must manage capacity—IT components and IT services. You've seen examples of both, but now it is time for a more specific definition of an IT service. The ITIL framework describes an environment in which your IT organization creates an overall strategy and then designs, implements, and manages a set of services that you offer to the wider organization you serve. IT services offer specific business value to help your organization achieve its goals. Each service has a definition, one or more quality measures called service levels, and potentially a cost to those who receive the service.

Using this definition, the reason for capacity plans based on IT services becomes clear. If IT were a separate company, your IT services would be the way you made money. Running out of capacity to continue a service would restrict your ability to generate more revenue. So clearly you will want to have a concrete, actionable plan to ensure that your IT services do not run out of capacity. If you have no more service to offer, why should IT need to continue to exist?

You know you need to create capacity plans for your IT services, but how do you put some boundaries around what a service entails? A typical IT service blends hardware, software, data, and labor effort in a unique way to deliver the service that the organization needs. For example, consider an IT service that sets up a new workstation when an employee joins the organization. You either purchase a new workstation each time or have some workstations on hand, so that is one capacity pool. Each workstation requires several software licenses for an operating system, an office product, and maybe other applications, and those licenses can represent additional capacity pools to be managed. But to complete the service, you also need technicians who can unpack the hardware, install the software, and deliver the package to the new user. The overall service can get quite complicated, so knowing where to draw the boundary of the service capacity plan can be difficult.

As a rule of thumb, you probably want to exclude labor components and focus on the hardware and software pieces that make up your service. Labor capacity is the domain of your human resources team and not really the subject of IT capacity management until you have a very mature capacity management program and a very good relationship with your HR team. After you have identified the most important hardware and software components, you need to define the relationships between them in a way that helps you understand the capacity of the service. These relationships should already be available as part of your configuration management system. Stop when you get to components that are really not integral to providing the service you are considering.

Of course, many of your IT services are delivered using shared components. A single server might be part of multiple different IT services, and network components are likely to be part of almost every service you deliver. If you have a way to allocate the capacity of a shared component to the different IT services it provides, then you can include these shared components along with the IT service. Otherwise, you need to create capacity plans for shared components separately from the plans for your IT services.

Component Capacity Plans

If you create capacity plans for each of your IT services, you will have most of your components already covered. So why would you define component-based capacity plans? These plans are needed only when you have components that do not participate directly in any specific IT service or for those areas where a component is shared among many or all of your IT services. In Chapter 5, "Establish the Capacity Management Information System," for example, you learned about the capacity management information system. Although capacity management, incident management, change management, and other IT service management systems are vital to IT, they are not directly related to any specific IT service that you offer to the wider organization. Because these systems are shared across all IT services, you should define a specific component-based capacity plan for them separate from your IT service capacity plans.

The scope of a component capacity plan is only slightly different than the scope of a service capacity plan. A component plan is more narrow because it needs to consider only a single capacity pool, or for a complex component perhaps two or three pools. Because of this more narrow focus, a component capacity plan is also more specific. Many times the utilization and total capacity information come directly from measurements done by automated tools, so the predictions in the plan of when capacity runs out can be much more precise than those of service capacity plans. In general, component capacity plans tend to be more technical and detailed than service capacity plans.

Sometimes it makes sense to link component capacity plans to IT service capacity plans. If a component is shared only between three or four different services, you might want to mention those services in the component capacity plan. It helps when reading the plan to understand that the capacity defined in the component plan is being allocated to a specific set of IT services.

Table 6.1 compares and contrasts IT service capacity plans and component capacity plans.

Table 6.1 Comparing Service and Component Capacity Plans

Service Capacity Plan	Component Capacity Plan
Variety of measurements	Single direct measurement
Unknown total capacity	Known total capacity
Contains options for capacity growth	Normally one known growth option
Utilization trends are estimated	Utilization trends are accurate
Contains business details	Contains technical details

How Many Plans?

The description of service and component capacity plans may leave you wondering whether it wouldn't be better to just create a single capacity plan after all. It might seem that managing this plethora of plans will cause extra confusion and added work, but that isn't the case. If you have really committed to managing IT as a set of services, you will have many other documents aligned by service, and the capacity plan will just be part of the entire set. For a very large organization or one with a high degree of complexity, the service owner manages the capacity plan along with other documentation for the service. In that case the service owner relies on the capacity management team for assistance.

You should also be aware that not every piece of your IT environment necessarily needs a capacity plan. Remember that capacity planning is all about making better decisions. There are likely to be areas where capacity decisions do not need to be made. For example, many organizations find that local area networks seldom have capacity issues, so they choose not to define or manage capacity plans for the LAN components. Similarly, personal workstations probably don't need capacity plans because shortages of workstation capacity do not significantly impact the IT organization or its ability to provide services to the business.

Your set of capacity plans is likely to grow over time as you get more experience in capacity planning and expand the range of decisions that can be made with solid capacity data. You certainly want to create plans for your most frequently used IT services first. Next you should define plans for those shared components that are most critical or that would have the most impact if they ran out of capacity. Finally, work on the less critical components and the less frequently used services.

The bottom line is that you should create capacity management plans with an eye to their value. If there won't be value in having a plan, don't create one. On the other hand, don't hesitate to create plans if you think you might need them. There is nothing worse than telling the business they need to wait a week or more for an important service because you didn't think you needed to manage capacity for that service!

Format of a Capacity Plan

The format of a single capacity plan is defined in Appendix J of the service design book. The format includes 11 separate sections covering all aspects of the unified capacity plan. In this section I expand on this basic format and provide some real-world experience that will help you to make your capacity plans complete, concise, and easy for your organization to read.

The Essential Elements

Although the service design book offers good advice for what makes a complete capacity plan, there are certain essential elements that should not be missed. Those elements are described here and depicted graphically in Figure 6.1.

Introduction

Of course, every capacity plan document should begin with an introduction. Somewhere in the introduction you should establish which elements the plan covers and what significant changes have taken place since the previous version of the plan. The introduction is also a great place to preview any significant issues that are described in the plan and to make a call for action if any action is necessary. Although the introductions to all of your capacity plans are likely to be similar, there should be enough differences and distinctions that the opening of the plan doesn't read like a template. If you find you are spending more than a page or so on the introduction, you are probably not summarizing well enough.

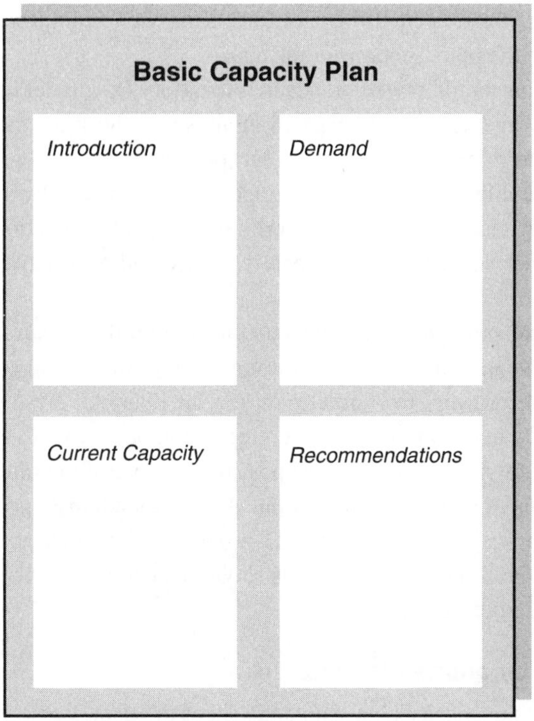

Figure 6.1 A capacity plan has four essential elements.

Total Available Capacity

After the introduction, the capacity plan should define the currently available capacity for the service or component. For IT services, this might include some theoretical information on what the upper limits might be and how they could be calculated. For a component capacity plan the task is much simpler because you can simply state the units of measure and define the real physical size of the capacity pool. For either type of plan, it is important to define the upper limits of capacity so that the rest of the plan, including any recommendations for expanding those upper limits, makes more sense.

In addition to total capacity, you will want to describe any capacity issues that are occurring with the service or component. If you have outstanding performance or capacity concerns, document them as part of the plan. This provides a strong base for the recommendations that you will make later in the plan.

Past Utilization and Future Demand

The majority of the capacity plan focuses on the current and anticipated capacity demand. It is this analysis of the demands facing a particular service or component that takes the most effort and provides the information needed for decisions. This section requires more detail and thus more organization than the other sections of the plan.

Your capacity plan should review trends in utilization. Document the long-term utilization trend, such as monthly averages for the past 18 months or at least for the past year. You should also document the trend in peak utilization if your tools are capable of gathering that. Often the peak utilization is more interesting than the average because you can learn more about what puts stress on your capacity. Understanding and working with peak utilization helps you to mix the right workloads together so that they can share capacity and each have available resources to meet their peak demand.

The capacity plan should also document shorter-term utilization trends. Profile an average day by showing the utilization for every hour during the day. Show an average and a busy hour by showing the utilization for every few minutes during the hour. All these trends provide the data needed to make capacity decisions about the service or component you are documenting.

The trend data show the history and one possible glimpse of the future, but you should also document any projected changes in utilization. As described in Chapter 3, "Understanding Capacity Demand," demand might come from IT projects or from business activities. Either way, whatever is known of the future resource needs should be captured in the capacity plan as more data with which to make decisions.

Observations and Recommendations

You should round off the capacity plan with analysis of the data. Look deeply at the trends and the upcoming demand, and see whether you can determine when new capacity is needed. Conversely, look at opportunities to save money by consolidating existing capacity, satisfying need with virtual servers, or even decommissioning systems that are no longer needed.

Don't simply observe these opportunities. You should also elaborate on them. Describe what should be done in sufficient detail that someone can create a project proposal or scope statement. Project potential cost savings or the capacity of a newly consolidated system. If you propose acquisition of new hardware, you should specify the configuration to be ordered and define how much new capacity will be created. Given the current trends, how long will that new capacity last?

The recommendations here should be reasonable and in line with the standards of your organization. Don't recommend purchase of a mainframe when a simple Unix box will do the job! Base your recommendations on the data presented in the capacity plan, and provide sound reasoning for why they are the right next steps.

As part of the observations and recommendations section of the capacity plan, you will also want to provide some follow-up on recommendations that were part of earlier versions of the plan. Did the recommendations get implemented? If so, did they resolve the concerns or head off any incidents? Review of past success strengthens your current recommendations, and review of past failures makes sure that you work harder on your current recommendations.

The Right Level of Detail

Now that you understand the basic pieces that make up the capacity plan, you might be wondering about the depth of detail that should go into the document. Although a capacity plan is fundamentally a technical document, you will not want to make it so detailed that it is impossible to read. You should strive for clear explanations without added complexity.

For a casual reader of the capacity plan, the introduction and recommendations are the most interesting. Casual readers are typically IT managers or executives, or perhaps even business unit managers who are particularly impacted by IT. These readers will be interested in knowing when capacity concerns will impact IT services and what the costs will be to alleviate those concerns. So the details in the introduction and recommendation sections should be sufficient to enable the casual reader to understand quickly and completely what the issues are and how they can be resolved.

The majority of the readers of your capacity plans will not be casual, however. They will be the technicians and engineers who provide and manage your IT capacity. These readers will want more than issues and recommendations. They will want to understand the details behind the current issues and the concrete steps to implement the recommendations. These readers will peruse the introduction and analysis, and then dive deeply into the current capacity and utilization sections. These readers may want details even beyond what your tools can produce. But remember that the engineers have real jobs to do and reading capacity plans is not their major focus. So, again, the rule is to be concise and provide the details that support the current position and recommended actions. Any details beyond those represent effort that you have wasted in writing the plan and that your technical readers have wasted in reading the plan.

There is one more audience to consider. The person or people who have to acquire new capacity will look at your plans with a completely different view. They aren't particularly interested in current capacity or utilization. They don't even care about the recommendations very much, other than those that drive new purchases. When new acquisitions do need to be made, however, this team will want enough detail to take action. There really isn't much purpose to a plan that says "buy another server." Instead, the plan needs to spell out exactly what model of server needs to be purchased and what features or components need to be acquired with that server. In other words, the procurement team needs to see a complete configuration that is ready to order. You don't want to end up with an approval to purchase new capacity and then waste time by not having the details of what needs to be ordered. Of course, planning in this light will also cause you to really consider the recommendations you make. Knowing that your recommendations need to go in front of someone to make investment decisions should cause you to really be sure the purchases are justified.

Maintaining Capacity Plans

Capacity plans are living documents. They need to be actively managed as your organization and its needs change. This section describes the procedures you can use to make sure your capacity plan is always ready to support the decisions that need to be made. By thinking about maintenance before plans are made, you will never be in a position to have to refresh dozens or even hundreds of out-of-date plans at the same time.

Periodic Reviews

The first issue to consider is how to keep capacity plans current as your organization's IT needs and projects change. Every organization goes through normal cycles when they need more capacity or less capacity. Therefore, every capacity plan is incorrect at least some of the time. You should conduct periodic reviews of each of your plans to bring them back in line with the actual issues, utilization, and capacity of your IT infrastructure.

Most organizations find a quarterly cycle to be best for capacity plan reviews. This allows enough time to go by for changes to happen, but doesn't let the plans get so far out of date that they are not effective when needed. Three months should be adequate time for most organizations to consider the recommendations made by the capacity plans and to implement those that are most critical. If your organization is particularly small or has very infrequent changes, you might consider a longer cycle, but certainly no more than every six months. Conversely, for very large or very dynamic organizations you might want to look at capacity plans more frequently. One very large client I worked with broke the capacity plans into areas by technology and had a monthly meeting for each area to review all the capacity plans that impacted that area. I cannot imagine needing a review any more than monthly.

After you've defined the review cycle, you need to establish a mechanism that reminds you when reviews are needed. With dozens or even hundreds of separate plans, you need to create a capacity plan review schedule that indicates which plans are up for review at what time. The best way to do this is with a document management system with built-in review policies. If you don't have a good system, you will most likely need to create an inventory of each of the capacity plans tracking their owner (more about that later), their last review date, and their next scheduled review date. Then as a capacity manager you are responsible for reviewing that inventory and setting up the appropriate reviews. Regular reviews must be a high priority because the expense of starting over again with capacity plans can be steep.

What should you look for as you're doing a review? You should review the pieces that change most frequently, which include the utilization and the analysis sections. The utilization either confirms or contradicts the analysis you have done in the past. If your predictions of the future were reasonably accurate, your analysis should still be sound. On the other hand, if you find that actual utilization has differed dramatically from what you predicted, you may want to read Chapter 3 again and find a more accurate way to predict demand. The entire validity of the capacity plan is based on the accuracy of your utilization predictions, so you should take every opportunity to learn to predict capacity demand more accurately.

The analysis and recommendations will likely change with every review of the capacity plans. If the recommendations were implemented, you will have new capacity and those recommendations can now be removed from the plan. For recommendations that were not adopted, however, you will want to review whether the recommendation is still valid, and if so, strengthen it to show why it should be adopted soon.

Capacity plan reviews should take place in a joint meeting between the technicians responsible for managing the capacity pool, the capacity manager, and someone with financial authority responsibility for the capacity pool. The technician is generally able to document how accurate the utilization predictions were, the capacity manager can describe any activities that have changed the total capacity or impacted the recommendations in the plan, and the financial manager can indicate which new recommendations are likely to get funded. This meeting does not need to take a long time or be extremely formal—the participants just need to touch base to agree together on the changes to be made to the plan.

In lieu of an actual meeting, it is possible for the capacity manager to update the plan with recommended changes and have the other two approve those changes through email. This removes some of the interplay that is likely in a meeting, but reduces the time commitment that each person must make. In many cases these "off line" reviews are needed because it can be difficult to organize everyone's time such that they can attend the reviews. Making your reviews organized and helpful to the attendees might help them prioritize their calendars to attend the reviews in person.

Coping with Major Changes

There may be changes needed in your capacity plans that are outside of the normal day-to-day activities that your IT group pursues. Some significant changes require more rework and deeper analysis than the norm. In this section we investigate some reasons you might need to significantly rework one or more capacity plans.

Of course, the initial cause of major rework is the fact that you don't have any capacity plans at all! If you haven't begun this discipline of documenting plans for each of your major IT services and significant shared components, you have a lot of work in front of you. By now, you should have learned enough to create the first drafts and get them into a regular review cycle. The value of capacity plans becomes greater as you mature them through many review cycles, so begin to draft your plans now.

You shouldn't ignore the value you can get from early drafts. Even though you know that the capacity plan gets better as it matures, you should not withhold early versions from your organization. The maturity you're looking for comes only from the wide exposure of people who will really use your plan. Don't wait for perfection because it will never come while the plan is still private.

Another cause of significant new capacity planning work is the initiation of a new IT service. During the planning for the service, you should have defined enough information to establish an initial capacity and some projections of how quickly that capacity will be used. The initial capacity plan should document those along with some projections of when it might be time to grow beyond the capacity initially deployed for the service. You should expect the first capacity plan for any new service to be flawed. Having a plan that you can revise leads to much better plans over time. Starting with nothing ensures that you never move toward an accurate and useful plan.

Of course, the opposite of a new service is the discontinuation of an existing service. Frequently, capacity demands are shifted when a service is discontinued. For example, imagine that your organization has decided to stop using Websphere Application Server (WAS) as an application-enabling technology and starts insisting that all developers use Apache Tomcat instead. You will create a sunset plan that removes all instances of WAS while moving critical applications over to Tomcat. This causes rework to capacity plans for both services. Eventually, you will retire or convert the last of the WAS applications and will be able to retire the WAS capacity plan, which means that the Tomcat plan describes sufficient capacity for your needs. There are many scenarios in which you will update two plans to show that capacity of one type is decreasing while capacity of another is increasing.

Another scenario that can create big changes in your capacity plans is a technology change. For example, if your organization was using VMware to host virtual Windows® servers but decided to change to Microsoft as the virtualization engine, you'd be facing a technology change. Although this probably doesn't impact the services you provide to your business, it certainly impacts utilization and available capacity. Most likely you will need to use a different tool to measure utilization, and you probably will want to reassess the number of virtual servers you host per physical server. Those ratios will affect the total capacity available to host virtual servers. This same kind of scenario happens anytime you change the technology that provides capacity to your IT services. When these changes happen, you almost need to begin from scratch to create a capacity plan that makes sense.

Storing Capacity Plans

As a final detail, we consider the options for storing your capacity plans. If you have an advanced document management system already in place, you may not need to worry about this detail. If you are still managing documents with a variety of local hard disks and shared file systems, read on. You'll learn some practical tips for keeping your capacity plans organized and available, and you may be able to use some of these same techniques for other documents as well.

Format of the Plans

Earlier in this chapter, you learned which elements are important to a capacity plan. Now it is time to consider the container that holds those elements. Most organizations settle on a capacity plan in a word processing document with tables and graphs representing utilization data. The free format of a document enables an introduction and recommendations to be drafted as part of the plan while the tables and charts convey the structured data related to the service or component being addressed.

Because capacity plans are simply documents, it is important to ensure that they don't end up sitting on someone's hard disk or in a file share somewhere. Those sources are notorious for being difficult to manage and restricting access. The best place to keep your documents is as attachments within the capacity management information system itself. If your CMIS software allows attachments, the issue is settled because that is where all capacity plans should be kept.

Of course, not all CMIS software packages allow attachments or can handle large blocks of unstructured data. If you find yourself in this situation, your next best alternative is to create a field in the CMIS that enables you to describe or point to the documents as they are being managed elsewhere. If your software allows universal resource locators (URLs), you can place those into the CMIS as links to enable users to launch the capacity plan in context while using the CMIS. The easier you can make it to find and read the capacity plans, the more they will be read.

As a final resort when nothing else is available, create your own index to the capacity plans manually. This could be as simple as creating a spreadsheet with a single line for each capacity plan that indicates the name of the plan, which element in the CMIS it refers to, and where the file containing the plan can be found. In the CMIS you can then create a field for each service and component that indicates the identifier of the corresponding row in the index spreadsheet. This kind of manual index can be laborious to maintain, but the effort is rewarded as you see your capacity plans becoming more integral to the way the organization manages capacity.

Over time, you should strive to define a set of data elements that exist in each of your capacity plans. If you can gradually move away from free-form text and toward structured text, you can do much more with the capacity plans. You may never arrive at the point where your capacity plan fits nicely within the columns and tables of a relational database, but you should definitely organize as much of the data as you can to help in searching, reviewing, and updating your capacity plans.

Maintaining Version Control

Regardless of where you store the capacity management plans, you must be sure to exercise control of changes. Nothing will derail your efforts quite as quickly as confusion over which version of a plan is valid or where to find the latest version. Since capacity plans undergo frequent revisions, you need to define a version management strategy up front to eliminate these problems.

The best practice for version control is to ensure that within each document is a table for tracking changes. The table should include columns to indicate who made the change, when it was made, and what the nature of the change was. This table should be updated as a habit whenever a change is made to any capacity plan.

If you have the luxury of having a team of capacity managers, you may also need a system to indicate who has control of each plan. In the best possible world you have access to a document or source code control system such as Documentum or Rational® ClearCase®. Those systems allow you to "check out" a document and ensure that two people cannot make changes concurrently. If you don't have a system that allows you to manage changes to documents, you can accomplish the same thing by using the index spreadsheet identified in the preceding section and simply adding a column indicating who controls the document at any point in time.

Whichever system is used, it is imperative that you control changes to the capacity plans. Only through careful management of the revisions will they become more accurate and more helpful over time.

Summary and Next Steps

Capacity plans provide the capacity management team with the opportunity to analyze the mountain of data they work with every day and make solid recommendations to the IT management team. This chapter has described capacity plans and provided some insight into how your organization can create them.

We started with an overview of what makes up a good capacity plan. You learned that, in addition to specific data elements such as utilization and capacity limits, a solid plan should also include predictions and analysis. You should create a separate plan for each major IT service and for each significant IT component, with each plan providing an in-depth approach for what to do when capacity is too high or too low.

We considered the way to format your capacity plans. You learned that although data can be in the form of a table or structured text, your analysis and recommendations will almost always be free-form text within a document of some kind. You should provide an overview for casual readers, but also provide technical depth to justify the recommendations you make within the plan.

We considered how to manage capacity plans and saw that they follow a life cycle that can be tracked through effective document management practices. Capacity plans should be reviewed regularly and updated when changes are needed. Minor changes can be bundled together into a regular release cycle for the document, and major changes should be planned and implemented as part of the major IT change that is causing you to rethink the capacity plan.

As indicated in Chapter 5, capacity plans should be stored in the CMIS. If your CMIS tool allows attachments, you should store the actual document there. If not, you should at least create some kind of index within the CMIS so that users of that repository can easily locate and view your capacity plans.

Now that we've addressed the two most misunderstood ITIL capacity management terms (CMIS and capacity plan), the next chapter returns to fundamentals. We explore how to define and staff the roles you need to create an effective capacity management team.

CHAPTER 7

Staff the Capacity Management Team

IT processes require discipline, and capacity management is no exception. Implementing capacity management and making it effective requires a team of professionals who are well trained and properly aligned to their roles. In this chapter you learn about the various roles, what skills it takes to fill those roles, and how to assemble a highly productive capacity management team.

When you think about staffing the capacity management team, you should consider all phases of the service life cycle. The skills and responsibilities needed to implement capacity management are not the same as those needed to operate the service effectively for the long term. The implementation team focuses on creating the new service, establishing a firm foundation, and reaching the goal of a productive, self-sustaining service. The operational team focuses on quality and process improvements while ensuring that the desired objectives are met day by day. In some cases the same people may move from an implementation role to an operational role, but in other cases you may have entirely different teams focus on these two parts of the service life cycle.

Implementation Roles

Let's begin with a deeper look at the roles involved in implementation. You obviously need to staff these roles first because without implementation you will never need an operations team. The implementation roles generally require people with more vision and deeper experience because creation of a new service is more difficult than operation of an existing service. As you think about and staff the implementation roles, look for people who can understand and create the value that will sustain your capacity management effort for years to come.

Capacity Process Owner

Every successful project has a successful leader. For implementing capacity management, that leader is called the capacity process owner or capacity service owner. One of the best practices defined by ITIL is that each process should be owned by a specific individual. The concept of process ownership involves the authority to make decisions on behalf of the process, the knowledge to oversee the implementation of the process, and the vision to continuously improve the effectiveness of the process. All these traits should come together in the capacity process owner.

The reason for the capacity process owner role is simple. Someone must define and oversee the implementation project. The capacity process owner is typically the most knowledgeable and experienced member of the team and normally is involved with the project from the beginning. If you're reading this book, you are probably preparing to be a capacity process owner!

The capacity process owner has many important responsibilities. The primary responsibility is to define and design the capacity service for your organization. Using deep knowledge of capacity management and familiarity with the needs of the organization, the capacity process owner documents requirements, designs the process, chooses the tools, and puts together a project scope, budget, and schedule that accomplishes the implementation goals. In other words, they are responsible for everything. This isn't to say that the capacity owner acts alone. As a leader, the capacity process owner should be collaborating with the team members, communicating with the project stakeholders, and providing ongoing updates to the project sponsors. All these are responsibilities of the capacity process owner.

To accomplish all these responsibilities, the capacity process owner needs a host of skills. From a technical perspective, the capacity process owner should be familiar with the major types of components that your organization uses to provide capacity. If you have mainframes, they will need to know mainframe capacity management. If you rely primarily on Unix or Windows servers, the capacity service owner should be familiar with managing capacity for those platforms. Familiarity with storage and networking helps as well since those components need to be managed by every organization. As you can see, the capacity process owner should be a technical generalist with a good understanding of the various pieces that make up a complete IT infrastructure.

In addition to technical skills, the capacity process owner should have solid leadership and organizational change skills. She must be able to lead a team of technicians and communicate well with managers and executives to accomplish the implementation project. The process owner should also have skills to help with process engineering and with project management as those are critical pieces of the project success.

The success of the capacity process owner during implementation is tied to the success criteria for the implementation project. As the owner of the entire project, the capacity process owner succeeds or fails with the project. Typically, you define success criteria for the project related to budget, schedule, scope, and quality, and then measure the capacity process owner by how well those criteria are obtained during the project. Table 7.1 summarizes the skills and responsibilities of the capacity process owner.

Table 7.1 Responsibilities and Skills of the Capacity Process Owner

Responsibility	Skills
Design capacity service	Capacity management skill Technical familiarity with managed components
Define capacity management project	Requirements management Organizational understanding Project management
Lead implementation team	Leadership
Communicate with project stakeholders	Communication
Support project with sponsors	Finance knowledge, leadership

The capacity process owner should, if at all possible, remain as part of the team after initial implementation. Thus, you will find this same role described again as part of the operations team.

Capacity Management Information System Designer

One of the key members of the implementation team is the CMIS designer. This person is an expert in capacity management tools and integration architectures. The CMIS designer helps ensure a successful deployment of the tools that automate the capacity management process. Because the tooling is both expensive and important, it makes sense to have an expert as part of the implementation team to make sure you get the best possible automated foundation to the capacity management service. If capacity management and the concept of a CMIS are new to your organization, you might need to engage an experienced consultant to be your CMIS designer.

The major responsibility of the CMIS designer is to plan and implement the capacity management information system. This typically includes helping the capacity process owner define tools requirements for both the CMIS and the tools that track utilization. In addition, the CMIS designer is responsible for creating an integration architecture that helps the CMIS gather data in an automated way from the various tools that detect and gather utilization and total capacity. The designer also assists the process engineer as they work to blend the process and the tools into an integrated service.

To achieve these goals, the CMIS designer needs to be an expert in capacity management tools. He or she must understand the features and functions available in the various commercial tool sets and must understand how to implement those tools in the real world. This typically involves experience in implementing one or more complete tool sets, or at least a good working relationship with the tool vendors or consultants who have implemented the selected tool set before.

The critical success criteria for the capacity management information system designer are all related to the success of the tool set. If the tools are flexible enough to meet all the requirements, complete enough to automate the majority of the process, and yet easy to use for the organization, then the CMIS designer has been successful. Because capacity management is not the full-time job for many of the people who use the tool set, the CMIS designer must select and implement a tool set that is as helpful as possible for occasional users. Table 7.2 reiterates the skills and responsibilities associated with the CMIS designer role.

Table 7.2 Responsibilities and Skills for the CMIS Designer

Responsibility	Skills
Define CMIS	Capacity management skill Application and/or data architecture
Select capacity tools	Requirements management Technology evaluation
Implement capacity tools	Technical understanding of software implementation
Test CMIS	Software testing skills
Design and build integrated tool set	Knowledge of software integration architecture

Process Engineer

The third member of the capacity management implementation team is the process engineer. This is the person responsible for defining and documenting the policies, processes, and procedures that are used to manage capacity for your organization. Whether you are fine-tuning an existing set of process documents or starting completely from scratch, it is a good idea to have a process engineer on your team. The process engineer makes sure that processes are documented rather than simply followed, and can help ensure the completeness of your capacity management processes.

The main responsibility of the process engineer is to define and help implement the capacity management process. Of course, the process is based on the one documented in the *ITIL Service Design* book, but that is like saying that all life is based on the carbon atom. There is much more to process engineering than simply copying the capacity management process out of a book!

The process engineer begins by understanding the requirements gathered by the capacity process owner. In reviewing these requirements and asking questions, the process engineer begins to understand the policies of the organization so they can be documented as the foundation for the capacity management service. Capacity management policies might include the frequency of collecting and summarizing utilization data, the number and type of capacity pools, and the threshold values that initiate decisions to increase or decrease capacity.

In addition to defining policies, the process engineer helps define the working procedures for each of the members of the operational team. Taking the basic outline of the process supplied by the ITIL best practices, these procedures are actionable steps that the team members execute as part of their daily jobs. It is important to ensure that the procedures are accurate because they form the basis of training at the tail end of the implementation.

The process engineer skill set is fairly generic. Although the process engineer needs some familiarity with capacity planning, the ability to interview experts and ask questions is really more important. Excellent writing skills and an appreciation of time management are important so that the resulting documentation can be easily understood and the final procedures are efficient. The process engineer should be a good communicator so that he can either conduct the final training or at least convey to the training team the important aspects of the process documentation. Most likely you have someone in your organization already who can fill the role of process engineer for your capacity management implementation.

You will know that a process engineer is successful if people feel comfortable following the process that is defined. When there are no unexpected or unexplained procedures, and everyone feels sure that they can follow the documentation to accomplish their jobs, the process engineer has been successful. On the other hand, if there are continual questions and the level of detail is insufficient to ensure consistent actions between team members, you know that the process engineer is not finished regardless of what the project plan says. Good process engineering should leave clarity and consistency in its wake. The skills and responsibilities needed by the process engineer are summarized in Table 7.3.

Table 7.3 Responsibilities and Skills for the Process Engineer

Responsibility	Skills
Document capacity process	Process design
Document capacity policies	Interviewing/analysis
Define and document capacity procedures	Time management Understanding of work flow
Interface with trainer/perform process training	Communication skills

Project Manager

Perhaps the most obvious role on your implementation team will be the project manager. Every significant project needs a project manager, and implementing ITIL capacity management is definitely a significant project. The project manager manages the project documents, coordinates team activities, reports status to project stakeholders, documents issues, and works with management to get them solved, and generally makes sure that the project keeps flowing. You might be tempted to have the capacity process owner or someone in another role assume project management duties as well, but unless your organization is very small, you should strongly consider a dedicated project manager to help make the implementation project a success.

Coordination is the major responsibility of the project manager. The capacity process owner documents the scope statement, and the project manager is responsible for bringing it to the various stakeholders and getting their concurrence. Similarly, the project manager negotiates the project schedule and budget, gathers feedback, and updates these important project documents until everyone agrees that they are correct. The project manager manages the schedule, resources, and scope of the project as changes occur, and ensures that all team members and stakeholders have access to the latest version of these critical project documents.

In addition to dealing with project documents, the project manager manages issues. When an issue arises, whether it is technical, schedule related, or financial, the project manager documents the issue by working with the appropriate team members. She then works with management and project team members to understand options for resolving the issue and chooses the best resolution to pursue. The project manager is responsible for tracking each issue until it can be resolved or until the team agrees that the issue can be safely ignored as a risk.

Another important responsibility of the project manager is coordination of people and activities across the project. As one team member finishes a work product, the project manager documents the completion and makes sure that the next team member in sequence is ready to carry on the work. If there is a delay, it falls to the project manager to understand how the delay will impact other team members. The PM is responsible for communicating all changes to the rest of the project member. In addition, the PM must make sure that the project members understand the impact of those changes.

Project management skills are well defined and well understood. No specific skills are needed to manage a capacity management implementation project. Strong communication and organizational skills are the hallmark of every good project manager, and these are exactly the skills required from the manager of the implementation project.

A project manager is successful when a project is completed on time and within its budget. The classical formula is that scope, schedule, and resources are all planned in advance and then achieved according to the plan. If the capacity management service is implemented as envisioned by the capacity process owner within the schedule and resources are allocated at the beginning of the project, then the project manager has done an excellent job. Table 7.4 shows a generic view of the responsibilities and skills needed by an IT project manager.

Table 7.4 Responsibilities and Skills for the Project Manager

Responsibility	Skills
Manage project documents (scope, schedule, budget)	Communications skills
Coordinate project activities	Ability to organize
Issue management	Communication and organizational skills

Operational Roles

The implementation team is temporary. They move in, get the capacity management service implemented, and then move on. If you make a mistake in hiring or staffing someone on the team, you can probably wait for the several months it will take for the project to complete, and then your mistake will be remedied.

The operational team is permanent. You need to carefully select its members because they will either deliver on the promises of capacity management or make your organization miss out on them. Any mistakes in staffing have to be dealt with because they are permanent. Although the implementation team is important, you should definitely take more care in staffing the operational roles.

Capacity Service Owner

Just as the implementation team needs a leader, so too does the operational team. The leader in both cases is the capacity service owner. Many organizations find it helpful to have the same person in this key role from the inception of the implementation project all the way through to full operational status. The skills required for implementation and operations are similar enough to make this plausible, and the continuity provided can be very valuable.

The capacity service owner is responsible for all aspects of the capacity management service during the operational phase just as they were during implementation. He keeps the team organized, looks for ways to improve the service, and responds to any issues that arise with the quality of the service. The many responsibilities required normally mean that the capacity process owner is a dedicated role, not a set of responsibilities assigned to someone who already plays other roles.

The capacity service owner is a leader and advocate for the capacity management team and service. This includes such responsibilities as representing capacity management to the rest of the IT organization, defining and tracking the value of capacity management to the business, and resolving any issues with the capacity management service. In their day-to-day role, the capacity service owner coordinates activities between the members of the team so that delivery of capacity management appears as a seamless service to the rest of the organization. This might include supplementing other roles when workload is heavy, stepping in to fill a newly discovered process gap, generating data to meet special requests, or even acting as a referee in disputes. The capacity service owner never lacks things to do!

Because the responsibilities of the capacity service owner are so varied, the skills they possess must be broad. As outlined earlier, the capacity service owner must have technical skills to understand the various issues that will arise. This includes some general knowledge of each of the kinds of platforms for which the team is managing capacity, as well as deep skills in capacity and performance analysis. In addition to technical skills, the capacity service owner needs strong business and leadership skills. In ITIL, the service owner role is enacted by the most skilled person in any given service area.

The success of the capacity process owner can be measured by the success of the capacity service. The best measurement is money saved through delayed purchases or equipment retirement. If the capacity management service is meeting its goal of saving money for the organization, it is because the capacity service owner is successful. In addition to monetary measures, you could also use service-level attainment as a measure of success for both the service and the service owner. There are many possible service levels, and some of the more common ones are covered in Chapter 11, "Produce Capacity Reports." Any of these service levels can be directly linked to the performance appraisal of the capacity service owner. Table 7.5 summarizes the skills and responsibilities for this role.

Table 7.5 Responsibilities and Skills for the Long-Term Capacity Process Owner

Responsibility	Skills
Lead the capacity team	Leadership and organizational knowledge
Improve the capacity process	Deep capacity management skill
Understand effectiveness metrics	Business analysis
Integrate capacity service with other IT services	Broad service management knowledge
Issue management	Organizational knowledge and problem solving

Capacity Analyst

Another important role on the operational team is your capacity and performance analyst. This is the specialist who can dive deep on any component or service to really understand the current utilization and total capacity. The capacity analyst normally writes the capacity plans for the resources she manages, and maintains that plan over time. It would be very rare to find a single individual who can perform the deep analysis of every IT service and every component in your environment, so typically you will have separate people playing the role of capacity analyst for different technologies and services. The role of capacity analyst is most often played by a system administrator who also builds and maintains a part of the IT infrastructure.

There are two key responsibilities for a capacity analyst. The primary responsibility is to perform analysis of the target environment. Normally, there is a monthly analysis that requires reading reports from your utilization-gathering tools and looking for thresholds that are being violated because there is too much or too little capacity. When the reports highlight an issue, the capacity analyst explores the issue and determines whether action is required. This action could be coordinated with the capacity plan or could be handled as part of an incident resolution for issues that were not predicted by the capacity plan. In either event, the responsibility of the capacity analyst is to provide the detailed data and recommendation needed to go forward.

The other responsibility for the capacity analyst is to manage the capacity plans. The capacity analyst initially drafts the plan and gets it approved by the capacity service owner and IT management. After this initial approval, the capacity analyst facilitates regular reviews of the plan and makes updates as conditions change. When new plans need to be added or existing plans are retired, the capacity analyst is instrumental in getting this work accomplished. Frequently, the capacity analysts begin their work as part of the implementation team to create the initial capacity plans and then continue as part of the operational team.

The capacity analyst must have very strong technical skills in the platforms they represent. They must understand the nuances of virtualization, memory utilization, input/output rates, and all the other technical performance measurements of their platforms. They are power users of the utilization gathering tools, often suggesting that the tools be changed in some way to gather even more details about the ongoing utilization and performance of the IT components. In addition to deep technical skills, the capacity analyst must have strong written communication skills to make the recommendations in the capacity plans as useful as possible.

A successful capacity analyst is one who can avoid surprises by looking forward. Through better analysis of the environment and more accurate capacity plans, the successful analyst has a good idea of where the hot spots are and can quiet them down before trouble strikes. As he becomes more successful in providing just enough capacity as it is needed, the recommendations that the capacity analyst makes are treated as absolute requirements and implemented with fewer questions or objections. The successful capacity analyst is seen as a master of his domain, and IT managers and the capacity process owner trust him to handle the job without interference. Table 7.6 shows the responsibilities and skills of the capacity analyst.

Table 7.6 Responsibilities and Skills of the Capacity Analyst

Responsibility	Skills
Perform deep capacity analysis	Technical platform knowledge
Respond to capacity and performance issues	Problem solving
Create capacity plans with recommendations	Capacity management skill Written communication
Manage capacity plans	Organizational knowledge

Capacity Data Manager

The role of capacity data manager is necessary because of the need for the capacity management information system. The CMIS is a very large database, and any large database requires someone to manage the data. Many organizations call this position a "logical database administrator." The capacity data manager handles changes to the schema of the CMIS, works with any issues surrounding data load or data extracts, and helps to manage the quality of the data in the CMIS. If you already have someone who manages the data in the configuration management system or another IT service management database, that person probably can also manage the capacity management data effectively. Data management is a very specific skill that can be applied to many domains, so you should definitely look for a data manager rather than specifically someone with capacity management experience.

The most important responsibility for the capacity data manager is to maintain accurate data in the CMIS. Data accuracy is impacted by integration with other capacity management tools and also by the degree to which team members follow the defined processes. The data manager should follow standard data auditing practices to identify and handle inaccuracies in the data.

In addition to data management, the capacity data manager is also responsible for managing the schema for the CMIS. Process and tool changes often dictate changes to the schema, and the capacity data manager should understand and communicate the impact of these proposed changes. After a schema change has been approved, the capacity data manager will implement the change and take necessary steps to ensure that preexisting data is reformatted as necessary to fit the new schema.

The capacity data manager must relentlessly pay attention to details. The key skills for this role are an ability to manage large amounts of data and a drive to perfect that data. The capacity data manager should understand how to collect sample data, compare actual data to that stored in the CMIS, detect any exceptions or inaccuracies, and work through how to resolve those inaccuracies. The capacity data manager should be quite skilled in using the CMIS tools and any additional query tools that help review the data in the CMIS.

A successful manager of capacity data should be nearly invisible. As long as the capacity data is accurate and reliable, the capacity data manager is doing a good job. If the number of inaccuracies grows and users begin to question the validity of the CMIS, the capacity data manager is not being successful. Table 7.7 summarizes the responsibilities and skills necessary for the successful capacity data manager.

Table 7.7 Responsibilities and Skills for the Capacity Data Manager

Responsibility	Skills
Understand and support data interfaces to CMIS	Data architecture
Prepare and conduct data validity audits	Data management
Evaluate proposed CMIS schema changes	Good understanding of data relationships
Implement changes to CMIS	Solid understanding of CMIS tools
Support ad hoc data queries	Working knowledge of query tools
Provide regular CMIS reporting	Working knowledge of query tools

Capacity Planner

Whereas the capacity analyst provides deep expertise and analysis of a specific IT service or component, the capacity planner offers a wide view across the enterprise of all capacity needs. The capacity planner is the one person who turns the many recommendations from various capacity plans and incident responses into a comprehensive budget moving forward. The capacity analyst scrutinizes the environment and digs up specific details, which the capacity planner then summarizes into a high-level view of the capacity needs across the organization.

The capacity planner is essentially a business analyst who can understand the technical recommendations and put business context around them for the IT management team. This business context involves the balance of cost with risk. The cost of acquiring new capacity is balanced against the potential costs of inadequate capacity. The capacity planner lives in a future world trying to understand and manage the incoming demand against the planned capacity increases.

The capacity planner maps the individual capacity plans into the overall IT budget by being the liaison between the capacity team and the IT financial team. Specific responsibilities of the capacity planner include preparing budget requests, working with the business to understand capacity demand, getting quotes from vendors for proposed capacity acquisitions, working with the purchasing team to track the shipment dates for ordered capacity, and tracking the financial value of capacity actions.

Many organizations try to assign the capacity planner role to the capacity service owner. This works if the organization is small enough, but for larger organizations the person in this dual role focuses increasingly on the demands of the financial planning and less on the important tasks of team coordination and service improvement. If you find that your capacity service owner is overworked, you probably want to consider adding a capacity planner role to the team.

The capacity planner needs strong financial analyst skills. This person must be able to build sensible business cases and document the financial impact of proposed actions. The planner needs to help prioritize among competing capacity needs and support the prioritized needs to your executive team. It is important that the capacity planner have a good understanding of demand management and a working knowledge of the different technologies used by your organization to provide capacity.

A successful capacity planner has numbers to back up her success. She will show the amount of money saved through strong capacity planning, and reflect the amount needed in the budget to achieve the goals of capacity management. Over time, a good capacity planner should gain the respect of the leadership team because she will always ask for only what is reasonable, and whatever she asks for will turn out to be beneficial to IT in general. Table 7.8 summarizes the skills and responsibilities of the capacity planner role.

Table 7.8 Responsibilities and Skills of the Capacity Planner

Responsibility	Skills
Read capacity plans to extract budget information	Financial analysis
Interface with procurement team to order new capacity	Organizational knowledge
Work with the business groups to forecast demand	Understanding of future projects
Prioritize capacity requests to fit available budget	Financial management
Define the financial value of capacity management	Financial metrics and analysis

A Word About Skills

Building an effective capacity management team is more than simply filling in the various roles described earlier in this chapter. You need to consider the balance of skills, experience, and personalities that compose a highly effective team. In this section you will find some additional information to help you in building the strongest possible capacity management team.

Skills, Roles, and Staffing

It is easy to read through this chapter and imagine that you need exactly four people on the transition team and four people on the operational team. This would be too simple, however. For a very large or complex organization you might need more people, and for a small organization you can probably get by with fewer people.

The relationship of roles to people is not always one-to-one. There are many reasons that a single role can be filled by multiple people, and why a single person might fill multiple roles. In a large organization, for example, you might have separate capacity analysts for the mainframe platform, the Unix platforms, and the Windows server platform. In this case you might not be able to find (or afford!) a single person who has skills in all three areas, so it might make sense to have multiple people play the capacity analyst role.

In other cases, you might find that the responsibilities of a single role are not enough to keep a person busy full time. In this case the person might fill multiple roles. The multiple roles might be all within capacity management, or might also span other areas of IT. For example, if you have someone who is very strong in storage management technologies, that person might be both a storage architect whom designs new solutions and the storage capacity analyst. The one person can use complimentary skills to fill both roles.

The best way to map roles to people won't be immediately obvious. The management team needs to understand the strengths and weaknesses of the people on the capacity management team in order to best assign responsibilities to individuals. Over time, these assignments might need to be rebalanced in order to keep the team functioning at a high level. Don't be afraid to make changes as time goes by and people acquire deeper skills in certain areas.

Developing Capacity Management Skills

Although capacity management has been an acknowledged discipline in the mainframe arena for many years, there is still a great shortage of people who can manage capacity effectively for distributed servers and for IT services. Because there aren't a lot of people with this skill set, you might have difficulty hiring people to fill the capacity management team. Maybe you could find people but your organization prefers to work with your existing IT people and develop capacity management skills from within the organization. This approach preserves organizational knowledge, and there is a huge benefit to having a capacity management team that already understands the ebb and flow of change in your organization.

The best way to develop capacity management skills depends on the starting point of the person you choose. If you want to take a technical person and grow him into a capacity process owner, you need to help him develop the ability to work across the management and executive teams, to coordinate and lead teams of people, and to understand budgets and project schedules. Because this person comes from a technical background, you probably will not have to spend much time helping him understand the technologies of your organization or how to measure capacity for those technologies. Focus instead on process and leadership training to develop a technical person into a capacity process owner.

To develop a capacity analyst, on the other hand, the training required is mostly technical. The analyst must understand the details of how the technology works in order to best recommend ways to measure and manage capacity for that technology. The principles of capacity planning are fairly easy to understand after this person understands the technology being managed.

If you choose to train your current IT people in capacity management, a great introduction is the ITIL foundations training followed by ITIL-specific capacity management training from a qualified training organization. Those classes generally prepare a person to understand the processes and concepts behind managing capacity according to the ITIL framework.

Skill Maturity and Team Composition

You want to make sure you have a mixture of different maturity levels on the capacity management team. Ideally, the capacity process owner has the most experience and serves as a mentor to the other team members. Assuming that your organization is large enough to have multiple people focused on capacity management, the other team members should not all be complete novices, nor should they all have years of experience. In general, you will find that a mix of experienced and new capacity management people generate more fresh ideas while still providing a balanced, measured approach.

Try to develop people as part of their assignment to the capacity management team. Capacity analysts can aspire to step into the capacity planner role. Capacity planners can aspire to be capacity process owners. The process owner should work to make team operations so smooth that they are no longer needed. This notion of a team in which everyone is growing in experience and skill provides a work environment where people are glad to do a great job.

Summary and Next Steps

Unfortunately, no one can tell you how to build the perfect IT organization. There are variations and exceptions to every rule. What I've tried to do in this chapter, however, is at least share the general rules with you so that you can begin to create the perfect capacity management organization for yourself. In this chapter you've learned the roles that other organizations have found useful and you've found some guidelines for staffing those roles.

You learned that the implementation team is led by the capacity process owner, who should be your most experienced capacity management expert. In addition, you need someone to design your capacity management information system, someone to design and document your process and procedures, and a project manager to keep the team focused in the right direction. This implementation team should be designed and staffed specifically to build the strongest possible foundation for your capacity management service.

But a firm foundation won't last without maintenance. In the second half of the chapter, we explored the roles you need for your operational capacity management team. The leadership stays with the capacity process owner, who is now called the capacity service owner. This strong leader builds and often manages the team of capacity analysts who do the day-to-day work of understanding the capacity of your IT components and services. As the name implies, the analysts do more than generate data—they explore that data and make recommendations to the rest of IT. You also learned that a strong operational team includes a data manager who can manage the intricacies of the CMIS and a capacity planner who can summarize the recommendations of the various capacity analysts and bring them to a wider business audience.

I finished the chapter by giving you a few insights I've gained over the years about staffing, skill development, and maturity. These aren't insights from a human resources professional, but from someone who has been in the trenches with the capacity management team and understands how the team can succeed if all the parts are in place.

In the next chapter we continue our survey of the best practices in capacity management by looking more deeply at the capacity management process and how to implement it. You'll find that the process is what will bind your team together and keep them moving as a unit when difficulties arise.

CHAPTER 8

Implement the Capacity Management Process

Like any significant IT endeavor, effective capacity management requires a well-designed process. In many areas the ITIL books provide a good high-level process that you can start with, but capacity management isn't one of those areas. The very simple process described in the ITIL Service Design *book is not really sufficient as a foundation for your capacity management program.*

Fortunately, there are solid process foundations available. You could use the IBM Tivoli® Unified Process (ITUP) as a base, or any of a number of other sample capacity management processes. Whatever your starting point, however, you need to customize the process to apply to your organization and define more specific process artifacts like policies and procedures to guide your team as they provide the capacity management service. This chapter describes the various process artifacts you need and helps you understand how to deploy them successfully.

The High-Level Process

A high-level IT process is a lot like the outline on a child's coloring page. It helps provide a starting point and keeps the boundaries clear, but it isn't very interesting by itself. You need a high-level capacity management process that helps explain to your organization which elements are parts of the scope of capacity management and which elements are not. The high-level process does not provide detailed instructions for executing necessary tasks, but it does provide the team with a broad understanding of capacity management as understood by your organization.

This section describes a high-level capacity management process and how you can tailor it to fit your needs.

The ITIL Process

In ITIL version 3, capacity management includes four process steps and three defined subprocesses. Figure 8.1 depicts the four process steps from the *ITIL Service Design* book. The process steps begin with reviewing current capacity utilization and the performance of your IT services and components. This is an ongoing activity that should be occurring continuously. You will most likely have automated tools in place that constantly monitor the performance of your IT infrastructure by looking at metrics such as CPU wait times, memory page spaces, disk I/O buffers, network latency times, and a myriad of other factors. Most organizations find it convenient to take averages of these technical factors over some period of time and use those averages as their monitoring threshold levels. In other words, reviewing the capacity and performance of the systems happens as the average utilization is calculated, and that capacity and performance is highlighted when that average reaches a predetermined threshold. This is the first fundamental part of the capacity management high-level process.

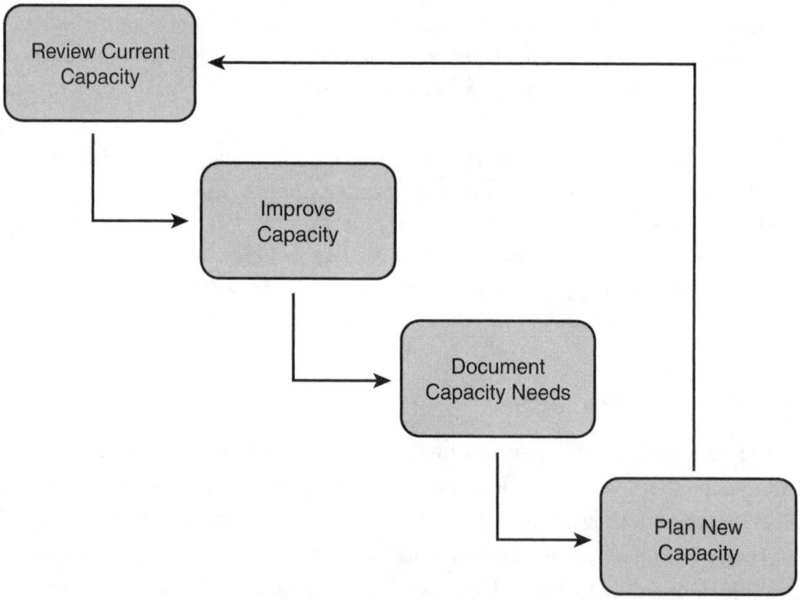

Figure 8.1 The basic ITIL capacity management process is quite simple.

The second ITIL process step is to improve the current performance and capacity of your existing IT services and components. This is known as tuning. You look for ways to maximize the performance of the individual pieces and parts of the infrastructure in order to get the most effectiveness for the IT services you provide. This tuning generally involves understanding a bottleneck that is inhibiting peak performance, adding more resources to bypass that particular issue, and then measuring again to see whether you've made a positive difference. This cycle can be repeated frequently until you get the desired effect, and should be a continuous process managed by the technical team of capacity analysts.

Many organizations are already doing steps one and two in some way. They might not be defined as a separate process or implemented consistently by a capacity management team, but you are most likely already reviewing your capacity and performing some degree of tuning in your environment.

Whereas step two focuses on small details and small improvements, step three in the ITIL process takes a broad view. In step three you look across capacity pools and IT services to forecast future capacity expansion. You assess what you have and document new capacity requirements. The assessment should take into account the various ways to forecast demand that you learned in Chapter 3, "Understanding Capacity Demand." Using those forecasting techniques, you produce a comprehensive view of future needs that can form the base of your capacity plans.

Step four is to produce the actual capacity plans. As described in Chapter 6, "Define and Manage Capacity Plans," you will define plans for each of the major capacity types that you manage and then manage those plans through ongoing reviews. Like all the other steps, planning new capacity is an ongoing process rather than a single event.

As long as patterns similar to these four steps are included in your high-level process design, you can assert that you are aligned with the best practices of ITIL. As your process discipline matures, you will want to start thinking in the three dimensions that ITIL envisions—component capacity, service capacity, and business capacity. The high-level process will be effective across all three of these dimensions, but your policies and procedures will likely need to be tailored separately for each.

Adopting and Configuring a Process

Process engineering is a complex and somewhat confusing discipline. In this section you learn just enough about this discipline to choose (or create) a high-level capacity management process and then begin to configure it for your organization. Although the capacity management team won't look at the high-level process very often, it is still important because it provides a foundation that holds all the policies and procedures together. Time spent on the high-level process yields rewards in a clearer understanding of the job roles for each team member.

The first question to consider is which process to adopt. There isn't a shortage of available processes. Carnegie Mellon University has developed the Capability Maturity Model Integration (CMMI) for Services. This framework offers the Capacity and Availability Management process area, which can serve as a foundation for your high-level process. As described earlier in this chapter, ITIL offers a Capacity Management process model that can be your starting point. IBM provides public access to the IBM Tivoli Unified Process, which includes a capacity management process with well-defined roles and responsibilities. All these process foundations are viable starting points, and each offers something slightly different for your organization. If you haven't already adopted one of these process frameworks, I would strongly suggest that you engage an independent consultant to help you find the one that meets your organization's needs the best.

If your IT organization has been working with mainframe computing or is mature in process discipline, you might already have a high-level capacity management process. It might have been adopted from an earlier framework or simply developed for your own use from scratch. If you have an existing process, one of your options is to align it to the best practices defined by ITIL. You can do this by comparing the high-level process steps from your process to those of the ITIL framework. If you are missing any of the four fundamental steps, consider adding them to your process. If you have additional steps, determine whether they add real value to your organization, and if they don't, remove them. Of course, the authors of the ITIL process did not know or understand your organization, so it is quite likely that your high-level process has some things that those authors didn't include.

Another option is to create your own high-level process. You can look at the various processes available to you, combine those with an understanding of your organization, and create a brand-new high-level capacity management process. The advantage of defining a new process in this way is that your organization will be deeply invested and this will make the process implementation easier. The disadvantage is that new employees or service providers coming into your organization will not be familiar with the process foundation as they might if it were based on one of the well-known frameworks.

With so many options, how do you choose the right high-level process? To make the best choice, you need to understand what your requirements are. Many organizations are adept at creating functional and nonfunctional requirements for business applications but fail to use the same discipline for choosing or creating business and IT processes. This is a shame because carefully crafted requirements can bring the same clarity to process selection as they do to application development.

To create requirements to guide your process selection, simply ask key stakeholders a series of guiding questions:

- What areas should the process manage?
- Are there important measurements that should be made?
- What management control points need to be included?
- Is there a need to audit at any point in the process?
- What are the key decisions to be made?
- Who will make those key decisions?
- Are there time-sensitive activities to be performed?
- Who are the key people or groups involved in capacity management?

After you have documented the answers to these and similar questions as a set of process requirements, you can evaluate which starting point meets most of your needs.

After you've adopted (or created) a high-level process, it is time to begin tailoring it to your specific organization. Most of the tailoring happens at lower levels as you define policies and procedures for your organization, but there are some steps you can take at the higher levels.

One easy step to tailor a high-level process to your organization is to reconcile the vocabulary used by the process with that used by your business. One of the key benefits of ITIL is that it uses terms consistently, and before throwing that benefit away, you should at least consider whether the terms make sense to your teams. On the other hand, don't get stuck on using the correct ITIL terminology if it won't be helpful to your organization. Work through the high-level process and make sure that terms like incident, configuration item, service desk, IT service, and component are understood by everyone who needs to use the process. Either educate your team on the appropriate definition of these terms or change your process document to use the words they are already comfortable with.

A second step in customizing your high-level process is to look at control points. While capacity management is primarily an operational process rather than a control process, there will undoubtedly be points at which you want to assert some level of organizational control. For example, you will want to understand who reviews and approves the recommendations that are part of capacity plans. Identify all the control points associated with the high-level process and then define which part of your organization actually exercises control and the degree of control they want to execute.

Finally, you can tailor the high-level process by defining the roles to be filled. Chapter 7, "Staff the Capacity Management Team," describes some of the roles you might want to consider, but there are likely additional roles that make sense for your organization or perhaps valid reasons that your team should not include all the typical roles. It is essential at the high level that each process step indicates a role that executes that step. This allows the lower-level process artifacts to start with an accurate picture of how they will work.

Attributes of a Good High-Level Process

It is impossible to determine the best or most useful high-level process for your organization if you don't understand what attributes are important in a high-level process. So let's briefly consider what differentiates a good process from a bad one.

The first attribute of a good process is that it must take understood inputs and produce consistent and useful outputs. Look at your potential high-level process and make sure that it defines inputs that your organization can produce. If your capacity management high-level process depends on having complete business plans as an input but you know that the organization does not produce complete business plans, you will never be successful in implementing the process. Similarly, if the process dictates an output, make sure that your organization can produce that output consistently and that the output is useful. A capacity management process that produces really pretty reports that nobody reads is not the correct process.

A second attribute of a good process is that it is complete. If there are key decisions that need to be made but aren't reflected in the process flow, then your process is definitely not complete. If there are significant steps that you know the organization must do or will continue to do, they must be included in the flow somewhere. It is certainly acceptable to defer details to procedures or lower-level process flows, but the high-level process must at least contain enough detail that people working to drive down to the next level of detail know where to insert those details. A complete process is essential at the high level because without it the cost of rework is very high.

A good high-level process is also convincing. You should be able to use the high-level process to explain capacity management to anyone who doesn't understand the scope of the effort. A good high-level process allows someone to understand the activities to be performed and why they are necessary. If the process is confusing or unclear to someone new to the subject area, it might be too detailed or too technical. A good high-level process should be brief, but should include enough detail to explain the process without confusing its readers.

Figure 8.2 is a simple graphic showing the three attributes of a good high-level process.

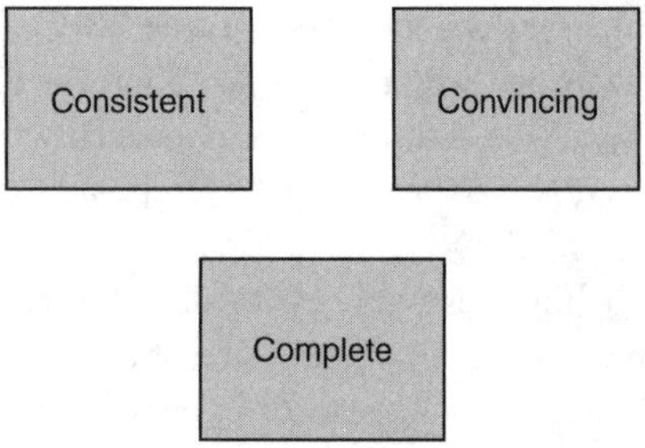

Figure 8.2 Good high-level processes follow the three Cs.

Defining and Documenting Capacity Policies

An important part of process engineering is helping your organization define the policies it will use in the capacity management area. Policies are decisions that you choose to make once in the controlled setting of the process work rather than making each time the process is executed. Of course, not all decisions can be made this way, but it is surprising how many decisions can be made once rather than many times.

These policy decisions should be documented either as part of the high-level process or lower-level procedures, or in separate policy documents. If your organization is not accustomed to creating and managing policy documents, simply document the policies within the other process documents. Regardless of how you document the policy decisions, it is important that you review them regularly to understand whether the decision still makes sense.

Capacity Monitoring Policies

One set of policy decisions involves the steps you use to monitor capacity utilization. Your process needs to define the steps for collecting utilization data for both components and services, and there are many questions that can be settled with a one-time decision rather than letting your teams make these decisions separately.

One key decision is the capacity monitoring interval. The Heisenberg Uncertainty Principle states that taking a measurement always impacts the thing being measured. This is definitely true in capacity management tools. The tool used to measure capacity itself requires some capacity to run. Thus, taking a snapshot of used capacity every 30 seconds provides much more data but requires much more overhead on your infrastructure than taking the same snapshot every 30 minutes. The more frequently you want to view the utilization, the more resources it takes. The frequency of data capture is an excellent decision to make during the process-definition phase of your project, and should be revisited periodically as your capacity management discipline matures.

Of course, your monitoring frequency policy might recognize different frequencies for different components and services. Measuring the used bandwidth of a network line requires little overhead, so you might measure it very frequently, whereas measuring the utilization of a complex IT service might be very difficult and consume many resources. Thus, the policy would differentiate between these two types of monitoring and specify different data collection intervals. It is perfectly reasonable for a policy to specify some variations, but if your policy starts to have many different exceptions and decision trees associated with it, you are really just defining a procedure for making the decision rather than a policy.

Another policy you should consider is where you want to set capacity thresholds. These thresholds are values you use to create warnings when capacity is reaching dangerous levels. Most organizations find that identifying two levels of warning makes sense. The first threshold indicates that someone should pay attention to the situation, and the second threshold indicates that an incident is likely to occur if action isn't taken soon. Of course, these thresholds could be set to provide warnings both as capacity grows and as capacity shrinks. Capacity management should see as much warning in a resource being 5% utilized as it does when the resource is 95% utilized. Both are signs of a serious mismatch between allocated and used capacity, although the politics involved in fixing underutilization are often very different from those involved in responding to overutilization.

As with capacity monitoring intervals, your threshold policy might have some variations as you define different thresholds for different types of resources. Be sure to explain the rationale associated with these decisions so that future reviewers of the policy can determine whether the settings still make sense.

In addition to intervals and thresholds, you might decide that some components or IT services do not need monitoring at all. If a resource type is nearly static, it might be sufficient to do an occasional manual observation rather than implementing a monitoring tool and maintaining thresholds. You might even find that some resources are really not worth the effort of managing capacity at all. In such cases, your policy should state why you made that determination. A policy statement that indicates resources that will not fall under capacity management will save many hours of debate later.

Capacity Acquisition Policies

Acquisition is another area that benefits greatly from predetermined decisions. The policies you make around acquisition of new capacity help add clarity to the capacity management process and simplify many tasks.

The most common policy indicates how many free resources to maintain. This can be quite a complex decision, but creating a policy can help to simplify it. Imagine that your monitoring indicates that free disk space on a storage area network is down to 2TB (terabytes). If the entire SAN is only 4TB and your growth rate is less than 1GB per month, you will most likely decide that no action is needed. On the other hand, if your entire storage array contains 200TB and your growth rate is 1TB per week, you need to acquire more disk space almost immediately. In fact, you might be too late and some projects might experience delays because you won't have disk space to allocate to them.

The preceding example shows how policy statements can be useful. You should establish a policy that indicates how low you will allow a resource pool to become before you acquire more resources to add to the pool. The policy can be based on the percentage free, or on absolute units. Your purchase reorder point might be the same for all services and components, or it might vary based on the criticality and expense of a given capacity pool. The important thing is that you have a policy that makes your acquisition decisions more consistent and balances the need for more capacity with the need to delay purchases until they are needed.

Another important part of your capacity acquisition policy should deal with the amount of capacity to acquire when you are running low. Going back to the example of storage space, if your entire current capacity is 4TB and your usage trend is fairly low, you probably won't want to purchase 2TB at a time. That would cause you to have a large amount of unused capacity before you really need it. On the other hand, if a 1TB drive costs only a bit less than a 2TB drive, you might decide that it makes more sense to purchase extra space now even if you won't use it for a while.

The capacity acquisition policy should take into account the rate of technology obsolescence, the price for various amounts of new capacity, and the length of time it takes to get the new capacity fully ready for use. Remember that the details of exactly what capacity you acquire will be part of your capacity plan for each service and component. The policy should try to define the rationale behind the capacity plans, indicating why new capacity is needed and why you purchase specific amounts. Policy statements almost always help to explain the reasons behind steps you take in the process.

Finally, your capacity acquisition policy should state your preferred means of getting new capacity. For large organizations, you might have other locations that are constantly acquiring and decommissioning equipment. For such an organization, your capacity acquisition policy might state that you always look to reuse equipment you already own before you acquire new. Although this approach seems obvious, it is amazing how often large organizations purchase new equipment rather than redeploying existing gear they already own. Even smaller organizations can make a decision between purchasing new capacity directly from its original manufacturer and trying to find older equipment from one of the major IT resellers. Older equipment costs less to purchase, but if it fails frequently, it might not cost less to own. Your capacity acquisition policy should specifically state whether you pursue used equipment or insist on new equipment.

It is important that you also align your capacity acquisition policy with your enterprise architecture team. The architects should be providing standard ways of expanding your infrastructure, and your policy should reflect those standards and the involvement of the architecture and design team in capacity decisions.

Policy for Capacity Incidents and Changes

The procedure for handling capacity and performance incidents is particularly difficult for many organizations, and thus it is a great area in which to define policies that can help add clarity. The difficulty often lies in determining when a slowdown in a particular service or application should be defined as an incident. If your organization does not have a process to establish the baseline or expected performance of your services, you often have no recourse but to declare an incident each time a user calls to report his perception that the service is slow. These incidents can be difficult to resolve because the symptoms are often fleeting, and by the time the technician is checking on the issue, the slowdown might already be resolved.

Rather than reacting to every reported slowdown, you can establish a policy that dictates what conditions really constitute a service disruption or incident that needs to be explored. If you are fortunate enough to have a performance baseline for each major service and component (as recommended in Chapter 9, "Relate Capacity and Performance"), you can establish a threshold for deviation. For example, if your manufacturing design system normally retrieves a product design drawing in four seconds, as indicated by the baseline, you can say that anything over six seconds indicates an incident that should be investigated. That way, a product designer who is having a bad day won't be able to raise an incident just because the response time is five seconds.

Along with a policy that determines when an incident is necessary, you can establish a policy for which kinds of capacity additions and subtractions should fall under change control. Many organizations, for example, determine that adding memory or CPU power to a running virtual server presents such a low risk that the change control process is superfluous. You might decide the same thing for other routine actions like adding more disk space to a drive already provisioned on network attached storage, adding more print queues to an existing print server, or relocating a virtual server to a new host for load balancing. Some of these actions could even be automated, although all of them affect the capacity pools involved.

Change and incident management processes are just two of those that can be integrated through specific capacity management policies. Many other examples are provided in Chapter 15, "Integrating Capacity Planning with IT Processes."

Policy for Capacity Planning on New Projects

Capacity planning can be much easier if the appropriate decisions are made during the project planning process. All new IT services and many IT components are deployed as part of a project. You should establish a policy that dictates the level of capacity planning done during the project so that you can expect consistent results when projects are delivered.

Many organizations specify via policy that all projects that implement a new IT service need to create a capacity plan as one of the project deliverables. This makes great sense because the project team knows exactly what the projected need for the service or component will be. Creating a policy like this helps remind project teams of the need to plan ahead for capacity, and help to institutionalize the capacity planning discipline.

Even if you don't believe that your project teams are ready to create fully developed capacity plans, you can still ask that they at least provide some kind of forecast of the capacity that is needed by the new service. Without this forecast, the capacity management team is unable to guarantee the availability of resources to meet the needs, a sure way to make sure that a new IT service fails!

This section has provided just a few ideas about areas where you might want to establish capacity management policies. As your organization matures and understands capacity management better, you are likely to find dozens of other ways to help reduce confusion and variability by creating policies. You'll find over time that capacity policies become an integral part of how your organization operates.

Creating Capacity Procedures

The high-level capacity management process helps your organization to see and understand the goals of the program. The procedures, on the other hand, help team members to know how to play their own distinct part in achieving those goals. Both are equally important because without an overall scope your program will be aimless, but without detailed steps your program will never reach its goals. This section describes procedures in general and recommends specific procedures to develop to support your capacity management program.

Process Steps Create Procedures

A typical process document contains a flowchart describing the process at the highest level of detail. The flowchart contains a combination of rectangles representing process steps and diamonds representing process decisions. Procedures are concerned with the rectangles.

If two people in your organization intend to execute the same process rectangle but get two different outputs, you know that the process is not spelled out in sufficient detail. The correct answer to this dilemma is to create a procedure. Procedures take the single-process step defined at a higher level and create an entire flowchart that describes how to accomplish that one process step. That flowchart will also have rectangles and diamonds, and if any of the rectangles fails to pass the consistency test, they can be further defined by procedures of their own. In this way you should keep driving a procedure to lower levels of detail until all people in your organization who must execute the procedure do it the same way.

The goal in creating procedures is consistency and predictability. You don't want to leave your capacity planning activities open to debate. You want the same results each time regardless of the skill of the person executing the procedures. This consistency allows you to have meaningful measurements for the process and allows other ITIL processes to rely on the outputs of capacity management. The rest of this section focuses on some of the procedures that organizations need to define to achieve consistency in capacity management.

Procedures for Capacity Reviews

You undoubtedly need to define procedures to help your team consistently measure and track the utilization of your components and services. Capacity tracking is a fundamental part of your overall capacity management program because it feeds your capacity plans and forms the baseline for capacity forecasts. Because the utilization data is important, you need to define procedures that are sufficiently detailed to ensure that data is provided consistently.

In a typical IT environment you have multiple hardware platforms, each running its own operating system. Normally, this causes you to implement and use different tools to measure utilization. The differences between tools, whether large or small, cause variation in the procedures you use to measure capacity. These variations can normally be handled as decision points in the procedures, but if they are really significant, you might want to have separate procedures.

Your procedure should define who will take actions and what actions they take. In the capacity monitoring procedure that means you describe a role for someone to either log in to the various capacity monitoring tools or review the automated data that is captured. Depending on the degree of automation available, this person might need to summarize data from multiple tools to calculate the utilization of your IT services. You might have the same person gathering data and reporting on that data, or there might be multiple roles involved. Even if you know that the organization has a single person who takes care of all the capacity monitoring tasks, it is still a good idea to write down those tasks as a procedure so that person can take vacations and in case that person one day leaves the organization. Without documented procedures the loss of a single person can cause your entire capacity management program to collapse!

Document any procedures necessary for collecting, storing, reporting, and reviewing utilization data. You will find it useful to read through the capacity management portion of the *ITIL Service Design* book to appreciate some of the procedures that might be involved. Most organizations end up with a monthly cycle that gathers (or calculates) the utilization for every component and service, then updates trend and forecast information and reviews the entire package with the appropriate management teams. As long as you have defined how those activities get completed regularly, you have defined enough procedures for capacity monitoring. Like all procedure documentation, be sure there is agreement between what you've documented and what is being practiced. Especially in regulated environments, this agreement is critical.

Procedures for Improving Capacity

Most organizations have at least rudimentary procedures for collecting utilization data from the IT components they manage. Whether they call this capacity management or simply an extension of systems management, it is a relatively common practice to keep watch on the CPU utilization, memory allocation, and disk space for computing resources.

A disciplined, systematic approach to improving capacity and performance is quite another story. Very few organizations have documented approaches or procedures for improving their capacity posture. This is unfortunate because most of the financial benefits of capacity management come from these capacity improvement steps. Leaving these steps up to individual system administrators or capacity analysts will deprive your organization of some of the benefit it could be getting if these procedures were documented and executed consistently for all your resources.

Capacity improvement procedures should begin with the assumption that utilization data has been gathered and is available. Without accurate information on the current state of services and components, it is difficult to determine whether your actions are improving or degrading the performance and capacity.

A typical procedure for capacity improvement would involve the following steps:

1. Choose a specific component or service to be improved.
2. Establish a specific capacity measurement to be improved for that component or service.
3. Document the baseline values for that measurement to establish the starting point.
4. Analyze the options or settings that might improve the measurement.
5. Choose one option and implement it.
6. Repeat the measurement to document any improvement that has been made.
7. If the improvement is not sufficient or more improvement is desired, repeat from step 4.
8. When you have improved the component or service, you are finished!

Of course, you need to supplement these simple steps by including the role of the person performing each of these steps and enough details to ensure consistency in the procedure. This simple outline helps you get started, but as your organization matures, you'll find that the better your capacity improvement procedure gets, the less you will overspend on new hardware and software. Chapter 9 has much more to say on the topic of improving performance through a disciplined approach.

Procedures for Capacity Planning

Another set of procedures that are often neglected are those for capacity planning. Whereas capacity improvement focuses on one service or component at a time, capacity planning spans all of your resources and tries to create a bigger picture of where the organization is heading.

You learned about creating a capacity plan in Chapter 6. But capacity planning involves much more than simply documenting the plan. To create a useful capacity plan, someone needs to use the techniques from Chapter 3 to understand the future demand, and then explore the utilization numbers to estimate when demand exceeds the total available capacity. This forward-looking forecast must then be updated regularly so that its accuracy can be improved over time. All these steps should be documented in your capacity planning procedures.

Create procedures that are detailed enough to ensure consistency, but not so detailed that you write volumes nobody will read. If you're inexperienced with procedures and the right level of documentation, just keep it simple. It is always possible to capture more detail in your procedures later, but you can never recover the time spent creating low-level details that aren't useful.

Managing Capacity Process Assets

This chapter has described three kinds of process documents—a high-level process, policy statements, and more detailed procedures. As you work through these three levels to define your capacity management process, you will create several documents that need to be managed and controlled.

If you already have a governance process and are experienced in managing the various assets associated with IT processes, you can probably skip the rest of this section. There is nothing about the capacity management process in particular that should change your current practices in this area. If you aren't accustomed to creating and working with process assets, however, this section provides some bonus information that can apply to all the process areas you choose to define in the future.

Document Format and Storage

The first question you need to deal with is how the documents will get created. Will you have one huge document that contains the high-level process, all the policies, and all the procedures? The advantage to this approach is that there is just one document that describes everything someone would want to know about capacity management. The disadvantage of a single document is that any change to any part of the process, policy, or procedure causes a change to the whole document, which can make reviewing and change control more difficult. It is also harder to manage with a single document if different people are creating and updating the policies and procedures. Unless you plan on very little documentation or an extremely simple process, it is best to begin with separate documents for your high-level process, policies, and procedures.

On the other extreme, some organizations document each procedure and each policy in a separate document of its own. I've actually worked with one customer who was trying to manage 80 separate documents just for the capacity management area. When multiplied across all the IT process areas described by ITIL, this resulted in a mountain of paper to deal with! I would recommend that you stick with three documents—one for the high-level process, one for all the policies, and one for all the procedures. You'll most likely find that you work on the high-level process very infrequently, the policies only occasionally, and the procedures at least monthly, so having them in separate documents supports independent updates on different cycles.

The documents should be stored where they can be reached by everyone who needs to update or read them. If you have an enterprise architecture or document management system that includes the capability to log who is accessing the documents, control who is able to update them, and manage multiple versions over time, then you have reached repository nirvana. If you don't have such a sophisticated system available to you, at least establish a repository that does some degree of logging so that you can see who is making changes to your process assets. Collaboration tools such as IBM Lotus® Domino® or Microsoft SharePoint® generally work well as document repositories because you can control read and write access and keep track of who is making changes to the document.

Reviews and Process Approvals

You should have gotten the impression from this chapter that the process documents are in a constant state of flux. Documents that don't change are seldom accurate because the organization should be growing and maturing, and as the organization learns more, those lessons should be captured in the procedures and policies for capacity management.

But change simply for the sake of change can lead to people who are confused or operating under older procedures. You need a carefully controlled change mechanism that ensures that the right people have an opportunity to understand the proposed changes and decide whether those changes really improve the process.

Your organization needs to understand that a change to the process or procedure is much more than an update to a document. Each change that is accepted is a commitment by someone or some group in your organization to change their behavior. There are few things that undermine the strength of your capacity management program faster than discrepancies between your process document and your teams' behavior.

Each of your documents should be reviewed on a regular basis as well as when they are changed. When a change is made to the process document, the review should determine whether the people who must execute the procedures are informed and ready to change the way they execute. If you review documents only when changes are made, however, there is a danger that the organization will change without updating the procedure. Therefore, you should also review processes, policies, and procedures that have *not* changed for a while. These reviews should validate that the way the teams are acting is still consistent with what the procedure or policy says.

Both types of reviews should specify people who can approve the change. Typically, the process owner is one of these approvers, but other roles might also be involved. Experience shows that holding reviews without designated approvers is a good way to ensure low attendance. If it really isn't anyone's job to sign off on the process documents, everyone tends to assume that someone else is doing a detailed review. This usually results in nobody doing a detailed review.

Making Updates and Tracking Revisions

One of the important parts about changing your process documents is helping people be aware of exactly what has changed. When working on processes, policies, or procedures, you should get very familiar with the revision-tracking capabilities of your word processing software. Be sure to track the changes, and then incorporate those changes into the base document after they are approved.

Within each document you should also provide a table that lists the version number, the reason for making the changes, the date the changes were made, and who made them. This kind of table allows readers to track the versions of the document over time, and helps to determine when someone has an older version of a procedure or policy document.

Most of these document management strategies are common sense, but failure to follow this common sense can lead to real problems as you try to sort out the mess and keep your capacity management program on track.

Summary and Next Steps

This chapter described the steps involved in documenting and implementing a capacity management process. Starting with the high-level process flow adopted from ITIL or another process framework, you learned which attributes are important in a high-level process.

We next explored policies, which are aids in making decisions while following a process. I described several categories of policies and provided some guidance on how to define your policies within each of these categories.

Next you learned about procedures, which are more detailed steps that you document so that your team can follow the high-level process consistently. You learned about procedures for capacity reviews, procedures for improving capacity, and procedures for capacity planning, all fundamental steps in the ITIL capacity management process.

The chapter ended with instructions to help you manage all your process work. Processes, policies, and procedures need to evolve as your capability matures, and you need to have a plan to manage that change as it occurs.

In the next chapter we continue our survey of best practices by considering the relationship between capacity management and performance management. In thinking about your high-level process, you need to determine whether performance management is simply a subset of capacity management for you or whether it has enough scope to warrant a high-level process of its own. The next chapter helps you to make that decision.

Chapter 9

Relate Capacity and Performance

One of the difficulties in managing capacity is that computer systems operate so quickly. There may be plenty of capacity one moment, but then a process runs amok or a virus takes over and suddenly all the available capacity is used up. Thus far we've ignored the dynamic nature of capacity management, but now we address it directly. This chapter helps you understand the similarities and differences between capacity and performance.

As you've learned, capacity management aims to have just the right amount of computing resources available when they are needed. Capacity managers tend to focus on the "when" part of that equation, forecasting over the long term when resources run out, and implementing plans to get more resources before that happens. Performance management focuses more intensely on understanding what the "right" amount of resources should be. In this chapter we consider techniques for performance management and provide a better understanding of how performance management and capacity management are related.

Performance Is Capacity in a Moment

Performance management cannot be understood without reference to time. We measure performance with rates such as bits per second or transactions per minute. Even processors are measured by the clock speed or instructions per second. Performance management is the management of computer capacity over some typically short period.

This section explores this basic definition of capacity and builds on it to help you understand how performance management can be an integral component of your capacity management program.

Definition of Performance Management

The central concern of performance management is how quickly IT systems can satisfy the needs of their users. This is a very real concern because the speedy response of IT systems is important in many aspects of our daily lives. Some IT systems are described as real-time because they control real world events that are time-sensitive. When an operator issues a command to close the oil-flow valves at a refinery, the delay must be minimal. When a clinician views the current status of a patient in a critical care unit, they expect the data to be current to less than a second. Even in day-to-day business systems, performance is important. Nobody likes to wait in line or on the phone only to hear a customer service person say, "The computer is slow." These examples show how important the discipline of performance management is.

Unfortunately, however, performance management concerns are often at odds with the goals of capacity management. The performance manager wants to have extra capacity available so there are no slowdowns waiting for computer resources. The capacity manager wants to minimize the amount spent on IT and does this by trying to eliminate extra capacity wherever possible. Performance management longs for more space, more memory, and more CPU power while capacity management longs to see all these resources close to fully utilized. ITIL tells us that the capacity and performance management process should seek a balance between these two desires. Although this is perhaps an oversimplification, the important point is that there are competing goals between capacity and performance management.

The relationship of performance and capacity management can also be seen in service-level management. Very few organizations have service levels related directly to capacity management. Maintaining IT service utilization above 70%, ensuring that disk space is never more than 30% unused, or making all servers at least 40% busy are not goals that most organizations aspire to. Instead, the service levels are normally defined in terms of the performance of systems. Average user response times of less than some number of seconds are very popular service levels. Other examples include system time to process a specific batch workload or the size of a maintenance window needed to run the backup process. These performance-based service levels all depend on having the resource capacity available to achieve the desired performance.

Another dimension of performance management is cost. You've learned that a major focus of capacity management is cost reduction. Performance management reduces costs only indirectly, and only in the long term. Most organizations find that hiring or training the skilled resources, building environments to support performance testing, acquiring and maintaining specialized performance testing tools, and conducting ongoing performance tuning are more costly than the savings. On the other hand, good performance management practices produce some savings, particularly in incident management. If system performance is well documented and ongoing tuning is taking place, the likelihood of performance-related incidents is reduced, and the duration of those incidents that do occur is greatly reduced.

Time Scale for Performance Testing

One question that often arises when organizations begin to consider performance management is the time scale that should be used. By time scale we mean both how long to test and how much other activity should be considered as part of the test. For example, should an application be tested to run for one typical business hour, or for one day during the busiest day the organization has experienced?

Best practices coalesce around the idea that the best way to begin a performance test is with an idle system. This means that all other applications and as many processes as possible should be stopped in order to run the performance test, and the test should just measure the impact of a single user performing typical work. This single-user system test can then be used as a basic case in future performance management work as the best performance that can ever be hoped for when the system is used by more than a single user.

After the impact of a single user on the system is understood, you should schedule a variety of tests that gradually increase the workload on the overall system. This works best if you have specific performance requirements defined for the system and you can test to see whether the system will achieve them. If you don't have specific requirements, you should estimate the average workload on the system during a typical business day. Use this estimate to test the system at half of this typical load, right at typical load, at double the typical load, and then at three times the typical load. The results of these tests should give you a good idea of how the overall system will behave as you increase the number of transactions or users in the future.

One of the challenges with reading the result of performance tests is that you are forced to deal with averages. In the single-user test you can measure absolute speeds and response times, but to make sure your numbers are more accurate, you should run the test more than once. To get the best possible picture, you then average the absolute numbers and you can tell what the average response time will be. For the single-user test, the standard deviation, or difference in the absolute numbers, is fairly small, and the average is a good indicator of the expected response of the system.

After you begin to test with higher loads, however, you will most likely want to take the response time for each simulated or actual user across a series of different transactions and a number of different test runs. To get to the expected response time, you average these numbers, which might vary significantly, but this decreases the precision of the number you can set as an expected response time. You will end up with an "average of averages," which can sometimes introduce a range of 30% to 40%. So instead of a response time of 2 seconds, you say that the response time will be between 1.2 and 2.8 seconds 90% of the time. A typical user hears 1.2 and expects that response every time rather than understanding it to be the best possible result. You can alleviate this concern by expressing your results differently, saying that a typical user gets a response in 2.8 seconds 90% of the time, ignoring the lower end of the range.

Performance Management in the Capacity Management Process

You've learned that performance management is important, and that it is sometimes at odds with capacity management. This raises the question of whether ITIL is mistaken in grouping performance and capacity management into the same process area. Let me assure you that ITIL is not mistaken. Although performance management and capacity management focus on different aspects, they are really two sides of a single coin. They both involve making sure there are enough resources at the right point in time to optimally provide the services that IT has committed to the organization.

Although capacity management and performance management are related, you should avoid the mistake of assuming that capacity managers can also be performance managers. It would take a person with an unusually broad skill set to play both roles successfully. Capacity managers need to be stingy misers who look for every way to eke more out of the resources available. Performance managers need to be tireless problem solvers who constantly look for ways to make services and components run just a bit faster. The capacity manager needs strong administrative and management skills, while the performance manager needs deep technical analysis skills. If you can afford only two people on your whole capacity management team, one should be oriented toward performance management and the other toward tracking and analyzing capacity.

Although performance management requires different skills than the rest of capacity management, it is a vital part of any capacity management process. The capacity management process provides a broad vista across months or sometimes years. Without the discipline of performance management included, there is a very real possibility that your capacity management team will ignore too many details. Performance management provides a very deep dive into the workings of an individual component or the small set of components that makes up an IT service. Performance management by itself runs the danger of getting lost in the details and minutiae and missing the bigger trends. Figure 9.1 provides a visual reminder of the two different dimensions that these disciplines use.

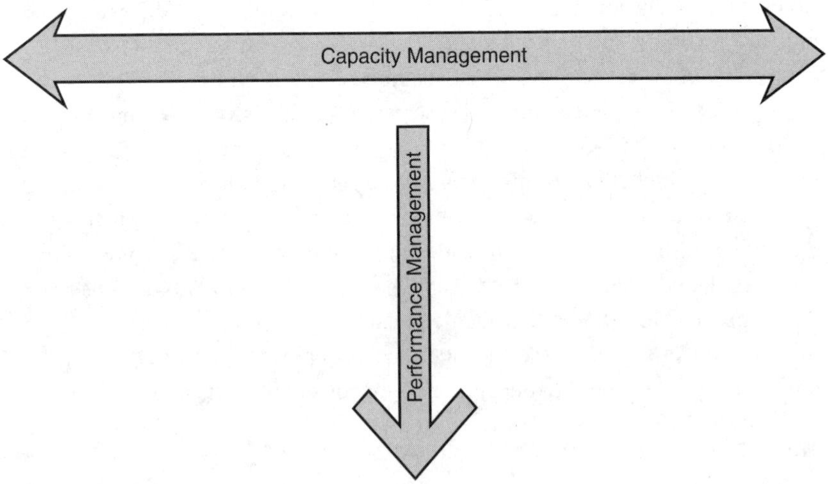

Figure 9.1 Capacity takes a broad view while performance focuses on a deep view.

Expand Capacity to Improve Performance

Since performance is measured as the capacity available at a specific moment in time, it is logical that most performance issues can be fixed by adding more capacity to the system. Although this is always the easiest fix, it isn't necessarily the least expensive, or even the best fix in most situations. If you don't take time to really analyze performance, then adding capacity may mask the true issue, or even worse, may have absolutely no effect at all on the performance of the system you're trying to improve.

In this section we take a deeper look at the discipline of performance management. You'll come to understand how to measure and improve performance, and learn how to really diagnose a performance problem so you can implement an effective solution rather than simply implementing the easiest solution. The goal is not to make you a performance management expert, but instead to enable you to find an expert and understand the performance management role as an integral piece of your capacity management program.

Techniques to Measure Performance

Of course, we are all familiar with the most popular method to test performance. You get out your stopwatch (digital stopwatch if you prefer high tech) and hit the Enter key to submit a transaction. When the response screen has finished painting on your screen, you stop the watch and you now have a measurement of the response time for a specific transaction. Of course, this method doesn't have very much precision and doesn't really take into effect what else might be going on at the same time. This means that if you use the manual method to measure response time a dozen times, you may get a wide variety of numbers in response. Averaging these numbers gives you a single number but really doesn't provide anyone a reasonable estimate of what response they might expect.

A much better method to measure performance is to use a performance analysis tool such as Rational Performance Manager, BMC ProactiveNet Performance Management, or CA NetQoS SuperAgent. These, and tools like them, create instrumentation that enables you to measure response times at the user interface, but they also enable you to break that time into the discrete pieces of the transaction such as data query time, application server processing time, web page display time, and network transit time. This gives you much more information about the overall response time and enables you to focus any improvement efforts on the right point in the overall system. Most tools of this type also capture statistics from the operating environment, such as number of logged-in users, CPU busy time, amount of memory in use, and paging rates. This data can help you make accurate and fair comparisons between different measurements taken at different points in time. With this data in hand, you can create a normalized response time that accurately predicts what your users can expect when they interact with the system. The downside of many of these tools is that they stumble badly when data is encrypted and they introduce an overhead into the transactions they attempt to measure.

The next step for measuring response is the completely scientific approach. Rather than simply taking measurements on a running system, you can use automated tools to simulate the load you desire. These tools generally use one or more "driver" workstations to simulate the actions of dozens or even hundreds of users. By controlling the specific actions that these simulated users perform, you can measure each transaction type in various conditions and create a very accurate picture of how the overall system performs under a variety of loads. Most performance managers start with a very light load to get the best possible response, and then ratchet up the load to find out if there are breaking points where software or network timeouts cause the system to be unusable. This is generally called "stress" or "load" testing.

Whether you are stuck with a stopwatch and keyboard or you have the latest performance test suite from your favorite vendor, it is important that you have people familiar with measuring the performance of the systems you want to manage. Your capacity models may show that systems are underutilized, but if you remove resources from a system, the only way to know that you've gone too far is by measuring the performance. As long as performance remains acceptable and the system is not consistently running out of capacity, your removal of resources can be considered successful.

Techniques to Improve Performance

Now you know how to measure the performance of a system, but what do you do if the performance isn't adequate? The second half of the performance manager job description is to take steps to make performance better when the measurements or user experience show that it isn't good enough.

The first task of performance improvement is to define which part of the overall system you are trying to improve. You may decide to add two more virtual processors to a virtual server, but if the performance is slow because of lack of memory, your new measurement won't show much improvement, and you will have allocated resources that could be used elsewhere. If your performance measurement included tools that are able to break the overall response time into discrete segments, you can start by focusing on particular segments that contribute the most to the overall response. If you don't have a tool that helps in that way, you may need to rerun your performance measurement and simultaneously measure various capacity utilization numbers. For the virtual server mentioned earlier, if you can measure the response time of several transactions and note the CPU utilization and memory utilization at the same time, you would likely see that the memory is heavily utilized while the CPU is not. This kind of information helps you determine where to make improvements.

After you have isolated one or more components that seem to be contributing to poor performance, the next issue is to decide what to do with them. In most cases the answer is to provide more resources. There are a wide variety of ways to provide resources, ranging from changing some parameters within a virtualized system to purchasing and installing new hardware and software. The performance manager at this point might consult with an architect or other hardware and software design person who can help evaluate the different alternatives for improving performance because different alternatives have different costs involved. The architect and the performance engineer work together to identify several possible ways to improve performance and then choose the best one to implement.

Tools can also help in the selection and implementation of performance improvements. Many performance management tool sets include the capability to build or detect a model of the system and then introduce changes to that model before you implement them in the real world. The changes you introduce in the model then simulate what the result of that change is likely to be when you make it to the real system. These tools and the skills to use them effectively are very rare and quite costly, and most typical business organizations won't need or use them. For work on certain systems, such as automated control systems that determine people's safety, this level of expense and extra rigor is warranted. Your organization can certainly spend as much as it wants to get the very best in performance management, and as part of implementing your overall capacity management program, you should consider which costs will provide a commensurate benefit to you.

Diagnosing Performance Problems

You've learned techniques to measure and improve performance. Now it is time to put those techniques into context by examining the full life cycle of a typical performance issue or problem. Although each individual performance issue has its own unique set of challenges, it is useful to have a predefined procedure ready so you can manage through them as they occur. This section introduces a procedure that has successfully resolved many performance problems. The procedure is shown in graphical form in Figure 9.2 and then described in the rest of this subsection.

The first step to working a performance problem is to pull out the baseline that you've made in advance. A baseline is really a profile of the typical performance across specific times of day or days within the business cycle. For example, a performance profile of your corporate e-mail system might include performance expectations for 9 a.m. on a typical Monday (the busiest time), for 2 a.m. on a typical Saturday (the lightest load), and for 9 a.m. on the Monday after a major holiday (the peak throughout the year). By looking at this kind of performance profile, you can determine whether there really is a problem. If the performance being reported is close to the performance expected according to the profile, you have a perception problem instead of a technical one.

You should build a performance profile for any application, service, or system that is important to your organization. Ideally, your release management process should be building these profiles when a new service is implemented and then updating them as new versions come out. If you don't have these profiles, you will want to make sure that you at least take several measurements of the system reporting the problem and consider that a worst-case profile because you know that when performance fits that profile, someone will consider the system to be broken. After you have the situation under control, make sure you run the measurements again to create a new baseline to use when the next situation arises.

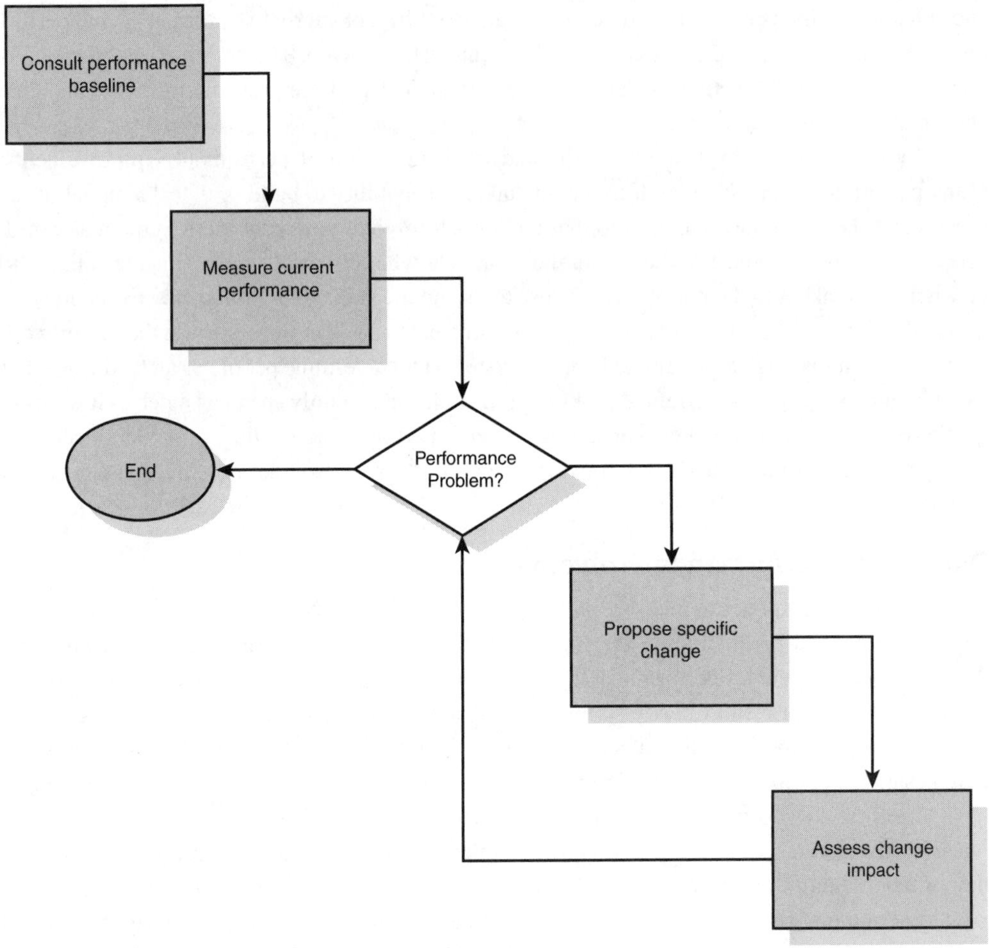

Figure 9.2 These are typical steps for resolving a performance problem.

After you have a baseline in hand for the system that is experiencing a performance problem, the next step is to measure the current performance. Use the techniques described earlier to measure the performance and find out how far off the system is from its baseline. If the difference is slight, you can probably explain it away and close the performance problem. If the performance is significantly different from what your baseline says it should be, you need to dig deeper. If you have a performance management tool, it helps you correlate performance measurements with capacity utilization measurements. If you don't have an automated way to do this, you still want to consider all the available measurements of utilization to better understand if the system is running out of some resource. A shortage of some computing resource like memory, disk space, or CPU space is typically the cause of a performance issue, so look for those symptoms first.

The next step in the problem resolution process is to propose one specific change that can be made to improve system performance. You might be able to think of several changes that could each help, but the best practice is to implement only one at a time so you can really understand what helps the problem. The change might be something simple that can go in almost immediately, or it may be something more complex that requires planning and testing before you can implement it in the production environment without undue risk. Make sure you consider all the opinions about what the real cause of the slowdown is, and select a change that repairs the most likely cause.

Before you implement the change, you should conduct an impact analysis. Involve the technical people who support the system and will implement the change. Involve the users or those who benefit from the system. The goal of this analysis is to determine whether the proposed change has a good likelihood of resolving the incident. When everyone agrees, implement the change in the target environment. This might involve starting with a test system and then promoting the change through a series of environments. If this is your normal procedure, don't short-circuit it because the change is only targeted at performance. Any system change has the potential for causing issues, so be sure to go through all the discipline that your change management process involves.

Finally, you should recognize that performance problems can be quite difficult to resolve completely. They often consist of multiple layers, and each change may make only part of the improvement that you really are seeking. This is especially true for organizations that are just beginning the discipline of performance management. When you advertise that your IT organization does performance management, you are likely to get reports of performance problems from users who have been dissatisfied with the response of your IT systems for years. When you attack this kind of performance problem, be ready to go through multiple changes to gradually bring the system performance closer to what you and the users want it to be.

Although resolving performance problems can be difficult, after you have this procedure in place and your organization becomes effective in using it, you will find that problems become less frequent and their resolutions come faster. Performance management eventually becomes a part of developing and deploying your IT services rather than a reactive discipline that fixes problems in existing systems. This natural evolution makes your users and customers much more satisfied with the services your IT organization proves.

Understanding Peaks and Valleys

Every IT system is less busy at some times and busier at other times. The humans using the system come in to work, making the system busier. Then they go home and the system gets less busy, or maybe a complex batch processing cycle kicks off and the system gets even busier. Even during a typical workday, different numbers of people are using the system, and the people who are logged in may be actually hitting keys or they may be thinking. Systems management tools such as virus scanners, resource monitors, and even capacity utilization trackers run in the background at various times and also contribute to the system being more or less busy. Most important systems are so complex and have so many different things that happen at unpredictable times that it is nearly impossible to say how much work needs to be accomplished at any point in time.

All of this variability in usage creates peaks and valleys in utilization. For some systems the peaks may be quite close to the valleys, as the system usage remains relatively stable. For other systems, however, the peak utilization might approach the total capacity of the system while the valley might approach a completely idle system. Unfortunately, it seems that the more critical a particular service or component is to the business, the more complex it becomes and the wider the difference between the peaks and the valleys. Performance management is made much more difficult by these systems, with a wide variability between the peaks and the valleys.

In this section we consider performance management of systems with this wide range of utilization. You learn how to document the usage over time by creating a performance profile and then explore some ways to manage capacity and performance for these challenging systems. More than anything else, this area of managing peaks and valleys separates the good performance analysts from the great ones. This brief section won't enable you to become a great performance manager, but it will at least give you a better understanding so you can have discussions with your performance manager when he tries to describe why he can't give you a single number describing the performance of a critical IT system.

Creating a Performance Profile

Performance profiles were mentioned earlier in this chapter, and the general concept was defined. When you're working on systems with peaks and valleys, however, creating a performance profile is both more critical and more complex.

The best approach to creating a performance profile is to define the most important things that the system under consideration is expected to do. These things might be specific transactions, specific batch jobs, specific system management tasks, or some combination of all three. What is important is that these be tasks that the system will repeat frequently or that have significant importance to the services IT is trying to provide. This list forms the basis of individual things you want to measure to create the profile.

If you have automated performance management tools, you will next define these specific tasks to the tools so they can either monitor the various components that are required to complete the tasks or even automate the execution of the tasks to accomplish load testing. If you don't have the luxury of performance tools, you need to determine how to measure both the time required to perform each task and the utilization of various resources like memory and CPU while the tasks are running. In other words, you'll figure out how to manually gather the data the performance tools would give you.

Having prepared the specific tasks and measurement techniques, you will next determine times to run the tests. Because you know there will be peaks and valleys, you will want to run each task at least 15 to 20 times at different times of day and different days of the year. If you have some educated guesses that help you determine the least busy and most busy times for a particular transaction, use those as times to create measurements. The more different times you execute the task and take measurements, the more complete your performance profile is, but the more expensive your testing process is. Of course, with an automated testing tool you can perform many tests almost as easily as you can perform a few.

As you run the various tests and gather measurements, you should prepare the graphs that form the backbone of the performance profile for a complex system. Use the data points you gather and curve fitting logic to define the intermediate points. Figures 9.3 and 9.4 provide two examples of graphs that are part of the same performance profile for a complex workflow management system. Figure 9.3 shows the peaks and valleys of CPU utilization for the database server as it responds to user activity. Figure 9.4 shows the response times for a typical approval transaction measured over the same time periods. These graphs are a small part of a complete performance profile for the overall system, but when a user calls to say that approval transactions are taking too long, we can focus on these graphs and determine whether the behavior is really outside of the norm for this system.

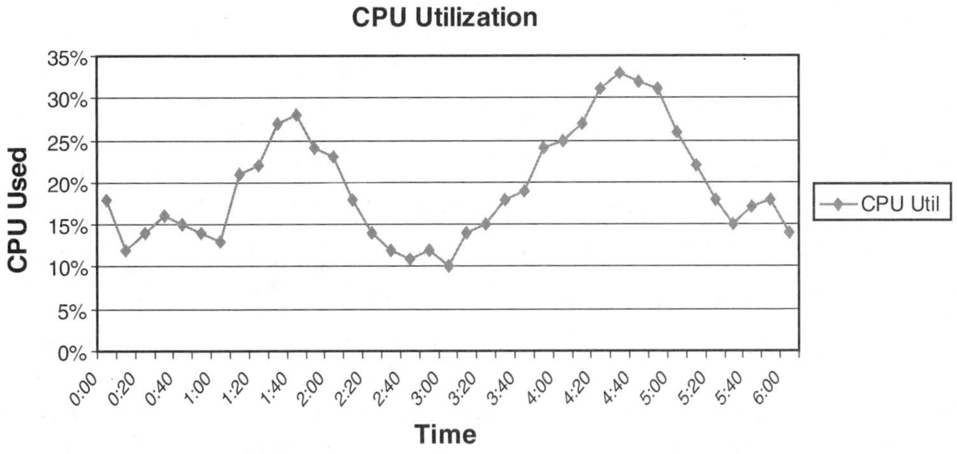

Figure 9.3 CPU utilization over a period of time for a complex workflow application.

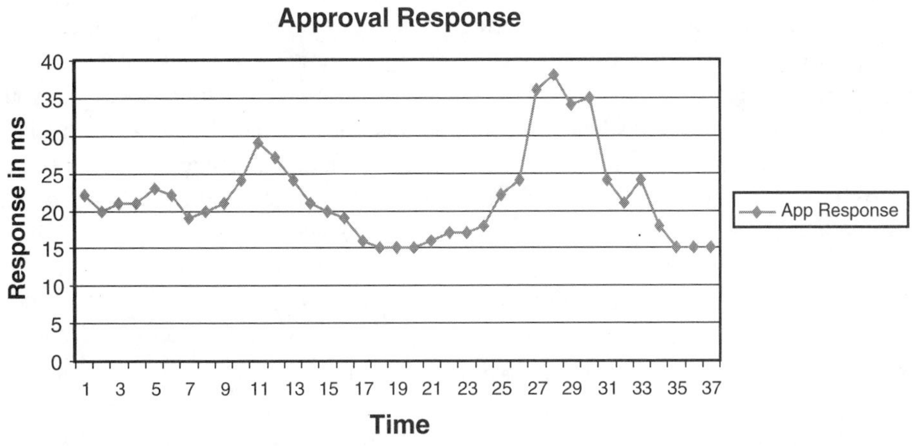

Figure 9.4 Approval transaction response time over the same period for the same application.

Measuring Performance Trends

Creating a profile is a great first step, but it is hardly enough to ensure that your critical systems keep performing their best. For these highly variable and highly valuable systems you need to be able to manage the performance trends continually rather than as a one time event. You need to measure and manage performance trends much as you do capacity trends.

Of course, trend management is much easier if you can instrument the components and the entire system with performance measurement tools. Then you can gather regular performance numbers such as response times and transaction throughput at the same time you gather regular capacity utilization metrics. The two can be blended together and you can easily plot trends over various periods of time so that you can predict with some accuracy what the performance is at any time of day or any day of the year.

If you don't have access to performance tools or the budget to acquire them, your performance engineer should establish a regular schedule of manual tests. The schedule should include times when the system should be very busy and other times when it should be less busy. But don't rely simply on guesses to schedule the performance readings. Sprinkle a few random reading times into the schedule as well to get a more complete view of the performance of the system. Using manual techniques, the engineer can gather the necessary performance and utilization readings that go into the trending graphs.

Integrating Performance into the Capacity Plan

You can probably see the pattern emerging. You define measurements, schedule them on a regular basis, and plot the results as trend graphs so that you can make predictions about future behavior. This pattern applies to long-range capacity management where the trends are often over months, and it applies equally well to performance management where the most interesting trends are often over a 24-hour period. Using past behavior as a predictor of future behavior is a good practice through all parts of the capacity and performance management process.

Another good practice to follow is to plan for the most likely future possibilities. For important systems whose performance is variable, you will want to include performance contingencies in the capacity plan just as you do with capacity contingencies. Using the trend data over time, you can anticipate where the peaks and valleys in performance will happen, and you can document specific steps to take when the performance of the system is likely to be unacceptable to your users or fall below the service levels you have committed. Document what course of action to take so you can avoid having to react after the performance has already dipped below the desired level.

Although it is possible to create separate capacity and performance plans for the same IT service or component, it makes much more sense to maintain a single combined plan. In one document you will see the relationship between capacity and performance and will be able to define synergistic solutions that can alleviate performance concerns without expanding capacity beyond what is needed. This synergy is lost if you have separate plans because the performance manager always asks for more resources and the capacity manager always tries to get by with less.

Virtualization's Impact on Performance

One hot discussion among performance managers today is the effect that virtualization has on the performance of an overall system. Intuitively, the hypervisor needs some resources in order to accomplish its function, so there must be fewer resources left over for the virtual servers it supports. But those virtual servers are allocated virtual resources according to the way they are specified, and the hypervisor load is not considered in that specification. So, theoretically, a virtual server with two virtual CPUs should be getting as much CPU time as a physical server with two physical CPUs.

The challenge with managing performance in a virtual environment is not the overhead of the hypervisor but its actions. The program used to create virtualization is constantly working to change the allocation of resources to the virtual servers. It attempts to balance the load of all servers it supports by taking resources away from less busy systems and giving it to busier systems. In general, modern hypervisors do a good job of this, but sometimes a performance manager wishes she had more control of the process. In this section we consider some of the implications of virtualization for performance managers.

How Hypervisors Improve Performance

The job of the hypervisor in a virtualized server is to allocate physical resources to the virtual servers. To do this effectively, it closely monitors the real resources of the system and the utilization of those resources by the virtual servers. The hypervisor adjusts the allocation of physical resources as necessary to ensure that each virtual server comes as close as possible to receiving the resources it is permitted to have.

Because it is constantly monitoring resources, the hypervisor quickly spots unusual situations. Of course, the hypervisor cannot allocate more resources than you've told it to, but it can be sure that the map between virtual resources and physical resources is close to a one-to-one ratio. In other words, the virtual server can be running very close to the same processing power as a similarly configured physical server. Hypervisors acting in this way can respond to unexpected demand to improve the performance of the server without any action from a system administrator.

Most modern hypervisors allow you to set boundaries for the virtual servers they govern. You can typically set upper limits on processing power, memory, and disk consumption, and the hypervisor never allows the virtual server to exceed those limits. In many systems you can also set lower limits, so the hypervisor never gives so much resource to other virtual servers that it cannot guarantee that these lower limits are available. As the hypervisor works within these administratively defined limits, it has latitude to balance the capacity and performance of the virtual servers. It is important that you understand how your hypervisor uses the limits you define so you can maximize its ability to manage systems on your behalf.

How Virtualization Automates Performance Management

The biggest advantage of virtualization for a performance manager is that the system takes automated action within a set of bounds specified by the administrator. Depending on the hypervisor technology, these actions might include dynamically adding and removing CPU resources, memory resources, or even disk resources. The performance manager may have to work with the system administrator to set the minimum and maximum range for these resources, but after they are established, performance management measurements become much less important. The hypervisor is constantly taking measurements and adjusting resources in a way that even the most diligent performance manager would never be able to do.

Of course, virtualization works best in an environment where you can place many variable workloads together under the supervision of the same hypervisor. When an individual load is less, its resources can be used by the other workloads. But when the demand grows again, the hypervisor can return those resources by taking them away from workloads that are less busy. The net effect is that real system resources are kept busy more of the time, increasing the overall utilization of the server. This makes the capacity manager quite happy because one of their key missions is to ensure full utilization of the resources your organization has already acquired. But at the same time each individual workload has access to more resources than it normally would during its peak load. This makes the performance manager happy because there will be fewer performance complaints from the users of the system. Virtualization is a great technology that should be a part of every capacity management program.

Summary and Next Steps

Performance management is a very detailed and demanding topic. This chapter has presented a broad overview of the subject with lots of simplification to help you understand the general theory. In the first section we looked at a general definition of performance management, and you saw that performance is really a measure of system capacity at some point in time. The next section described techniques for measuring and improving performance, along with a general procedure for attacking any kind of performance issue. The next section examined performance management for systems that exhibit considerable variability in their busyness, such as you would expect from business systems whose users work on only a single shift. Finally, we explored the relationship between virtualization engines and performance management and decided that, in general, virtualization helps automate performance management.

The next chapter covers capacity and performance management tools. You learn about the various categories of tools, what characteristics are important in each category, and the likelihood of finding good tools in each category. Rather than telling you which tools to buy, the next chapter gives you the information you need to make the best selection for your organization.

CHAPTER 10

Choose Capacity Management Tools

Now for the moment you've all been waiting for.... Maybe not, but if your organization is like most of the ones I've worked with, there is some belief that if you could just find the perfect capacity management tool, all your worries would be over. Let me start this chapter by saying there is no perfect capacity management tool, and if there were, your organization wouldn't be ready to use it because there are no perfect organizations.

Tools play a vital role in any healthy capacity management program. It would be foolish to think you could manage hundreds of IT services and thousands of components with a simple notebook or even a very complex spreadsheet. On the other hand, tools only automate the process. They do not create the process for you, nor do the tools have the discipline required to execute the process effectively. The good news is that you can have a very effective capacity management program with only rudimentary tools, but no matter how excellent the tools might be, they cannot rescue a poorly designed or implemented program.

This chapter describes capacity management tools you might want to consider as part of your program. As with every IT investment, you should do research, document your requirements, quantify the value to be gained, and then search for tools that provide the best match to your requirements and the best value for the lowest total cost of ownership. This basic approach is the foundation for this chapter. I won't tell you which tools to buy. Instead, I offer an approach that helps you evaluate capacity management tools and identify which tools you do and do not need as part of your program.

Tools to Track Component Capacity

The most fundamental tool in your capacity management toolbox is one that tracks the utilization of each IT component in the environment. Component utilization tracking tools are vital because without knowing the utilization of your existing environment, you will never be able to define the trends that make prediction possible. This section talks about component tracking tools and which ones make most sense for your organization. See Table 10.1 for an overview of tool characteristics in this category.

Table 10.1 Component Capacity Tracking Tools

Tool Category	IT Component Utilization Tracking
Common Requirements	Covers broad range of components Small resource usage Integrates well with other tools Can customize which attributes are tracked
Tool Availability	Lots of tools are available in this space, including operating system utilities and vendor-specific tools.

Specific Requirements in This Class

The primary requirement for any component capacity tracking solution is coverage of all of your components. The tool must track the key elements for each component as you have defined them. If you believe that a key measure of the capacity for a router is the number of IP broadcast packets it can filter per second, you need a tool that can measure and track that statistic. Whatever you have decided to track must be tracked by the tools you choose.

Many people get this requirement backward—rather than specifying the items they want to track and finding tools that track them, they instead pick tools they like and then leave all the default settings and accept whatever the tool tracks as their requirements. This is a bad practice for several reasons. First, the software publishers typically add in every feature that is easy for their programmers to implement. They want to sell more software, and long feature lists sell more software. But settling for the defaults collects information you won't ever need or use. While drowning in details you run the risk of missing out on what's truly important for managing capacity. The second reason to be careful about the data you capture is that accidental data capture probably won't meet your needs in managing IT services. If you don't specifically plan out what characteristics you'll manage for IT components you will have little hope of capturing and managing useful data for your complex IT services. Don't let your capture of capacity data be driven randomly by your tool selection, but instead choose a tool that specifically captures the data you need.

A second important requirement for component capacity management tools is to minimize the amount of resources they take up on your systems. Although it seems obvious, many organizations have chosen tools with lots of function only to realize that running the tool takes 5% or more of the capacity of the systems they are measuring! Although no tool can claim to take zero resources, you should specifically look for tools that don't steal the very resources you're trying to manage. Look for tools that have a very lightweight agent, or whose agent can accomplish other useful functions in addition to tracking capacity. Be very aware of the mix of system management tools on your servers and how much of the capacity of those servers is taken by your tools.

You will want to consider the integration capabilities of any component capacity tracking tools you investigate. Because the utilization information these tools gather is an essential part of a capacity management information system, you need to be sure it is easy to pull data out of the tool. Because it is difficult to find a single tool that tracks the utilization of all IT components, the tools must be able to integrate with one another well enough that reporting won't be a nightmare. Spending 20% less for a tool is foolish if you just end up having to spend thousands of hours later creating reports from it. In general, you will want to look at tools that offer accessible database formats or web services programming interfaces since those are two of the best integration methods. If your organization chooses to integrate in some other way, you should specifically require that your component tracking tools be able to support your means of integration.

You should also consider your needs and ability to customize the tools you choose. As already mentioned, software publishers provide tools that can track all sorts of attributes of the components they run on. You will want to be able to turn those attributes off so you don't end up swamped with useless data. You will probably want ways to customize thresholds to alert you to both high and low utilization. Although the capability to customize tools is important, the best tools also make that customization easy and secure. Make sure your tools allow you to track who modifies the settings.

There are certainly many other areas to consider as you document requirements for component capacity management tools. The important point to remember is that you need to document the requirements before you get involved or emotionally attached to specific tools or vendors. The more thoroughly you can document your needs, the higher the probability that you can choose a tool to meet those needs.

Available Tools

There are many tools that track the utilization and capacity of IT components. You will most likely end up with multiple tools established in your environment because each has its own strengths and weaknesses. The more diverse your environment, the more tools you are likely to have.

The most basic tools are those that come with the operating systems of your devices. Routers from Cisco allow you to track network packets sent and received on each of the device interfaces and also provide response times for network traffic. Servers running the Windows operating system can use Performance Monitor, and mainframes running the z/OS® produce SMF records that can be used to understand capacity and utilization. Almost every major operating system today provides at least a rudimentary way to track the resources used by that operating system.

These OS utilities can be a part of your IT component tracking tool set. In most cases they need help from other sources such as scripts or external tools to really accomplish the whole job. The operating systems generally don't help you filter the records or store them in an accessible database. In many cases more advanced tools simply rely on the operating system tools to gather the data but then supplement them to notify you of threshold breaches or to generate trend data. Because the operating system is so heavily involved, you should be sure that your system administrators have the time to manage your capacity reporting tools.

Beyond the operating system, there are many vendors who sell tools for managing computer systems. Vendors like Tivoli, HP, Microsoft, and CA provide system management suites that include event monitoring, software distribution, inventory scanning, and capacity tracking all in the same set. Normally these system management suites come with a proprietary database of some kind to store not only capacity data but configuration and event data as well. Systems management suites are almost essential in the data center environment today, and if you already have one or more of them installed, you already have the capability to collect and report on IT component capacity and utilization.

The downside of broad system management suites is that they may not focus very heavily on capacity management capabilities. Desiring to do everything in the data center, the tool publishers often focus on basic capability in each area instead of advanced functions specific to particular process disciplines. If you followed my advice and documented requirements for component IT tracking tools, you are in a good position to assess whether your system management suite is really capable of handling capacity management the way you want it handled.

Specialized Tools Approach

One approach to component capacity management is to purchase specialized tools for each type of capacity you want to manage. If you use VMware as your hypervisor, you would use Virtual Center for component capacity management. If you run Linux servers inside those virtual machines, you could use the built-in tools of Linux with some custom scripts to really track exactly the attributes you want to measure. If your network routers and switches come from Cisco, you would deploy Cisco Works to track their utilization. If you run HP servers, you could deploy HP System Insight Manager to help you understand the detailed usage of those servers. This approach introduces lots of tools with specialized features custom-fit to your environment.

After all these tools are established and running to track their individual environments, you need to integrate them into a single capacity management information system. This might involve extracting data from each of their databases and moving it to a central database. It could involve something as complex as a systems management service bus with each tool publishing its data as a web service and a reporting tool subscribing to all the services to generate aggregated reports and trend graphs. In any event, a specialized tool environment needs a strong integration strategy.

The benefit of specialized tools is that they often capture data that cannot be captured by the more general system management suites. Because there is an affinity between the tool and the specific hardware or software it tracks, the tool is able to dive deeper to get more precise data than other tools are capable of. This is especially true if you stay current on your operating systems and hardware. As vendors introduce new features, only their tracking tools can track those features for a while. Eventually, the independent system management tools catches up and tracks the same characteristics, but if this lag is important to you, then you will be best served by the specialized-tool approach.

Of course, using specialized tools for each environment you support has a downside as well. The complexity created by this management strategy can be difficult and expensive to manage. You need to acquire and track software licenses for many different tools. Your organization must have the knowledge to manage and use the different component tracking tools you've acquired. There is frequent change as new versions of tools are tested and deployed through release management. Dealing with this complexity generally requires a larger, more skilled staff, so smaller organizations generally should not try to maintain a specialized tools environment.

Generalized Tools Approach

The opposite approach to specialized tools is to deploy one single systems management suite that covers your entire set of IT components. You could, for example, deploy IBM Tivoli Monitoring as a single tool set with agents for virtual hosts, mainframes, databases, application servers, and so on. Other vendors also offer tool sets that can cover most platforms that are likely to exist in your environment.

The advantage of this single-tool approach is that you need only one skill set to manage the tools. Although agent changes may be needed for new versions of operating systems, changes to the basic platform is much less frequent if you have only one tool. The simplicity offered by this approach lends itself to smaller environments quite well and even in larger environments generally results in less cost than the deployment of many specialized tools.

Although there are advantages to a single-tool approach, you need to be sure it is really possible in your environment. If you have some less traditional environments such as an HP Open VMS platform or an IBM iSeries® server, you might not be able to find a generalized suite that covers them. Many of the general tools fail to provide agents that can adequately track the capacity and utilization of your storage devices and network equipment. So although you might begin with a strategy that says you'll use a single tool, you will find that other tools begin to creep into the environment to cover the gaps.

Most small organizations can adopt a strict one-tool approach and manually manage devices for which they cannot get an agent. Medium-size to large organizations more likely have a primary tool that they use for most occasions with a small number of additional tools that make sense to gather component utilization for those areas where their main tool is weak.

Tools to View Service Capacity

You've seen that finding a tool to measure component capacity is like choosing a tree from a forest—you have plenty of options to choose from. Choosing a tool to measure and track the capacity of IT services is more like finding water in the desert. There are very few tools specifically designed for IT service capacity management, and the ones you find might not be completely satisfying. This section describes some of the desirable characteristics of service capacity management tools in the hopes that software vendors will want to differentiate their products by offering some of these capabilities. Table 10.2 describes characteristics of tools in this category.

Table 10.2 Service Capacity Tracking Tools

Tool Category	IT Service Utilization Tracking
Common Requirements	Can group IT components into a single view Can perform "what if" analysis by component Integrates into an overall CMIS
Tool Availability	There aren't very many options to choose from in this category.

Specific Requirements in This Class

Managing the capacity of IT services requires tools that go well beyond simply reporting on the utilization of individual components. You need to define means to aggregate those individual components into the overall service. The capacity manager must deal with multiple resources at the same time and understand how the capacity of that entire pool affects the overall capacity of the service. In many cases managing an IT service involves creating a model of the service using mathematical modeling techniques and then adjusting the capacities of various components within the service to evaluate the impact of component capacity on overall service capacity.

Given this background, the most important characteristic to look for in a service capacity management tool is the capability to organize specific components into a single service view. The components themselves might be dedicated to just one service, or they might be shared across multiple services. Therefore the tool should have the capability to understand dedicated components and shared components, and enable you to allocate shared components to multiple services.

In addition to grouping components together, a good service capacity management tool enables you to conduct "what if" analysis. You should be able to adjust the capacity of various components and have the tool tell you how that will impact capacity of the service. You should be able to integrate the projected growth in utilization of one or more components and see the resulting growth in utilization of the entire service. You will require a tool that enables you to build the mathematical model in such a way that you can rely on these analysis techniques to accurately project how changes you make to component capacity impact service capacity.

After you have data and can project the trends, you will want to store your IT service utilization and models, so another requirement for your service capacity management tool is that it must enable you to store data in the overall capacity management information system. One possibility is that your IT service capacity management tool is also the foundation for your configuration management database, in which case the format of the data will be handled for you. If you instead need to pull data from the service capacity tool into a separate tool for your CMIS, you need to specify that the service capacity management tool must have an open data format so that you can create the integration with the CMIS.

Available Tools

Chapter 2, "The Geography of Managing Capacity," declared that managing the capacity of IT services is much more complex than managing the capacity of IT components. That difference is certainly highlighted by the wide disparity between the number of component management tools and the number of service management tools. There are very few tools that claim to satisfy any of the requirements stated previously.

One tool that looks like a promising start is Neptuny Caplan. Created by a set of academics, this tool enables flexible modeling of complex IT services and enables the user to perform both trending and "what if" analysis. Another player in this space is BMC Capacity Management, a tool set that provides some of the mathematical modeling capability but fails to really recognize the important distinction between component management and service management.

More tools are certain to emerge into this important space as software publishers recognize the value of IT service management.

Build or Buy

The lack of really good options for IT service capacity management leads many organizations to decide between building their own tool and buying a tool and hoping to cajole the publisher to improve its capabilities through active participation in user groups and industry conferences. We are beginning to see the larger publishers enable users to get the best of both worlds. For example, with IBM Tivoli you can implement a broad suite of system management tools that includes component capacity management functions. By implementing the Tivoli Data Warehouse feature and integrating with Tivoli's Application Discovery and Dependency Manager (TADDM), you can create reports that mathematically combine the various components into business services as discovered by TADDM. This is a far cry from having automated trending and being able to adjust components to see the impact on the service, but it will at least get you started toward understanding service capacity.

For those who really want to build their own tools, you should begin with a solid data warehouse capability. Essentially, the CMIS is a data warehouse, so beginning with tools designed for data warehouse construction makes perfect sense. If you want to then add specialized forecasting and prediction tools, you can build them separately and integrate them with the data in your warehouse-based CMIS.

This approach is definitely not going to provide the lowest cost, but it will at least meet all of your requirements for an IT service capacity planning tool.

Performance Management Tools

Another class of tools comprises those that help you with performance management. As you learned in Chapter 9, "Relate Capacity and Performance," performance management is not the same as capacity management, so there should be no surprise that it requires specialized tools. Fortunately, many publishers offer very strong performance management tools. This section guides you through some of the features and functions and help you understand which tools really add value to your overall capacity management program. Table 10.3 describes the characteristics of performance management tools.

Table 10.3 Performance Management Tools

Tool Category	IT Performance Tracking and Management
Common Requirements	End-to-end performance tracking Can relate performance to capacity utilization Ability to simulate various loads Clear and concise reporting with graphics
Tool Availability	Most software development tool vendors have offerings in this space, along with several systems management tool vendors.

Specific Requirements in This Class

Of course, the most important requirement for a performance management tool is that it is able to measure what you really want to track. Although this seems obvious, it is amazing how many organizations purchase tools only to find out later they cannot track what is most important to them. As an example, assume you have a business application that consists of a web page, a workflow processing engine, and a database. You want to track end-to-end response time from when a user presses a key to when the screen displays the results of various transactions. This means you need a tool that runs on the user workstation and accurately detects key presses in the application, as well as determines when the screen update is complete. A tool that simply runs on one or more of the servers won't be adequate because it won't account for the time spent inside the web browser or between the workstation and the server environment.

Another important requirement for performance management tools is the capability to link performance observations with utilization information. Knowing the response time to a specific action is relatively meaningless if you do not know how heavily loaded the IT components involved may be. Intuitively, responses should be faster when the system is lightly loaded and slower when the system is heavily loaded, but if your performance management tool doesn't correlate system load with response measurements, you won't be able to observe this relationship.

You should also look for performance management tools that enable you to test under a variety of conditions. Tools can simulate load by creating automated users running specific numbers of various transactions. These tools enable you to model the activity within a system very precisely and then measure the performance of the system under those conditions. If you want to go down this path, be aware that the tools can be very complex to set up, and you need an environment that mirrors production so you can get the best possible results. This kind of load testing is not easy and is quite expensive, but if you have applications or services that absolutely require high performance, the tools and testing may be worth the investment.

Much of the work of performance management involves presenting complex information clearly and concisely. Your performance management tool should help with this by allowing you to create a variety of graphics- and text-based reports. Don't simply choose the tool that provides the most reports—look at the reports available and choose a tool that generates reports that real people can read. Some tools provide customizable dashboards that enable you to customize various graphics to present a summary view of performance across environments. You should specify your reporting needs to enable you to find a performance management tool that most closely meets those needs.

Available Tools

Many different performance management tools are available. Most of the large publishers that provide software for application development offer a tool to measure and test the performance of those applications. In addition, some of the system management vendors have produced tools that help track performance. The performance tools are often classified as active and passive, wherein active tools automate an actual transaction and measure the performance of that transaction, and passive tools simply measure the response of the system to the various transactions that are already taking place.

Performance Measurement Tools

The most common tools for performance management are those that simply measure the performance of a component or service. Many of the same tools that measure the capacity or utilization of a component also measure performance. IBM Tivoli Monitoring, for example, measures the CPU utilization (capacity) and the response time between the Tivoli endpoint and the closest gateway (performance). Many other tools provide both performance and capacity metrics in a single tool.

Less common, but still plentiful, are the tools that actively monitor performance by repeating a single transaction on a recurring basis. These tools create synthetic transactions and use those transactions so they can measure exactly the same user actions repeatedly. Typically, you train these tools by capturing mouse and keyboard events while a real user performs a transaction. After the transaction has been captured, you configure the tool to replay that same transaction on some predefined schedule. Each time the transaction is replayed, the tool takes a series of measurements, including the response time for the transaction. In this way you can compare performance under different loads and different times of day. Of course, you must schedule the synthetic transaction carefully so that it does not create undue overhead on the system being measured.

Performance Testing Tools

Another class of tools supports performance testing. Tools in this category generally enable you to capture multiple kinds of transactions and then build a model that mixes those transaction types together across a number of simulated users. The tool then executes that workload mix, perhaps escalating the number of transactions and users over time, while measuring the utilization and performance of the systems. These tools are normally run as part of an application or system development project before the system is promoted into a production environment. Ideally the tools will also enable you to enter performance requirements and will alert you when the requirements cannot be met by the performance of the system.

Integration with Capacity Measurement Tools

The ideal performance management tool integrates both capacity measures and performance measures. Since performance management is really a measure of capacity at a point in time, having both measurements together is critical to a sound understanding of the environment. The best performance management tools are those that let you see performance in the context of the amount of capacity being used at that point in time.

Tools for a Capacity Management Information System

Perhaps the most elusive tool in the entire capacity management realm is one that helps you implement a complete capacity management information system. There are tools that hold component data, some that enable you to model complete IT services, and plenty of tools that produce and hold performance data. But thus far I haven't found a single tool that can manage component, service, and business capacity data and also enable you to define, store, and manage capacity plans. All this is part of what ITIL calls a capacity management information system, as described in Chapter 5, "Establish the Capacity Management Information System." This section describes some options you might use as a foundation for building your own CMIS, or features to look for should true CMIS software become available in the market. Table 10.4 shows the characteristics of this tools category.

Table 10.4 Capacity Management Information System Tools

Tool Category	Capacity Management Information System
Common Requirements	Ability to store data on components and services Can store and manage capacity plans Integrates well with service management tools
Tool Availability	You are not likely to find any tool that meets all your requirements in this area.

Specific Requirements in This Class

The key requirement for the CMIS tool is that it can store the component and service capacity data that you want to track. You'll find that some tools can store only specific components, whereas others can store a variety of components and services but need to generalize them with averages or some other technique before storing them. To be effective as a CMIS, the tool should store all your data without losing precision or summarizing.

Another key requirement for a CMIS tool is the capability to store and manage capacity plans. Since plans frequently use unstructured data such as graphics or word processing documents, your CMIS tool should be adept at handling this unstructured data. Look for a tool that not only enables you to store the plans in whatever format you use but also tracks metadata about the plans. At a minimum, the CMIS should keep track of the author and date the plan was last updated. You should also be able to "check out" a plan to indicate that it is being worked on by someone outside the CMIS.

The CMIS tool should integrate well with your other service management tools. You should be able to link incident records to specific capacity plans, tie capacity plans to configuration items, and link utilization and performance numbers to specific application release records. As your organization gets more mature in your ITIL implementations, you will see a thousand ways that capacity information can be integrated with data from other ITIL processes, so your CMIS should support integration with other systems.

Available Tools

As already stated, there are no complete tools that implement everything that capacity management information systems should be. The most promising tools are those that track IT component and service capacity and performance all within a single tool. Tools like Neptuny Caplan or TeamQuest Model show promise in this area, although they don't yet store or manage capacity plans.

Another approach to the CMIS issue is to use a typical component capacity tracking tool coupled with an analytic tool that can help document the trends and a data warehouse model to store data and capacity plans. IBM Tivoli seems to be heading this direction with its latest versions of monitoring. Until full CMIS tools are available in the market, your best bet is to build your own CMIS.

How to Choose the Best Tools

At this point you're probably wondering how much money you'll need in order to acquire all the various tools described in this chapter. The answer is that you can spend as much or as little as you like. The question is not the amount you spend, but the amount of value you receive.

This section describes a simple tool called the trade study that helps you determine which tools really add value and which ones you can avoid. The trade study is a simple systems engineering technique that has been used for many years but that is often forgotten in the debate concerning which tools are best. The trade study tool helps you remove the emotion from the decision and avoid costly mistakes in your tools acquisition strategy.

At a high level, the technique for choosing between various competing alternatives is not new to anyone. We determine a workable set of desirable characteristics, assign a relative weight to each characteristic, and then compare all the alternatives by assigning a score for each alternative to each characteristic. The results, visible in Figure 10.1, compose a matrix of scores. Totaling these scores shows the degree to which each alternative fits your needs.

To choose the most appropriate capacity management tool, start by deciding which characteristics or attributes of a tool are important to you. You can use the requirements areas in this chapter as your guide to select the characteristics against which you'll evaluate each potential tool.

Capacity Management Tool Trade Study									
		Tool 1		Tool 2		Tool 3		Tool 4	
Need	Importance	Raw Score	Weighted Score	Raw Score	Weighted Score	Raw Score	Weighted Score	Raw Score	Weighted Score
Characteristic 1									
Characteristic 2									
Characteristic 3									
Characteristic 4									
Characteristic 5									

Figure 10.1 A trade study helps you choose the best tools for your organization.

When all the desirable characteristics are known, it is time to prioritize them. Assign each characteristic a weight. I like to use a 5-point scale, in which 5 means that we absolutely must have that feature and 1 means that it would be nice, but we can live without it. Three-point scales tend to not differentiate enough, whereas 10-point scales are overly complex. Assign each characteristic a weight that reflects how important it will be in your tool selection process. After you have weighted characteristics, it is time to score each potential tool. In most cases you'll want to use two different passes. In the first pass you take all the tools you can find and evaluate them using just the marketing literature provided by the software vendor. This can often be done using a web site or publicly available literature without having to engage the actual marketing team. The advantage of this quick first phase is that you won't ignore tools that might potentially be useful, but you won't spend a lot of time talking to sales teams that don't have what you need. Evaluate each characteristic by assigning it a score (again, I like a scale of 1 to 5) based on how well it meets the characteristic. Five might mean the tool automates this feature and requires virtually no effort on your part, and one might mean that you could write some custom code to make the tool meet the characteristic.

After providing an individual score for each characteristic, you can simply multiply the score by the weighting factor. This provides a weighted score, which gives you a good idea of how well the tool will meet your needs in that particular area. If you continue this work across all characteristics, and then add all the weighted scores, you get a single raw number to indicate the overall "score" of a tool. This number isn't particularly important by itself, but it can be compared to the score of other tools to help you assess which ones are stronger candidates for your organization's use.

After the first pass, choose the top two or three candidates for a deeper assessment. This is the time you bring in the vendors and allow them to demonstrate their tools for you. When possible, ask the vendor to demonstrate against your set of characteristics, using the weights you assigned to determine which things are most important for you to see in a demonstration. In some cases you will also want to get an evaluation copy of their software so you can conduct an even deeper "hands on" evaluation.

Most likely, there will be some attributes of the tools that don't fit neatly into the matrix. Cost is certainly one of those. So although you can use a trade study matrix to evaluate certain things, your overall choice of tools should use the raw scores from the trades study as only one decision point. Speed of implementation, reputation of the vendor, references from others who have successfully implemented, and cost of implementation should also be taken into account.

Summary and Next Steps

This chapter considered four kinds of tools that can help manage capacity in your organization. It described component capacity tracking tools and IT service capacity tracking tools and contrasted these categories with one another. There are many different tools that track components but far fewer that combine those components as IT services and track the capacity of an entire service.

You next looked at performance management tools. These run the gamut from simple performance reporting tools to sophisticated tool sets that simulate many users running a mix of transactions to enable you to do sophisticated performance testing before putting a new service or application into production.

You briefly considered capacity management information system tools, only to learn that there aren't any strong offerings in this space. The CMIS is a relatively new concept, and the software publishers haven't yet figured out how to build a system that meets all the requirements specified by ITIL.

This chapter described how to use the trade study technique to determine which tools are most appropriate for your organization. By putting some numeric values behind the importance of your requirements and the degree to which various tools meet those requirements, you can quantify the degree to which each tool fits your needs.

Chapter 11, "Produce Capacity Reports," focuses on reporting as the final piece of an operational capacity management program. You learn about the different kinds of reports that are typically used and gain some insight into which ones will be essential for your program.

CHAPTER 11

Produce Capacity Reports

There are two ways people will recognize your capacity management program. The negative way is when lack of capacity causes an important service to fail or exhibit dismal performance, or when the organization realizes that they are using less than 20% of the hardware they have purchased. The positive recognition comes when your well-defined and clearly formatted capacity report demonstrates the value your team is providing. Of course, nobody loves to read IT reports, so it is important that you choose to produce a few high-quality reports rather than generating reams of information that only the most die-hard fan would ever wade through.

In this chapter we survey a variety of reports. In the first half of the chapter, we consider reports about the capacity and performance of your IT environment. You learn about various reports that help explain how much capacity is being used and how much is left, and I provide some tips on making these reports as effective as possible.

The second half of the chapter describes ways to measure the effectiveness and maturity of your capacity management program. If you cannot measure your program, you won't know how to improve it, so these management reports and effectiveness metrics help you create the basis for your continuous improvement program.

Capacity Reports

The challenge with capacity reporting is to pull useful information out of reams of data. Most capacity and performance tracking tools produce an avalanche of statistics, measurements, graphs, and data points. Although each of these has some value on its own, taken together they form an impenetrable veil that can blind readers to the information they need in order to make adequate capacity decisions. As you build your capacity management program, you need to understand the needs of your organization and be sure to craft reports that help people make decisions rather than overwhelming people with data.

Component Exception Reports

The perfect example of generating information instead of data is the component exception report. You could quite easily create a report showing the utilization of every IT component in your environment every few minutes of every day. In even the smallest organizations this report would be hundreds of pages long. Instead, you should build filtering logic into the report that selects only components that have extremely high or extremely low utilization. These exceptions require some attention, and make a worthwhile report. Obviously, you need to collect all the data to find the exceptions, but there is no reason to put all the data in a report for someone to wade through. You should run the exception report at least once a month to make sure you have adequate time to respond to the information it gives you.

How do you determine what components belong on an exception report? You use the thresholds that you learned about in Chapter 5, "Establish the Capacity Management Information System." For each capacity pool you should have established threshold values that define "too much" and "too little" in accordance with your policies, perhaps including dynamic thresholds that respond to conditions. Many organizations find that multiple thresholds make sense. A three-part threshold indicates how close you are to either 100% or 0% utilization. If you have multiple thresholds, you should use them on your exception report to sort out the really critical exceptions from those that are of interest. Thus, your exception report might have a top group of rows showing components that have breached the top threshold and are almost out of resources. The next set shows those components that are close to breaching the top threshold. The third group of rows shows those that have breached the first high utilization threshold. Next are those rows that have breached the first low utilization threshold, followed by the ones that breached the second low threshold, and at the bottom of the report are those components that have virtually no utilization and have thus breached your lowest threshold. This arrangement of data supports quick decision making for the components that might fail without more capacity and more leisurely decisions for those that are wasting money by being underutilized.

So now that you've considered what components to put in your report, you should next consider which data elements to represent for each component. Most modern capacity or performance management tracking tools enable you to see hundreds of elements for every component. CPU manufacturer, disk swap space, memory paging rates, network packets sent and received, and processor idle time are all attributes that I can get from our standard capacity tracking tool. Of these, we tend to show only the memory-paging rate because that is all that is needed to make the decisions our organization needs to make. You need to really understand the decisions that you're likely to be faced with in order to best choose which data elements to put on the component exception report. The most important lesson is that you shouldn't just fill the report with data because you can. Choose to convey information that meets the goals of your capacity management program. You want to choose those elements that provide the "canary in the coal mine" to help the organization detect larger issues.

In addition to careful selection of the rows and columns that make up the component exception report, there are some other things you can do to make the report useful to your organization. After your capacity planning discipline has matured a bit, you can introduce more logic into the component exception report. For example, many organizations find that certain components are always exceptions because their normal capacity is a breach of the thresholds. These components can be left off the report as long as you have alternative ways to make the organization aware when their capacity actually changes. You can also use the report to indicate trending by highlighting items that have moved from one threshold level to another differently than those that are new exceptions for this report. The goal is to keep making the report more useful so that eventually it can be used to find those components that really need someone to take action on.

Component Trending Reports

A second type of report you'll want to use to track capacity is the component trending report. The focus of this report is not so much on numbers as it is on movement. Is the component using more capacity than it was on the last report, or less? Is this movement a long-term trend or a short-term issue? The trends described on this report form the backbone for your capacity plans. You will want to add more capacity just before the trend says you will run out. Conversely, you will want to consider consolidation projects just when the component trend report indicates that you have excess capacity.

Obviously, the component trending report could get quite lengthy if it contains the trend for every IT component in your environment. You certainly need to track the trend for every component, but for most components, the utilization for the current reporting period is just another data point in a curve you already understand. You don't need to report on data that simply confirms what your organization already knows. Instead, you probably want to focus on two specific kinds of trends.

The first type is a trend that has shifted unpredictably. If you've seen the memory utilization of a component steadily go up for six months, and suddenly you have a data point that reverses the trend, you may want to investigate what happened. Even though the data point may not breach any of your thresholds, and therefore the component wouldn't be displayed on a component exception report, it still makes sense to understand why the trend has reversed. The trend shift does not necessarily need to be in a separate direction, either. If you've seen storage increases of 100GB very regularly for ten months and suddenly the increase is 400GB this month, that could also be a trend shift worth investigating. On your component trend report you want to display any components that have unpredictable shifts.

The second type of components to include is those that have the most dramatic trends. Your report should include the ten fastest-growing components and the ten fastest-shrinking components. Those components with the fastest percentage rate of change should be watched more carefully because they are most likely to be the source of any trouble. Your organization should decide whether you want to depict the top ten or some other number, but you should definitely highlight the components with the most dramatic utilization changes.

After you've chosen which components to include in the report, you next face the decision about which elements to include. Whereas the exception report provides technical details to indicate what capacity is running low, the trend report should provide trend data about the components highlighted. You should certainly include the average growth (or decline) over the past year, the growth or decline for the current period, and a reason why the component is important. Some data elements I have seen include the anticipated utilization for the next three months, the projected date on which capacity changes need to be made, and even the rate of acceleration or deceleration in capacity usage. Remember that a trend report is primarily a statistical exercise, so you should use statistics to best highlight the decisions that need to be made.

As your service management disciplines become more integrated, you can add information to the component trend reports to indicate reasons that the trends were different than expected. For example, if you had a long-running incident that caused one or more servers to be out of service for an extended period, the component trend might show dramatically reduced usage of those servers. By integrating incident data with capacity data, you can note this kind of correlation on the component trend report.

Service Trending Reports

The next logical step after you are routinely producing effective component trending reports is to focus on trending your IT service utilization. As you learned in Chapter 2, "The Geography of Managing Capacity," IT services can be composed of many different components, and calculating the utilization of a service can involve complex mathematics. If you have succeeded in defining the appropriate calculations to define how the various components make up the service, then you can code those calculations into a service utilization report so you can quantify the usage of your IT service each month. The configuration management database is invaluable here because it defines the dependencies between components that help you calculate the overall capacity and utilization of your IT services.

As an example, let's suppose that your organization supports a work-at-home program. You might offer a service that includes a virtual private network (VPN) client on the home PC, a secure authentication server, and a VPN concentrator in your data center, all woven together with an Internet connection and some firewalls. In this scenario, you will most likely track the utilization of the authentication server, the firewalls, the VPN concentrator, and the Internet connection. For the sake of simplicity, imagine that each of these utilization numbers can be expressed as a simple percentage. The Internet connection is for many other applications and services but shows 24% utilization for the month. The outside firewall reports that it has an average utilization of 18%, and the inside firewall is used at 12%. The VPN concentrator shows average utilization of only 7%, and the authentication server reports that it is 23% used. So how do you take all of these numbers and turn them into a single number that shows how much of the service is used?

The answer is that you create a synthetic formula based on your knowledge of the complete service. Realizing that the Internet connection and the firewalls are used by many other services, you assign them a lower value in the formula. The VPN concentrator, on the other hand, is used only by the work-at-home service, so it is assigned a high value. The authentication server is used by only one other service, so it is assigned a medium value. Combining these, define the complete work-at-home service as having 100 capacity units, with 50 of them coming from the concentrator, 20 from the authentication server, and 10 from each firewall and the Internet service. Simple mathematics shows that the utilization of the service is thus:

- 7% of 50, or 3.5, plus
- 23% of 20, or 4.6, plus
- 24% of 10, or 2.4, plus
- 18% of 10, or 1.8, plus
- 12% of 10, or 1.2

So you've determined that the total utilization for your service is just 13.5%, which pretty much stays in line with the low utilization you're seeing in the component parts. Of course, this method doesn't really calculate a percentage of utilization. Instead it assigns an arbitrary number between 0 and 100 as a score for the service. As long as you use the same calculation each month to produce the score, you can compare the score over time and understand the trend.

Using a similar technique, you can create utilization scores for all your IT services. Unlike with the component trend report, you will probably want all IT service trends to appear on a regular report, even if the trend is just a continuation of what you've seen in the past. There should be significantly fewer IT services than there are components, so the report is still manageable, and putting all services on the report enables your organization to have a better view of all the services IT provides to the business.

The data elements you display for each IT service are similar to those displayed for components on the component trend report. Average growth or decline in use of the service is important, along with predictions of when the service might need to be expanded based on the current trends. For a service trend report, you may also be able to include some additional directly measurable data elements. Returning to our work-at-home service, it is probably easy to get the number of user identities that have been defined for authentication specifically for VPN access, so you can include the number of users of the service along with the formula for how busy the service is. These additional elements help to confirm the trend and are extremely helpful for putting the service into a better context.

As your organization gets stronger at managing IT services, you will find the service trend report becoming more useful. It helps to explain your ability to achieve service-level agreements and objectives, it allows you to justify charging users for the service IT provides, and it helps you make more concrete plans for the expansion of valuable services or the discontinuation of unimportant services.

Capacity Management Reports and Process Metrics

The major purpose of capacity management is to ensure that your organization has just the right amount of IT capacity to provide the services it has promised. The capacity reports described in the first part of this chapter enable you to accomplish that goal. As with most processes, however, you want to achieve the goals of capacity management in the most cost-effective and time-efficient way. That is where process metrics come into play. The reports described in this section help you assess whether your capacity management program is effective and efficient. You could certainly manage IT capacity without these reports, but you wouldn't be able to say how well that capacity is managed, and you wouldn't have a basis for improving your capacity management service.

Measuring Capacity Trend Accuracy

Because trends play such an important role in predicting capacity usage, it is important that the trends be accurate. You can measure the accuracy of your trend reports by evaluating your predictions against reality over time. This report tells you whether you are getting better or worse at predicting future capacity needs and hopefully helps you identify specific reasons why your forecasts are not as accurate as they could be. The trend accuracy report improves your confidence in the entire capacity planning process as you learn to more accurately predict future patterns of capacity utilization. Note that trend accuracy is really a factor of how much data you have and how consistently your organization behaves. The trend accuracy reports do not measure whether you've done the math correctly, but whether your organization behaves with a consistent pattern.

You can produce a single trend accuracy report that provides information about both IT component trends and IT service trends, or you can choose to report these two trend types separately. Many organizations find that component trending is significantly more accurate than service trending, so they choose to report the two kinds of trends separately. Other organizations find that the same causes of inaccuracy arise from both kinds of trends, so reporting them together helps improve overall accuracy. I would recommend that you begin by reporting them together, and separate them only if you see more value in separate reports.

Because even the smallest organizations have thousands of IT components to report trends for, you will probably not want to report on the accuracy of every trend. Instead, you should produce a summary that shows the number of trends that achieved accuracy thresholds. For a medium-sized organization you might show that you have 23,149 IT components and 147 IT services. Of all of those trends, more than 18,000 might have less than 5% difference between the forecasted utilization and the actual utilization. Another 2,000 might be more than 5% different but less than 10% different, and only 218 might be more than 20% inaccurate. This kind of summary allows you to quickly see whether overall accuracy is improving each month and highlight the ways in which your IT consumption is unpredictable.

In addition to the summary, you might want to focus on those trends that are more than 20% different than you expected them to be. For those components and services, you might want to indicate whether they are already part of an exception report and are thus already being investigated. It may be that there is a problem with the way you report trends, and you need to change your method. Looking at these outliers can highlight those issues.

Over time you will most likely find that the trend accuracy report becomes less useful. It is really a tool to help you gain maturity, but when your capacity planning discipline is mature, your accuracy should reach a plateau and stay there. If you decide to implement a focused project to improve your trend accuracy and break through that plateau, you can start to produce the report again. When you get to the point that you can understand the unpredictable components and/or services without producing a trend accuracy report, the report has lost its value.

Tracking Capacity-Related Incidents

A second report that helps you assess the health and maturity of your capacity management program is the capacity incident report. When you first begin tracking capacity-related incidents, you will note that many different issues are labeled as capacity related. After your policy and tracking method improves, you should start to experience a decline in capacity-related incidents. Producing the report and reviewing it with your stakeholders should highlight this pattern and help you understand the state of maturity your program is achieving.

To begin tracking capacity-related incidents, you need to make a change in your incident-tracking procedures. Most organizations are already classifying incidents with some set of categories like hardware, software, or network. You simply need to implement another category called capacity. This first involves process work to define a policy indicating what a capacity-related incident refers to. You might choose to define only those cases in which lack of capacity created a service disruption or also track those cases in which capacity was critically low and your IT team had to take immediate action to avoid a service disruption. Try to make your policy fit the goals and purposes of your capacity management program because we all know that measurements influence behavior. In addition to the policy definition, you will most likely need to update the procedures used by the service desk and other organizations so that they know about the new policy and the new category.

After the process work is accomplished, you need to update your tools to include the new capacity category. Depending on your incident management tool, this could be as simple as adding a value to a drop-down field, or as complex as defining a new set of service levels and potentially even severity codes to correspond to the new category. The tool work that you do should reflect the process work—not the other way around. If your process calls for many decisions to be made based on the category of an incident, you will have more tool updates to make to accommodate that process.

Finally, after the process work is done and the tool has been modified, you need to be sure to train your teams on how to handle capacity-related incidents. Regardless of how clearly the policy is documented, you need to provide some kind of training to ensure consistent use of the new category. If the category is used inconsistently, your reporting is not very useful.

After the new incident category is put into practice, reporting on capacity-related incidents should be simple. You probably already have a report of incidents by category, so the new capacity-related incidents simply show up on that existing report. Extend the report distribution so that the capacity management team receives it, and you have accomplished your reporting goal. The capacity team should review the report and look for common issues that might be causing capacity-related incidents. As the team learns to anticipate capacity needs and meet them before they become critical, the number of capacity-related incidents should steadily decline.

As your overall implementation of the ITIL process areas becomes more mature, you can relate capacity incidents to specific configuration items and classes of configuration items to identify the specific capacity pools or capacity streams that cause the most issues. This information can help you fund and implement improvement efforts to better manage certain types of capacity. Over time, you should find that capacity incidents are easier to classify and become less frequent as your capacity planning skills improve.

Evaluating the Completeness of Capacity Plans

The major product of your capacity management program is capacity plans. As you learned in Chapter 6, "Define and Manage Capacity Plans," a good capacity plan includes a record of past utilization, a prediction of future needs, and a specific set of steps that describes what you will do to avoid a situation in which demand exceeds capacity. You should certainly create capacity plans for your major IT services and will probably want to create them for critical IT components as well.

A significant measurement of your maturity is the ability to produce capacity plans that are complete and specific. As you first begin producing plans you'll find that you don't have a very long history of utilization and the corresponding prediction of future demand will not be very accurate. Over time, your history will grow and your predictions will become more accurate. As this happens, you should turn your attention to making the third piece of the plan, the action steps, more helpful.

Unfortunately, this isn't an area that can be automated. As you actively manage capacity for your organization, you will inevitably need to use the action steps described in your capacity plans. When this becomes necessary, you should observe how accurate and complete those steps are. The first time you execute a capacity plan, you are likely to need an IT project manager to create the actual plan, which most likely includes ordering new capacity, scheduling the people to install that new capacity, and then updating your capacity management information system to indicate the availability of the new capacity. But after executing capacity plans a few times, you should begin to observe what makes a plan truly useful and how you can define the plan to help the project manager. Over time you may even find that the capacity manager can execute the plan without needing a project manager at all.

So what does this cycle have to do with reporting? You should create a monthly report that indicates how many capacity plans you actually needed to invoke and how much time was required to define the project because the capacity plan didn't have a complete definition. This is admittedly subjective, but the very act of compiling this data makes your organization more conscientious about building and maintaining capacity plans in the future. If you intentionally measure the completeness of your capacity plans, they will naturally become more complete over time.

As your organization takes advantage of technologies such as virtual servers and cloud computing, you may even be able to automate your capacity plans. Many of the emerging software products in data center automation, such as Tivoli Service Automation Manager (TSAM), enable you to define scripts in advance and trigger them based on conditions of utilization. The script automates your capacity plan action steps, and the utilization is measured directly through the Tivoli management infrastructure. You will still need to monitor the resources available to TSAM to ensure that it can implement the capacity plans you've defined, but in general this enables you to provision new resources exactly when and where they are needed. The capacity plans themselves are still vital and must be maintained, but automating their execution can significantly increase the value of your plans. If you don't have solid capacity management processes and a good maturity in your capacity management program, this kind of technology will not be successful in your organization.

You should continue to track the completeness and effectiveness of your capacity management plans as part of your overall continual improvement of the capacity management program.

Summary and Next Steps

There are countless other reports that could be created to track capacity and measure the effectiveness of your capacity management program. This chapter has introduced you to some of the reports that have been most helpful to the organizations I've been involved with. Based on what individual trouble areas you have, your set of reports might include all the ones I've mentioned or might include a completely different group.

The important point of this chapter is not which reports you end up creating, but why you create them. You learned that generating data is easy, but producing useful information takes more work. You should consider what decisions need to be made and create reports that help people to make those decisions. Don't put data elements on reports simply because you have access to a database with those elements in it. Instead consider the consumers of those reports and give them the information they need but no more than they need. In many cases the quality of a report can be greatly improved by reducing the amount of data on the report.

We looked at a set of reports that will help you manage the capacity under your control. You can produce a report that shows components with very high or very low utilization to help identify potential projects. A second report highlights the component trends to show where the utilization is growing or shrinking the fastest, which allows you to focus on things that might otherwise sneak up on you. We also considered IT service trend reports and looked in some detail at how to create artificial ways to calculate the utilization of an IT service. This whole set of reports provides high-quality information about the capacity you are managing.

In the second half of this chapter, we considered some of the ways you can measure and improve the effectiveness of your capacity management program. We looked at ways to measure the accuracy of your trends, because improving the accuracy of trends will help you predict more closely when you need to take capacity actions. We highlighted a way to track capacity-related incidents so that you can focus on reducing those incidents over time. Finally, you learned how to evaluate the completeness of your capacity plans. If your plans are complete enough, you can reduce the effort needed to implement them or perhaps even automate their implementation all together. All these reports help you to see your maturity as a capacity planning organization.

This chapter completes Part II, "Best Practices in Capacity Management." In this part you've learned all the best practices for managing capacity. You've learned about the capacity management information system and how it is the base for all your critical information about capacity. You explored capacity plans and learned how to create and manage them. This part also described how to staff the capacity management team and implement the process that your team will use. You discovered the interdependency between capacity and performance management, and I made a case for why performance management should be viewed as a subtopic of capacity management. Finally, you learned about desirable characteristics of capacity management tools and how to use some of those tools to generate capacity management reports.

The next chapter begins the final part of the book, Part III, "Common Issues in Capacity Management," which highlights some of the issues you are likely to face as you manage capacity for your organization. The first issue, highlighted in Chapter 12, "Business Capacity Planning," is how to handle business capacity management. Thus far I've been pretty quiet about business capacity management, but ITIL insists it is a vital component of a complete capacity management program. In the next chapter you learn how to address this component, and I give you some hints for how to adjust if your business doesn't want to be an active partner in managing capacity.

PART III

Common Issues in Capacity Management

In Part I, you learned the general concepts about managing IT capacity. In Part II, you looked in depth at how to implement a capacity management program and how to make it effective over the long term.

This third and final part of the book tackles several common issues and challenges that you are likely to deal with. The issues addressed in this part include business capacity management, models for procuring additional capacity, capacity management within a project plan, and integrating capacity management with other IT process areas.

These are certainly not the only issues you will face, but they are the most common questions and issues I've seen in working with many of IBM's largest corporate clients.

CHAPTER 12

Business Capacity Planning

Throughout this book, we focus on planning capacity for the IT organization. You've learned about managing IT components and IT services, and we've looked deeply at the interaction between these two. If you've followed the flow of the chapters thus far, you are now aware of everything you need to know to effectively manage capacity for most IT organizations.

But if you are only managing IT capacity, you're missing some of the benefits of ITIL capacity planning. The third part of capacity planning is managing the capacity of the business or wider organization that your IT organization is part of. Whether you work with a commercial enterprise or a nonprofit organization, there are significant benefits from close integration between IT and the rest of the organization. Rather than IT simply being a cost center that maintains the "plumbing," you can transform IT into a key business enabler that can provide agility and help your entire organization react more quickly to the market or constituency that you serve.

This chapter describes how to make that transformation. We look at the scope and definition of business capacity planning, and then you learn why truly managing business capacity is difficult. You learn some practical ways you can begin to reach into the business and get utilization data and link that data to your IT capacity planning process. Finally, we investigate how you can get by without business capacity data if your organization is not yet ready to overcome the obstacles associated with measuring and planning business capacity.

The Scope of Business Capacity Planning

ITIL defines business capacity planning in only the most general terms. Just as IT capacity planning tries to ensure that you have the right IT resources to accomplish the mission of IT, so business capacity planning works to ensure that you have the business resources to accomplish the primary mission of your organization. For a manufacturing organization, this is simply the measure of how many goods can be produced. For other kinds of organizations, the definition can become more complex.

This section describes the scope of business capacity planning to provide background for the rest of the chapter. In addition to covering a basic definition of business capacity planning, we explore the concepts of utilization and prediction of capacity needs as they apply to the business.

Defining Business Capacity

The total capacity of an organization to conduct business can be difficult to measure. Sometimes it is even difficult to define what you mean by the capacity of a business. Imagine that you belong to an organization that owns and operates commercial radio stations. What is the capacity of your business? Is it the number of hours in a day that you can fill with content? Perhaps you want to measure capacity as the number of watts of power that your transmitters can generate. Maybe capacity of your radio stations is measured by the number of minutes of commercials that you can sell to advertisers.

From the outset it is important to realize that business capacity consists of those elements that IT controls and many elements that are outside of the control of IT. When ITIL describes business capacity management, it is not saying that your IT group should measure and plan the human resource needs or the raw materials needs of the business. Enterprise resource planning and human resources groups manage those capacities, and IT need not be directly involved in the planning process. Instead, ITIL describes business capacity planning as a means of understanding how information technology resources contribute to the overall capability to conduct business operations.

Returning to the company that manages a string of radio stations, you can now see that there are several links between IT capacity management and the business. There will most likely be a scheduling business process that determines what content gets aired at what times, and this process is supported by an IT service called scheduling. The scheduling service might consist of three different servers that support the web interface, the application logic, and the content indexing pieces of the scheduling service. The capacity to schedule content from an IT perspective is thus based on the capacity of these three servers and one IT service. This organization also has business processes for payroll, equipment maintenance, advertising sales, and many others. Each business process supported by IT can be managed as an aggregate set of resources, and thus capacity for that business process can be planned.

So business capacity planning in the context of this book involves understanding how the IT services support and drive business activity. You need to learn to make IT plans such that no business process lacks the IT resources it needs to continue. ITIL capacity management cannot help with vacation scheduling, suppliers' late deliveries, or temporary facility shutdowns, but effective management of the IT capacity can ensure that your business never again sees IT as the reason it cannot operate at full capacity.

How to Measure Business Capacity Utilization

By defining business capacity management narrowly, we move closer to an idea of how to measure it. Since we are only speaking of the contribution of IT to the business, we can measure utilization by the same kind of formula we created for IT services. We can examine the various components and services that make up a specific business process and then use a formula that turns the utilization of the constituent services into a single number expressing how many of the available IT resources are used by the business process.

As an example, imagine a legal firm with a large law library. Being a progressive organization, the firm decides to put the entire library online. The IT group decides to create a library search service and a library management service. The management service consists of a storage area network (SAN) to support the large volume of data, a content server to manage the content in the library, and a management server to support checkout, acquisitions, and indexing functions. The search service consists of a pair of load-balanced web servers to provide the end-user interface and a search server that executes queries against both local resources and Internet-based law directories. The complete law library business process thus consists of five servers, a SAN, and two IT services, as illustrated in Figure 12.1.

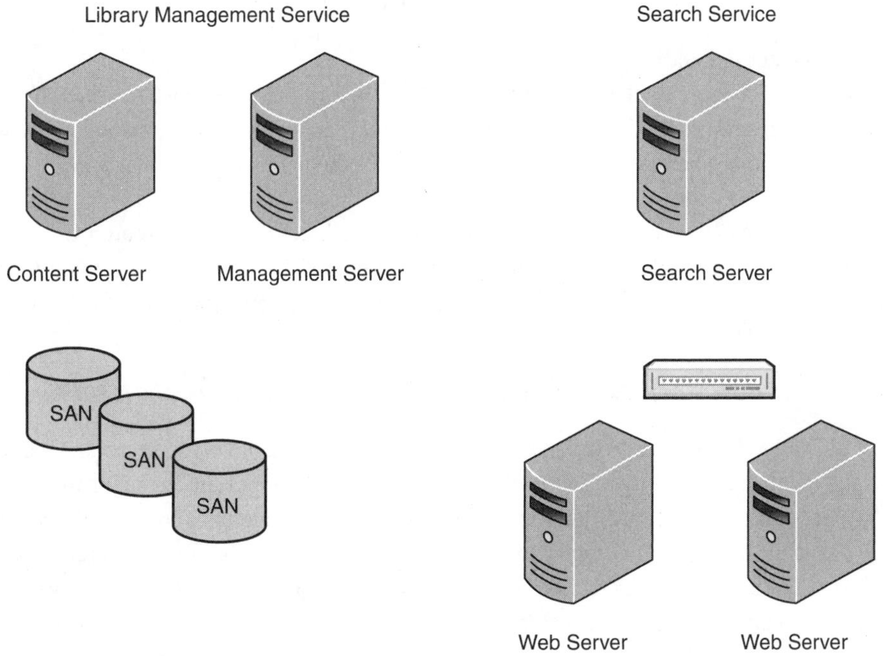

Figure 12.1 An example of a legal library management business process.

Given this set of components, we can assign priority and importance to each of the IT components in a way that the total adds up to 100% for each service. For our purposes, let's assign the SAN a value of 40, the content server a value of 40, and the management server a value of 20 because management transactions are less important to the overall management service than content transactions. To break down these numbers further, we assume that the value of the SAN is entirely made up of a single measurement for disk space, while the value for the servers is split evenly between CPU percentage and memory utilization. Given this breakdown, the utilization of the component server (CS) is thus

$$20 \times (CPU\% + MEM\%)$$

where 40 represents full capacity.

The utilization of the management server is

$$10 \times (CPU\% + MEM\%)$$

where 20 represents full capacity.

The utilization of the SAN is simply

$$40 \times \%DiskUsed$$

where 40 indicates that the disk is full.

So overall we can calculate the utilization of the library management IT service by adding together the utilization of the SAN, that of the content server, and that of the management server. The result is a number between 0 and 100 that expresses the percentage of total service capacity being used.

Similarly, we can assume that each web server contributes 20% to the search service while the search server as a single point of failure contributes 60%. Using the same logic that each server capacity is composed of half CPU and half memory, we can express the total capacity of the library search IT service as

$$20 \times (CPU\% + MEM\%) + 20 \times (CPU\% + MEM\%) + 60 \times (CPU\% + MEM\%)$$

where CPU and MEM represent the measurements from the three involved servers. Assume that the management and the ability to search the library are equally important to the business, and we can now define the overall capacity utilization of the library management business process as the average of the utilization of the library management IT service and the library search IT service.

Certainly this level of abstraction leaves lots of room for adjustment and improvement. As your capacity management practice matures, you will undoubtedly want to adjust the values in your formulas to more accurately represent the importance of the various components involved in your IT services. Just remember that each adjustment makes all previous measurements irrelevant because the change in formula means you are measuring a different quantity than you did before. Thus, changes to the formula terminate your old trend and start a new trend line.

Although this combination of mathematics and intuition seems abstract at first, you will gain confidence with it as you start to accumulate historic data and see how you can use these formulas to actually predict future business capacity needs.

Predicting Business Capacity Needs

The key to effective business capacity planning is to identify or predict future capacity needs. The most fundamental way to do this is to use your utilization formulas to establish trends and then use statistical methods to predict where the trend line will go in the coming weeks or months. This is exactly the same discipline as described earlier in the book for IT components and IT services.

Of course, the trend lines will tell you what will happen only if all factors remain equal. In most organizations, the last thing you want is for all factors to remain equal. You would like to see business growth driving faster growth, resulting in increased stress on the IT infrastructure. You may see quantum changes driven by mergers or divestitures. Increased advertising or promotion might cause a sharp increase in the number of transactions processed. All these business events have a direct impact on the utilization of your business processes and the IT services that support them.

If your IT organization is not well integrated with the business, you will simply need to observe these actions as they impact the IT services. In your monthly reporting cycle you can note increases and decreases in capacity utilization and discuss them with the business users who are supported by your IT services. These discussions often result in the businesspeople explaining what they did to drive the change. As this happens, you begin to forge a closer relationship with the business, and eventually they will see the value in identifying significant business events to you before they happen.

The first few times you are made aware of an unusual business event, you won't know how it might impact your capacity. But with experience, you will become more adept at understanding how business changes affect your infrastructure. As this knowledge grows, and the business sees you responding to events before they happen, you will become a true partner with the business and will no longer be seen as the anchor weighing down business agility. This is where the value of business capacity management really comes into play—you can grow or shrink your capacity as needed because of your close relationship with and understanding of the business units.

It is important that your capacity management team becomes very familiar with your business. If IT can have a good understanding of how the business operates, they will better understand which services are critical to the business and the relative importance of each to the reputation and revenue of your organization. This understanding helps you adjust your calculations so the business units more readily agree that you are providing the right services at the correct priority.

The Challenge of Planning Business Capacity

Now that you understand what business capacity planning looks like, you need to consider whether it makes sense for your organization. I'll say right from the outset that not every organization implements business capacity planning. Some organizations already have an enterprise resource planning (ERP) capability, and business capacity planning from an ITIL perspective is redundant and thus unnecessary. For other organizations, particularly smaller organizations, the benefit may simply not be worth the effort involved. Business capacity planning is difficult, but there will certainly be some organizations that find that the difficulty of implementing and maintaining the business capacity planning program is much less than the benefits gained. This section describes some of the difficulties involved and helps you overcome them.

Effort Versus Benefit

The first thing to factor in when considering any IT initiative is whether the benefit outweighs the cost. The cost of business capacity management is steep. There are lots of individual calculations to be defined in order to get reasonable utilization statistics. After the formulas are defined, they must be coded into a reporting tool so that regular data points can be generated. These data points are then plotted on a graph, and the trend lines established. All of this is very manually intensive work. Even a small organization can quickly consume half of a person's time to keep up with reporting on business capacity. Larger organizations may find that it takes more than one person to be doing this work.

In addition to the reporting costs, significant effort can be expended in gathering business event data to make capacity forecasts. You need to consciously reach out to the various parts of your organization outside of IT and cultivate ways to learn about significant events they are planning. In larger organizations there is often an "IT liaison" or "customer relationship management" function, but smaller organizations may need to specifically direct IT people to read business newsletters, talk to people from other business functions, and report to your capacity management team whenever a key business event will happen. This intelligence is critical to maintaining an accurate forecast of business capacity needs, but it is not easy to gather.

Another significant challenge is formatting the information you gather and calculate in such a way that the business sees value in it. IT people are often intrigued by statistics and graphs, but many people outside of IT would rather not see anything that reminds them of high-school algebra. Sometimes it takes great creativity to build reports that capture the attention of the business community and convince them that the capacity planning work of IT is really helping them. When IT reaches out to the wider business, there is always an element of marketing, and business capacity planning is no exception.

While business capacity planning is difficult and involves some expense, there are also benefits to be gained. You can start the analysis of potential benefits by reviewing your incident tickets over the past year or so. If you have a way to record capacity- and performance-related tickets, focus there first. If you don't have that capability yet, look for tickets on which the description field includes "slow down," "delay," or "response time." Assume that you could have eliminated half of those tickets through better business capacity planning and you can start to project what the benefit would be to your organization.

In addition to a reduction in slowdowns and tickets for nonresponsiveness, good business capacity planning practices can also help you avoid spending money. Most organizations without capacity planning use 15% or less of their IT infrastructure capacity. When you begin to manage capacity more carefully, you can drive that utilization up to 45% or more, getting three times more work done with the same amount of infrastructure. This represents a huge potential savings for capacity management in general. Business capacity planning helps you identify this opportunity over a wider range of resources because you are generally looking at a wider range of components when doing business capacity management than you are when working with IT services or individual components. The wider your point of view, the more opportunities you will see to add work load to existing infrastructure rather than buying new infrastructure components.

But perhaps the most important benefit of business capacity planning is that it improves the reputation of your IT group within your organization. You will recognize what the business units need and make sure they can continue to work without IT causing interruptions. As you do this more often, your business units will notice that IT has become more of a partner and less of an adversary. Over time, you will find that the efforts you put into understanding the business and its major events are rewarded with less time in meetings and much more cordial relationships when it comes time to ask for IT funding. In short, business capacity planning more closely aligns your IT organization with the business.

For a summary of the costs and benefits of business capacity planning, see Figure 12.2.

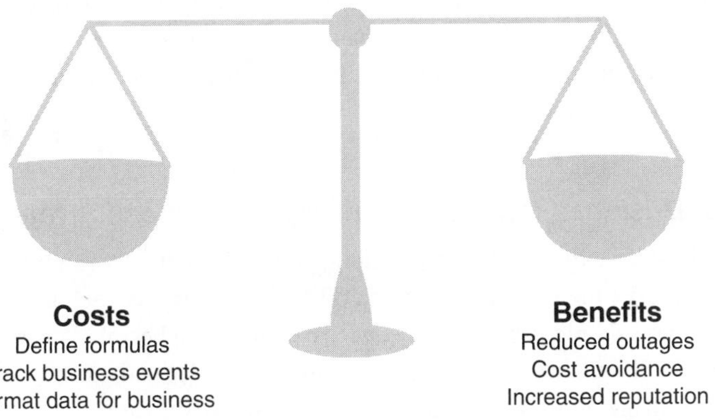

Figure 12.2 Costs and benefits associated with business capacity planning.

Getting Agreement on Measurements

One of the more difficult aspects of business capacity planning can be coming to an agreement on the metrics to be used. If you follow the advice I offered previously, you will stick with an abstract formula that simply expresses capacity as a percentage. This measurement won't have any meaning except in relationship to the same number during a different reporting interval. For the purposes of agreement with the business users, you simply need to say it expresses the fraction of total capacity that is used.

Sometimes you'll run into users who are more curious or want to have a more concrete measurement. That is where your troubles begin! If you are lucky, there might be a specific measurement you can take based on a business application that appeals to your users. For example, you might want to express the capacity of your payroll business process as the number of pay checks that are handled per hour. Of course, you can't offer that as a valid capacity measurement unless you can really measure it with your current tool set. Although it might be hard to measure in terms the business can understand, you can quantify financial benefits of capacity management in a way that the business readily accepts.

Bridging the gap between measurements that business users can understand and those that IT tools can measure can be difficult. Businesspeople don't care about bytes free or milliseconds of response time. IT systems can't generally measure patients served, widgets manufactured, or passengers transported. Stretching the IT systems is sometimes prohibitively expensive, so generally the business users have to settle for IT measurements and they go away feeling that IT might be talking about business capacity management but is really just managing the capacity of IT.

The best practice is to use a generic percentage as your business capacity indicator. As long as you are consistent in the way you calculate the percentage, you will accomplish your goal of having a trend and knowing roughly when you need to increase capacity to ensure that the business can continue. Of course, if your trend hits 100%, you may not actually be in trouble because the measurement could be off. On the other hand, you might actually run out of capacity when your derived formula tells you that you have 10% or even 15% more available. This is why you should tune your measurements over time as you get more experience in managing business capacity.

The Place of Business Capacity Planning in Business Strategy

If you actively pursue business capacity planning, you will eventually run into someone from the business side who asks the obvious question: What do you expect the business to do with this data? Ultimately, you should use business capacity planning to become a partner in the business strategy process. IT should become a strategic partner who fully understands what the business is trying to accomplish and who can help the business achieve its goals.

This may sound impossible, but it definitely is not. If you begin small by simply identifying the business processes and tracking how heavily they are used, you can start to gain some recognition from the business community. Move beyond simple trend tracking to making some actual predictions, and the business will really take your work seriously. Finally, you should be taking an active interest and helping the business achieve their goals without disruptions caused by running out of IT capacity. When you get to this point, you will be invited to participate in strategy sessions because you will have proven your ability to think long-term and follow through on those thoughts.

Capacity management doesn't normally drive business direction, but it should be very involved in determining the speed at which the business pursues the desired direction. If someone proposes a new program that doubles the utilization of some business process in a very short time, the capacity manager can suggest that the business might not be ready for that level of risk. If an initiative is proposed that will make significant amounts of capacity obsolete, IT can help to really define the total cost of ownership for that new initiative. You should certainly work to identify the IT resources that need to be added to meet the strategic initiatives in the timeframe the business desires. In all these ways, you will be a full partner in defining the business strategy for your organization.

Integrating Business Capacity Planning with IT Capacity Planning

Business capacity planning cannot be done in a vacuum. The best practices as described in the ITIL books tell us that business capacity planning is built on a firm base of IT component and IT service capacity planning. In this section we consider that hierarchy more fully and you'll gain an understanding of the implications of the linkage between IT capacity planning and business capacity planning. To get the most benefit from your efforts, the complete capacity planning process should be well integrated.

The Business Component Hierarchy

If you think about it very long, you'll realize that the world is made of ever-more-complex groupings of simple objects. In nature a series of cells makes a vein, a group of veins forms a leaf, a set of leaves populates a branch, many branches make up a tree, and a whole group of trees makes up a forest. The IT world is similarly organized, moving from small simple parts to complex assemblies and ultimately to complete business systems.

This concept of an organized hierarchy is important in capacity management. The smallest, most simple things are IT components, and we can directly measure and manage the capacity of an IT component. Groups of components work together to provide an IT service, and we manage capacity of services by considering the capacity of each component within the service. At the next layer, one or more IT services working together support a business process, which also includes some people and quite possibly resources other than IT resources. Because we have this almost infinite need to organize things in our minds, we can continue the hierarchy. A group of business processes organized together drives a business function. One or more functions can be grouped to create a business unit, and a set of business units under common leadership makes up an organization or a business. Groups of businesses with similar products or services are organized into an industry, and a set of industries in a single country makes up an economy.

So why is this hierarchy interesting to a capacity manager? It is simply because we can continue to abstract our management domain as far as desired. By following the hierarchy beyond business processes, we can assess the capacity of a business function, a business unit, or the entire organization. Of course, when we get to the organization level (or even beyond it), capacity is a very theoretical number. There are no direct ways to measure or assess capacity, so instead we use indicators to help us get some way to measure the abstract quantities. We use profit earned, revenue received, expenses incurred, taxes spent, or investments made as ways to assess the capacity of a business and understand whether we are utilizing that capacity.

Of course, at some point in the hierarchy, capacity management stops being an IT-specific concern and becomes instead a concern of the business leadership. But without understanding the hierarchy and how one piece fits with another, the IT capacity manager may miss the opportunity to support those business leaders with information that can help drive decisions at higher levels of the hierarchy. The enterprise architect is your best ally in defining and understanding this hierarchy.

The Line Between IT Services and Business Processes

The line between IT capacity management and business capacity management is not clearly understood. For most organizations IT has become so ingrained in the way business operates that no significant decision about the capacity or needs of a business unit can be made without considering the capacity of IT to support that decision. This is why the adept IT capacity manager always seeks to understand the business he or she supports and work to manage above the realm of simple IT.

This probably sounds quite theoretical at this point, so let's use an example. An airline is trying to decide whether to invest in new routes between Warsaw and Istanbul. Although there are many factors involved in making that overall decision, one of the important factors is whether their IT services can support the addition of new routes, or whether they need new IT resources. The IT capacity manager needs to understand how many passengers use the kiosks at the affected airports and whether more passengers can use them without undue delays. The IT capacity manager must understand the automated flight routing software and know whether it needs additional resources to track more routes than it handles currently. The IT capacity manager needs to know whether the current logistical business process needs more IT resources to handle tracking of flight attendants, ground crews, maintenance crews, and pilots at more destinations. These are very practical concerns that go into supporting the overall business decision. Without an adequate understanding of the hierarchy, from simple computers, disks, and networks up through business processes and business functions, the IT capacity manager cannot provide the needed information. You will often need to engage a software engineer or architect as well, because sometimes programming changes are needed to accommodate higher transaction rates in one or more of the affected business applications.

So although tracking IT components and services is the minimum you can do, there are some very good reasons for tracking business capacity as well.

Integrated Utilization

We've already looked several times at how to derive the utilization of business process capacity by using the utilization of IT services and IT components as a base. This is the first step toward integrating business capacity planning with IT capacity planning. These formulas that you create to define the business capacity automatically integrate the measurable IT capacity into your business capacity planning, but they are just the beginning.

Integrated Capacity Plans

The next step is to adopt integrated capacity plans. Recall from Chapter 6, "Define and Manage Capacity Plans," that capacity plans consist of a measure of the total available capacity, some sense of how that capacity is currently being used, and what demands are expected to use more of that capacity, and finally recommendations on steps to take to avoid running short of capacity.

In addition to capacity plans for individual IT services, you can create an integrated capacity plan for a business process. This plan has a broader scope but still includes trends of past utilization of the business process, forecasts for future utilization, and an estimate of when the future demand will exceed the available capacity. The business process capacity plan should then define steps that can be taken to avoid capacity shortages for the business process, and predict when those steps are necessary.

These business process capacity plans have all the same advantages of IT service capacity plans. They can be shared with the affected business units and serve as an excellent communication tool to help the businesspeople understand how IT supports them. Along with availability plans for the same business processes, they give a complete view to help the business understand the depth and breadth of service they are receiving from IT.

Managing IT Capacity without Business Capacity Information

Hopefully by now you understand the difficulties and the benefits of including business capacity management into your overall IT capacity management process. You may even be wondering why anyone would consider IT capacity management without at least attempting to manage business capacity as well. The short answer is that capacity management in general is so foreign to many IT groups that neither the IT team nor the business has the confidence to implement a business capacity management component of the program.

If your capacity management program is not very mature yet, or worse yet, if you have implemented capacity management poorly and thus lost the respect of the business community, you may have to manage IT capacity without business capacity information. This is really fairly simple since business capacity management is really a layer built on top of IT service capacity management.

The biggest change if you are forced into this situation is that you should be engaging the business units in an informal way with your IT capacity management program. As they see your success and discover the value you are bringing to IT, you can begin to talk to them about expanding to business capacity management. In this way you can win over the business by showing your competency in the IT realm first.

Summary and Next Steps

In this chapter we examined business capacity management in greater detail. You discovered why it is difficult, and you learned why it is valuable. Overall, ITIL recommends business capacity management as an integral part of your capacity management program, and I concur. The clients that have implemented business capacity management on top of a robust IT capacity management capability have found the reward to be well worth the effort.

We began by discussing the scope of business capacity planning, and you learned that it is different than IT capacity management but is essentially an extension of the same techniques. You learned how to define a formula to calculate the utilization of any business process based on the utilization of the IT services supporting it, and we looked at how to use those utilization numbers to predict future capacity needs for your business processes.

We looked at the cost-versus-benefit analysis for business capacity planning. Although there can certainly be challenges, in most cases the benefits are greater than the costs. Obviously, if this isn't true for your organization, you should be content with simple IT component and service capacity management until some factors change to make the benefit more valuable or to make business capacity management less costly.

You learned how to integrate business capacity planning with IT capacity planning and the value of building specific capacity plans for business units. And finally we touched on what to do if your business isn't quite ready for full-blown business capacity planning yet.

The next chapter tackles another topic that challenges some beginning capacity management programs. You learn the relationship between capacity management and procurement and learn some techniques to help you order capacity on time, but not too early. One of the major benefits of capacity management comes when you avoid ordering IT components that will sit around without being used. After you learn the techniques described in Chapter 13, "Smoothing the Order Cycle," you will have a much better chance of implementing a "just in time" ordering process.

CHAPTER 13

Smoothing the Order Cycle

Because a major goal of capacity management is to reduce IT costs, it is important that we link capacity management with IT spending. Capacity management doesn't affect your payroll directly, but it should certainly have a strong impact on your IT procurement.

In this chapter we examine the link between managing the capacity you have and purchasing new capacity in the form of hardware and software. You learn that managing capacity effectively can help you defer spending, and as your organization gets more mature at managing the existing IT capacity, justification for future spending is much easier.

Establishing Capacity Buffers and Reorder Levels

The most important step you can take to link capacity management with IT procurement is to treat your capacity pools as though they were separate items in a traditional manufacturing inventory. In a traditional inventory system, you manage the quantity on hand versus the quantity you reorder at one time and the length of time it requires for a new order to come in. By tracking these three quantities for each resource pool, you can place orders at just the right time so that new capacity comes in exactly when you need it. If capacity is ordered too early, you will have idle hardware or software and you will have spent money before you needed to. On the other hand, if your capacity is ordered too late, you will have to delay some new project or operate some IT service at less than optimal levels because you lack capacity.

Determining Capacity Buffers

A capacity buffer is simply the number of units left in any capacity pool. For simple capacity pools this can be very easy to determine. If you've purchased 50 single-user licenses for Microsoft Office and deployed 20 of them, your capacity buffer is 30. This can be tracked in your service asset tracking system or via a simple spreadsheet. Similar capacity buffers can be tracked for any individual use of capacity such as user workstations, cellular phones, office printers, or nonvirtual servers.

Capacity buffers become a bit more complex when the resource pool includes resources that have multiple uses. Imagine you've purchased 50 concurrent licenses of BMC Remedy for incident management. Now you can allow hundreds of people to use those licenses, but only 50 are allowed at any one time. Tracking the capacity buffer now becomes a very dynamic process, which is fortunately assisted by tools inside the software itself. But the same principle holds true for a server that is virtualized. You purchase a single large pool of processing, memory, and input/output resources and then proceed to create multiple servers from that pool. Modern virtualization engines enable you to actually assign more resources than are physically present, so it can be difficult to determine how much resource actually remains to be assigned.

For resources that can be used in multiple ways, you should define a set of standards for your organization around how they will be used. For a tower server that will be virtualized, for example, you should define a standard size for each new virtual server and a standard that indicates how many of those virtual servers to create per host tower. This enables you to define a reasonable capacity buffer based on the standards you created. You should understand that it is always possible to squeeze a little more out of a resource if you need to, but the standards provide a healthy guideline for the purpose of linking capacity management with procurement.

It is important that you manage the capacity buffer for each of your capacity pools where utilization is growing. In other words, if you are going to run out of capacity in a pool, you need to know when you are likely to run out. You know this by managing the forecasts and trends as described throughout this book. Your capacity trends tell you how fast you are depleting the capacity in any given pool. The forecasts you make will help you determine when surges may occur that increase your capacity needs. Together these tools help you to manage the capacity buffer for each pool.

Establishing Reorder Levels

Of course, knowing how much capacity remains is only part of the solution. The other part is to understand how much new capacity can be obtained and how quickly. This is called the reorder level. For each capacity pool you have a specific increment in which you add new capacity. Perhaps your standards say that you can create 20 virtual servers out of a specific hardware tower that you purchase. That means your reorder level for that resource pool comes in blocks of 20. For a software license pool you may reorder in blocks of 50 licenses because the vendor offers the best discount at that level. Each capacity pool has its own reorder level associated with it.

For simple capacity pools like individual nonvirtual servers, you may be able to reorder just one unit at a time. When this is the case, you should consider the rate at which you use the resource and the cost of any overhead associated with acquiring and deploying the resource. For capacity pools that are quickly depleted, you may consider setting the reorder level higher than one. In other words, you may choose to have some stock on hand simply for the sake of convenience. The less expensive the resource, the more likely it is that you will want stock on hand because of the larger overhead of making a purchase. You will very likely have a few extra laptops in inventory, but it is highly unlikely that you'll purchase an extra mainframe! Figure 13.1 provides a graphical view of the reorder point concept.

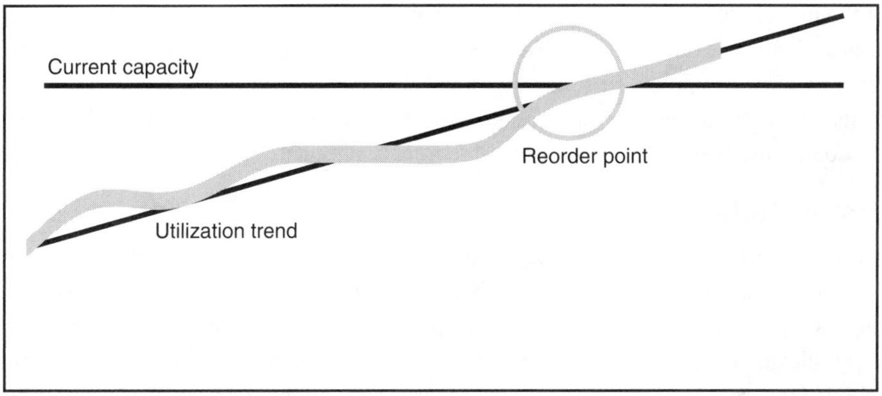

Figure 13.1 The concepts for capacity planning are similar to those for inventory management.

First Guesses and Fine-Tuning

Setting up capacity buffers and reorder levels takes some trial and error. You should begin with conservative reorder levels, by which I mean you should err on the side of having excess capacity instead of experiencing capacity shortages. As your skills in managing trends and forecasts increase, you can tighten the reorder levels to avoid purchasing more capacity than you can use quickly.

You could, of course, use a more rigorous approach based on queuing theory to establish more precise reorder levels. If you happen to have people on your staff skilled in that discipline, a rigorous approach might make sense for you. For most of us, however, just making initial guesses based on experience is more practical.

Over time, you should continue to fine-tune each of your reorder levels. Vendors may change, discount structures from your existing vendors will change, and the IT budget in general will change over time. All these are occasions for reworking the reorder level to take best advantage of when to order new capacity and when to wait just a bit longer. Your continuous improvement goal should be to try to deploy new equipment the day before you actually need to use it for capacity growth.

Factors Affecting Reorder Levels

Setting the correct reorder levels is important but it isn't always easy. There are several factors that must be considered to establish the correct reorder levels. In this section we consider those factors, and I provide some guidance on how to evaluate each factor in the context of capacity ordering.

Deployment Time

One of the first factors impacting your reorder levels is the time required to deploy new capacity after it is available to you. You should strive to shorten the cycle between equipment arriving on your floor and that equipment being ready for use. During this time, your organization has committed the money for the new equipment but isn't yet getting any benefit from it. The longer this delay becomes, the farther ahead you need to reorder equipment.

Process Maturity

A second factor to be considered is the maturity of your process. Simply put, the more mature your capacity management program gets, the more fine-tuned your reorder levels become. At the beginning of a capacity management program, you should estimate your reorder levels and then add a significant buffer to account for the fact that your estimate is not very accurate. For example, if you are running a VMware server farm, you might estimate that you can build 20 more virtual machines before reaching capacity. You know that you are building 3 virtual machines per week on average and that it takes 3 weeks to purchase and install a new VMware host. Logic dictates that you would place an order when you have capacity left to build 9 new machines. Rather than setting your reorder point at 9, however, you should recognize that the estimates may be off by as much as 50%, and set your reorder point to 15. This gives you a buffer that allows for inaccurate estimates.

Of course, setting your reorder point artificially high also causes you to spend money before it is really necessary, and in the preceding example you may well have a VMware host sitting idle for some number of weeks before it is really needed. This is why you need to use the process reports described in Chapter 11, "Produce Capacity Reports," especially the trend accuracy report. As you gain confidence that your capacity trend data is always accurate to within 25%, you can reduce this artificial buffer to 25%. In our example, you would order with four weeks of lead time instead of three and reduce the idle time by a week. This doesn't seem like a significant amount, but when you consider the effect over the dozens or even hundreds of capacity pools you will manage, it can have a major effect on your IT budget. These kinds of incremental changes also show the rest of your organization that the capacity management program is growing stronger and showing benefit.

The final goal should be to make your capacity trends at least 95% accurate and thus have a buffer of only 5%. This enables you to defer costs until they are really necessary. Operating at this level of accuracy helps you build and maintain the confidence of the executives to allocate the IT budget, and you will find that your budget requests get approved more easily because you can prove that you are managing the budget effectively.

Vendor Packaging

Another factor that impacts your reorder levels is the way vendors choose to sell to you. Whereas most organizations want to hang on to their money by delaying purchases as much as possible, most vendors want to get money from you as soon as possible. Many vendors offer discounts if you purchase more of their products than you absolutely need, and these discounts sometimes offset the cost of having idle capacity. Part of good capacity management is to understand and take advantage of volume discounts offered by your suppliers.

Volume discounts apply more frequently to commodity items such as workstation software and hardware, but there are other packaging strategies that vendors can use to entice you to purchase more than you need. For example, almost all software vendors offer enterprise licensing agreements that allow you to essentially purchase an unlimited supply of their software. An enterprise agreement can save money both directly in software license costs and indirectly in the costs for software asset management and capacity management. Be sure to let your procurement team know about these added cost savings so that they can fairly evaluate the enterprise license agreements offered by your vendors.

Vendor packaging also affects your hardware purchases. As hardware manufacturers strive to design the most attractive systems, they often put more capacity than you need in some parts of the system and less in others. One of the clients I've worked with had a standard "large" server with four quad-core processors, for a total of 16 CPU cores. When the industry shifted to hex core-core processors, they had to decide whether to change that standard to two or three processors. Two processors would provide 12 cores, which might be sufficient given the faster nature of the server in general. Three processors would provide more cores than needed, and in their particular case caused them to jump to a more expensive server frame. This is just one example of a hardware manufacturer directly impacting the capacity planner's job. The net result is that client actually chose to start acquiring servers with four hex-core processors and set their reorder point differently to reflect the fact that they could accommodate much more workload with these larger servers.

Virtualization Standards

Perhaps the largest impact on your reorder levels is the degree to which you have chosen to adopt virtualization. As you learned in Chapter 2, "The Geography of Managing Capacity," a hypervisor splits a single server into multiple smaller servers. The number of resources you choose to give to each virtual server is variable but should be established using some standards that your organization has set. Although those standards offer a guideline, it is possible with most hypervisors to oversubscribe your resources. In other words, you may have a guideline that says you can build two new mainframe LPARs given the resources you have, but there is no technical reason you couldn't build three new LPARs and just allow them to contend for resources when they need it.

Because of this principle of over-subscription, capacity reorder levels become less distinct. Instead of firm limits, you will use guidelines to indicate how much capacity you really have. You can adopt either a rigid approach or a flexible approach. To use a rigid approach, simply ignore the fact that your reorder levels are guidelines. Establish a firm number of virtual servers to build on each physical host, and stick to that number regardless. Your limit should allow for growth of the workload inside each virtual machine, but when the prescribed number of virtual servers is built, you will insist on using a different host for future build activity.

The flexible approach recognizes that not all virtual servers within a host are the same. Even if you start with standards, operational issues will arise that can cause you to allocate more CPU or memory to some virtual servers or to reduce the resources allocated to another. Using a flexible reorder level, you determine on a host-by-host basis (or cluster basis if the virtual servers can move dynamically between hosts) how many more virtual servers can be built. Each time a server is built, you reassess the host to update your number that can still be built and update your reorder level accordingly.

Most of the clients I've worked with have found that a rigid approach is the best place to start. Add the complexity of the flexible approach only when you find that you get significant benefit for the extra effort.

Cost-Containment Efforts

It may not seem obvious, but your capacity reorder points are also influenced by the prevailing economic conditions. When there is pressure to contain costs, you'll find that the consumption of resources slows down, and your reorder points are thus lower. When your organization seeks to expand its market and gain new business, the pendulum swings to more liberal reorder points to accommodate much faster IT growth. We've all experienced these economic cycles, but as a capacity planner you need to be sensitive to how they influence your ability to reorder.

Although the world and national economies can certainly impact your capacity plans, so too will your organization's own economic cycles. Most organizations have either an annual or a quarterly budget cycle, and almost all organizations try to juggle their cost and revenue to line up with reporting cycles. This isn't a book about financial management, so I will simply say it is important to consider your current financial constraints and tighten or loosen your capacity reorder levels based on their current state.

Figure 13.2 summarizes the factors affecting reorder levels.

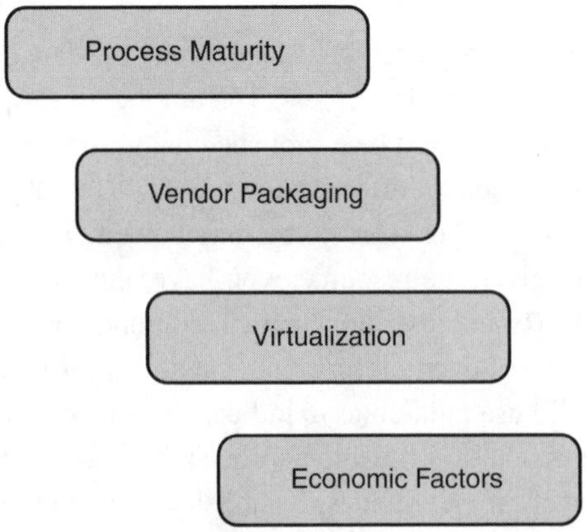

Figure 13.2 Multiple factors affect your decision on when to order new capacity.

Ordering the Right Amount

We began by covering the basic concepts of capacity buffers and reorder levels. Next you learned how to know when it is time to place a new order to add capacity to your environment. The logical next question to examine is how much capacity you should order at a time. If you order too much, you end up with idle capacity, which we've been trying to avoid for many good reasons. If you order too little, however, you end up having to order again very soon, and the overhead inherent in the procurement process causes other costs that you'd rather avoid. In this section we examine the question of how much capacity to order at a time.

Ordering Individual Units

The simplest order is for individual units of some product. An individual needs a new PC so you order a PC to fill the need. A new project requires an additional network firewall, so you order a firewall. These individual units are generally ordered in response to a project or special need rather than some trend that you are following as a capacity manager. Rather than predicting when capacity will run out, a project manager predicts when the item is needed by traditional project planning methods.

In an environment without capacity planning, ordering individual units is most likely the norm. There may be large projects such as workstation refresh in which you order many individual units, but the ordering is still driven by project managers and the need is predicted with project management methods. The problem with this method is that it doesn't take into account the growth of existing uses. You might order a new firewall for a special project, but without capacity planning and management you won't know when you should order a new firewall because the existing one is simply getting too busy.

Capacity plans may call for ordering individual units as well, but these orders generally come from a capacity plan rather than a project plan. When your storage area network is filling up, you may order another drawer of disks to augment capacity, or when a three-node server cluster is approaching capacity, you may order a fourth server to add more capacity to the cluster. These individual orders are still the simplest to understand because they involve ordering more of what you already have and understand.

Ordering Hardware for Virtualization

Things get much more interesting when you are ordering new hardware to build virtual devices, whether servers, storage, or even virtual networks. This scenario is more interesting because multiple variables are involved and the decisions are not nearly as simple. You need to consider the risk of ordering very large hardware that enables you to create lots of virtual partitions versus the cost of ordering smaller hardware that holds fewer virtual partitions but presents less risk when it fails.

Hopefully you have already considered this equation and established a standard configuration that you use for virtual resources. If not, you should consider the rate of consumption for the virtual resources you are provisioning. If you build a new virtual server every day and have thousands of them in your environment, you are likely to order very large hosts that can hold many virtual servers per host. On the other hand, if you provision a new virtual server every month or even less frequently, you should use smaller hosts because they cost less. That way you won't have a huge investment sitting mostly idle for months waiting to fill up. Figure 13.3 demonstrates the relationship between the order cycle and the size of virtual hardware.

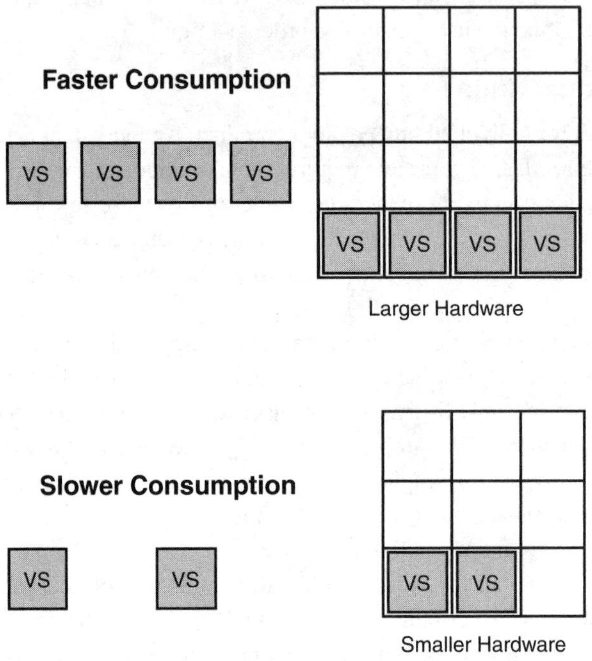

Figure 13.3 Faster resource consumption requires larger servers for virtualization.

The standard that you use for virtual resources needs to be reevaluated frequently. Hardware types change, your rate of consumption changes, and the economic factors around you change. All will have an effect on your choice of standards. You should establish a process to review your standard hardware orders at least once a quarter to determine which of these factors has changed and how your new standard should adjust to it. It may well be that you decide not to change the standard for a cycle or two, but at least it will be an informed decision rather than a default decision made because you neglected to think about the issues.

Fortunately, most modern hypervisors no longer demand that the underlying hardware platform be uniform, but if you are forced to use an older hypervisor that doesn't allow for disparate hardware, you will need to build a new virtual group each time you need to add capacity. If this is your situation, you will be forced to order a group of similar hardware at the same time. This forces you to order more than you initially need or to count on the manufacturers continuing to offer the same hardware for the next time you need to add capacity. In general, if you have a hypervisor that requires the same hardware type for each server you order, your next standards decision should strongly consider a new hypervisor standard.

Volume Ordering

As mentioned earlier in this chapter, it sometimes makes sense to order in volume to receive the best prices from your vendors. You need to avoid the temptation to order very large quantities, especially of items for which your consumption is quite low. Although the initial purchase price might seem very reasonable, you need to add the cost of warehousing the items, the cost of managing the overlarge capacity pool, and the cost of paying the money before you really needed to. If all of those factors are taken into account and you're still getting a good deal, go ahead and purchase in bulk.

Some vendors allow you to place a volume order but delay shipment of the order until you really need the items. This can save you the warehousing cost, and sometimes saves the manufacturer cost as well because the manufacturer can produce the items right before they need to be shipped. If quantity pricing is attractive, you should ask your vendors whether they support this kind of arrangement. You still need to manage the unused capacity so that you can understand your financial commitment and schedule the ship dates, but at least you can avoid the warehousing cost.

You should be in close alignment with your procurement people if you want to take advantage of volume ordering. The savings are not always what the vendor would have you believe, but there is a time when ordering in volume really makes sense, and you should definitely take advantage of volume ordering.

Finding the Right Balance

At this point you understand that capacity management is all about making sound business and technical decisions. This is also true when ordering new capacity. You don't want to wait too long to place an order because you may run out of capacity, crippling one or more IT projects or causing a service disruption. But you don't want to order too soon or you will waste money by having capacity sitting idle waiting for your consumption to catch up. This is the balance you must strike in defining your reorder levels.

You must also find a balance in specifying your orders. Order too little capacity and you are right back into the order cycle very quickly, incurring whatever overhead costs are associated with placing an order for your organization. But if you order too much, you will again have excess capacity that sits idle and thus waste money. It will take you some time to find the right balance between too soon and too late and between too much and too little. After you have found it, you need to keep focused because many factors cause the balance point to shift. This is one of the hardest jobs of the capacity manager.

Reclaiming Capacity Instead of Reordering

Throughout this chapter I've assumed that your organization is growing, and therefore your IT needs will grow. Although I'm normally an optimist, I certainly understand that steady growth may not be the pattern for all organizations. Even in organizations that are growing overall, projects are still cancelled, applications are retired, and infrastructure is refreshed. These typical activities that every organization undertakes shrink capacity demands rather than grow them. Thus, it is important to understand how shrinking demand impacts the procurement cycle.

How Reclaimed Capacity Affects Capacity Demand

When you decommission a server or uninstall software, you are reclaiming capacity that can be used at another time. Many other activities also provide added capacity, and as a capacity manager you need to be aware of how these activities impact your capacity demand.

One thing to think about with reclaimed capacity is that it directly affects your utilization trends. Consider disk space, for example. If a database is decommissioned or a set of files is deleted, space is reclaimed on the SAN. During the same period, new files might be created or databases set up, using space on the same devices. Thus, rather than a simple progression in which space continuously gets consumed, there is an ebb and flow that dictates how much a resource is used. This ebb and flow certainly applies to individual resources like the memory on a server or the bandwidth of a network line, but it can also apply to groups of resources like a pool of cellphones or software licenses. Any IT resource important enough to be tracked by your capacity management will most likely both grow and shrink in usage.

Growing and shrinking resource usage is expected and is tracked by your utilization trends. You won't really need to pay much attention until the trend shows a sustained decline in usage. When you see a resource declining regularly, you should update your capacity plan to include some kind of consolidation effort and eventually take hardware and software out of your environment. These activities save money, which is probably what your organization needs if the IT utilization trend is matching your revenue trend.

How Reuse Affects Reorder Levels

When your negative utilization results in removing equipment from your environment, you will find yourself with the opposite of reorder levels. Instead, you'll find a need to sell or dispose of unwanted assets. If the assets have residual value, you might be able to sell them on the open marketplace for some fraction of their original cost. If there is no residual value, or the market does not offer a solution for you, you most likely need to dispose of the asset.

For capacity pools that show a steady decline in use, you will want to set a disposal level rather than a reorder level. Essentially, this is a point at which the utilization of that pool becomes so low that you want to consolidate resources and dispose of some of the asset. The disposal level is tracked just like a reorder level would be, and as you approach the limit you have set, you will make a business decision on the cost of the decommissioning project versus the value gained by disposing of an asset. For hardware assets don't forget to consider the power savings, the datacenter or office-space savings, and the savings you get by no longer paying for maintenance.

Notice that decommissioning does not necessarily mean that your entire organization no longer uses an asset. It may well be that you can move that asset to another part of your organization or save it in inventory until it is needed again. Before you actually dispose of an asset, make sure you have considered all the alternatives because you certainly don't want to dispose of any hardware or software only to find that you need to purchase the same thing again a year later.

Creative Ways to Reuse Capacity

There are many ways to reuse capacity that has been set free. You should consider all of them before simply discarding any hardware or software.

If your excess capacity has computing power, consider creating a low-cost grid environment. One of my clients went through a significant workforce downsizing and had hundreds of unused personal computers left as a result. Rather than disposing of these, we installed Linux and some low-cost grid software on them and created a significant computing resource that has now become a key part of their computing infrastructure. The customer never would have considered buying several hundred computers specifically for this purpose, but seizing this opportunity created a strategic advantage for them.

For unused server hardware, consider giving it to your software developers. I haven't met a developer who couldn't use another development or test machine somewhere. Many of them would even love to support and maintain a server at home, and would spend their own time developing code that could someday be used in their business applications at work. Developers can be a strange lot sometimes, but many I've met would be very motivated by receiving their own server.

You can also consider using spare capacity to automate some of the peripheral functions of your organization that generally don't get a part of the IT budget. Does your organization provide a day-care facility for employees? Maybe that spare server could be used to create an automated check-in system. Do you have an employee fitness center? You could use some spare servers to create a media hub that allows employees to access music and video during their workouts. Of course, these projects have costs associated with them, but many times the benefits you get in employee morale and retention are well worth the costs.

Summary and Next Steps

In this chapter we've examined the link between capacity management and IT spending. You learned that for each capacity pool you manage, there needs to be a buffer of unused space. When that buffer becomes too small, you have reached your reorder level. Reorder levels are different for each kind of capacity you manage, and managing them is an important part of the capacity management program.

We looked at the factors that affect reorder levels and considered how your process maturity, vendor packaging, virtualization standards, and even the economy cause you to change the reorder levels from time to time. Keeping track of these changes and predicting just the right time to reorder hardware and software can be the hallmark of a well-run capacity management program. Failing to track the changes results in orders being placed too early, wasting money, or being placed too late, causing project delays.

You next discovered that how much you order at a time is nearly as important as when you place orders. There must be a balance between placing large orders with high costs and placing small orders that don't add sufficient capacity.

Finally, we briefly considered what might happen if instead of ordering you have declining utilization and need to retire some capacity. We thought about what this might mean to your reorder levels and how to track the need to retire assets, and as a bonus you learned a few ways in which you might use excess capacity creatively rather than simply getting rid of it.

In the next chapter we look at another issue that confuses many beginning capacity managers. We talk about how the capacity management team should interact with project teams and project managers. I describe how the capacity plan should be created within the project life cycle and when it should be updated.

CHAPTER 14

Capacity Management in a Project Context

The biggest changes to IT capacity happen as a result of projects that your IT group manages. Many of those projects add new capacity to your environment, and all will use capacity that you are expected to manage. The project will have a focus for a while, but when the mission is accomplished and the dedicated team dissipates, you will be left needing to manage the footprint that the project leaves behind. Fortunately, there are steps you can take during the project that can make managing capacity easier.

In this chapter we think about the influence that capacity management can and should have on IT projects. We specifically look at how a capacity plan should be part of the overall project plan, and how that plan should be created by the project team and turned over to operations.

Capacity Plans as Project Deliverables

Nearly every IT project starts out with great intentions for doing the right things. Study after study, however, shows the IT projects end up doing the wrong things, taking longer than expected and costing more than budgeted. Unrealistic expectations, economic pressures, unexpected personnel situations, and competing priorities often derail projects. This isn't a book about project management and I don't know how to fix the issues with IT projects, but this section attempts to describe how to at least ensure that you can manage the capacity that your IT projects end up delivering.

Capacity management cannot be an afterthought toward the end of the project or a checklist item that the team considers right as they are wrapping up the project. Throughout the solution development life cycle, careful attention must be given to how much capacity is produced by the project and how much capacity is consumed by the new service or application that is deployed as part of the project. You should work with your project managers or program management team to ensure that each project leaves behind the right capacity management plan.

Adding Capacity Requirements in Project Definition

Integrating capacity management thinking into a project begins as the requirements for the project are being defined and refined. Project teams and their sponsors naturally think of functional requirements to enhance the way the resulting service or application are used. You might need to prod them to think beyond functions to service, and especially to capacity. Good capacity and performance requirements are extremely difficult for most project teams to define, but are essential if the solution they develop is going to provide good service for its users.

Good capacity requirements generally start with two simple words: "how many." Ask the project team various questions: How many people use their application or service? Will they all use it at the same time, or will the use be distributed? How many users should the new service handle at its busiest time? How many different interactions or transactions are users able to perform? How many of each kind will they perform in a minute, an hour, or a day? How many users are in the same location as the servers? How many will be distributed and to what locations? How many different kinds of information need to be saved? How many of each kind? How many other applications need to connect with this service? How many things need to be printed? As you can see, you can and should play the "how many" game for a very long time. The more times you can ask the project team "how many" and get reasonable answers, the more complete your capacity requirements will be.

Whereas capacity requirements stem from asking "how many," performance requirements come from asking "how long." How long should it take to log in? How long should a normal printing event take? How long should it take to do a search? How long can it take to save a transaction to disk? Keep asking all the questions you can think of about how long various operations in the service or application should take. Don't focus only on those that are automated, but also learn how long process steps should take if they are executed by people. These performance requirements help the project team to set better expectations for their users and help you to know the right things to manage after the project finishes. Figure 14.1 reminds you of the two questions that need to be asked relentlessly to get good capacity and performance requirements.

Be sure the project team documents all these requirements before starting in on the design of their infrastructure. Without adequate capacity requirements, the infrastructure team is left with no choice but to create very large servers and hope they are big enough. That means you as a capacity manager have to consolidate the project or shrink the team's infrastructure because they didn't take the time to really define their needs. Remember that those follow-on projects normally need to come out of the operational IT budget and probably won't get funding from the project team. So be sure that the project spends its money to do the right thing for capacity management up front.

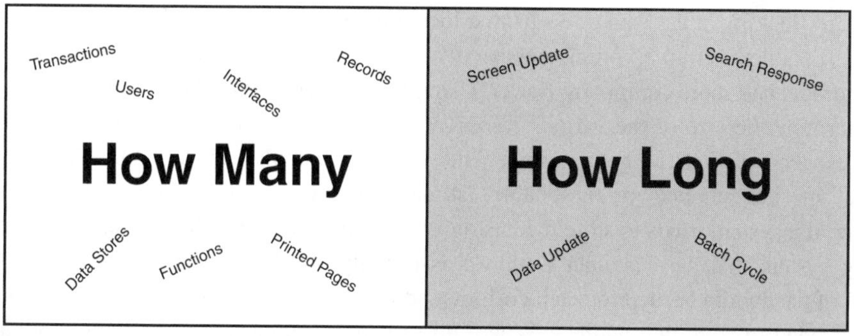

Figure 14.1 You have two key questions to ask when discovering capacity requirements.

Considering Capacity and Performance in the System Architecture

After the project team has settled on its requirements, there is a design phase in which the new solution is planned and designed. One of the outcomes of the design phase of every project should be a system architecture that describes the complete system, including the infrastructure that the system uses. This architecture should describe the software that is required, the computing resources, the storage needs of the project, and the network layout where the computing and storage resources are located.

Many projects put together this architecture by making guesses about how much computing power, storage space, and network bandwidth are required. If the project team hasn't taken the time and effort to define capacity and performance requirements, you will most likely have to use that same approach. But if the team has gathered good requirements indicating how much capacity and performance are needed, the architect has a better option available as the designer of the system.

The architect begins creating the system infrastructure by looking at patterns of data usage. Notice where the data needs to be stored and how much needs to be stored there. Observe from the requirements where data originates and where it flows. Taking a data-centric view of the system to be developed helps the architect understand network placement of the system more than any other method.

Normally the architecture has some fixed constraints associated with it. If your organization has invested in centralized storage area network (SAN) infrastructure, you will most likely need to place the long-term data stores wherever that SAN hardware is located. If all your computing power is located in a single data center, you will obviously use servers in that data center as part of the architecture. These constraints help the system architect to establish the boundaries, but should not define the entire architecture.

After looking at the data flows from a location perspective, the architect should next consider the data flows from a volume perspective. Larger amounts of data need more bandwidth, more storage, and more computing power. Using the answers to the "how many" questions, she can determine the size of the various resources that are needed to fulfill the capacity requirements. Correctly sizing a computing system that hasn't been built yet is difficult. Where the architect has specific numbers or reasonable estimates, she can perform some calculations. For example, if a system needs to store the customer's address and the architect can find out from an existing system that the customer's address is roughly 160 bytes, she can calculate both the amount of bandwidth needed for each customer address transaction and the amount of disk space that is needed to store that address. Where no reasonable numbers are available, the architect needs to rely on experience designing and operating similar systems. If you have good capacity trending data from other systems that use the same middleware and operating system environment, you should be able to provide the architect with a good estimate of the resources needed for the new system.

As you review the design for a new system, insist on understanding how the architect came up with the sizes of hardware resources needed. Were they based on calculations? If so, the calculation and the raw data that went into it should be defined in the architecture document. Were comparable systems used as a basis for the estimate? Those too should be documented. As the capacity planner, you should be reviewing each new system architecture document and insisting that those documents be based on accurate and timely capacity data. Ideally, the size of a new system would be based on simulation or modeling tools that are already part of your capacity management toolkit. If such tools are unavailable, your organization should at least develop a repeatable method for estimating the capacity required by new systems.

Defining and Executing Capacity Test Cases

If the project team has defined good capacity and performance requirements and the architect has designed a system to meet those requirements, then all that remains is for the project to verify that the requirements are indeed met. Performance and capacity testing can be difficult and time-consuming; so for many IT projects the choice is made to test functionality and integration between systems but ignore performance and capacity testing. If your capacity management program has shown value to the organization, you need to insist that project teams find ways to include this vital stage of testing in their projects.

Good testing begins with building good test cases. A test case is nothing more than a specific set of circumstances and actions that the system executes under controlled conditions. For capacity and performance testing this might be a specific number of users performing a prescribed set of transactions. It could also be a simple transaction such as saving or retrieving a large file. The test cases should reflect real actions that the system is expected to perform in production. Many development organizations perform stress testing in which they ratchet up the load on a system to determine when performance or capacity is fully consumed. That can be helpful, but it isn't nearly as important as testing with a normal load to make sure that the system behaves acceptably during typical utilization.

These test cases can also often validate the usage estimates, and serve as a preproduction warning if SAN or other resource pools are too small.

Just as the capacity planner should review the architecture, so too should you review the test cases. Just looking at what the project team plans to test helps you understand what they feel is important in the finished system. If the tests look too weak or don't appear as if they will really provide an adequate test, the capacity planner should raise an issue and try to get some more stringent test cases written. In some organizations the capacity planner actually writes all the performance and capacity tests for systems. If you are staffed to work this way, you can certainly make projects more effective in their test efforts by having qualified capacity managers focus on ensuring that capacity and performance test cases are complete and thorough.

Building the Capacity Plan at Project Time

In an organization that is serious about managing its IT capacity, the capacity plan is a vital document. When implementing capacity management, you need to create capacity plans for each service and component that does not already have one, which is likely to be all of them. After you have implemented your program, however, and have been managing capacity for a while, you should shift the responsibility for creating capacity plans to the project teams that are implementing new services or components. The project team has the best knowledge of what the new system can do and how much capacity it requires, and if they are educated on the value and importance of capacity plans, they should be in the best position to produce a complete and accurate plan. This section describes some of the ways you can help your project teams leave behind capacity plans that your capacity management program can then manage.

Testing and Estimating Capacity Utilization

The basis of any good capacity plan is a trend report showing how the capacity has been used for some period. Because a project is likely creating a new service or adding a component, there is no history to use for a trend line. The solution is to use the data gathered during the capacity and performance testing phase of the project.

A typical capacity or performance testing cycle starts with good test cases as described earlier in this chapter. After this set of scenarios is developed, monitors are put on the system to assess performance and utilization. Normally, these monitors are the same as those used for capacity management when the system goes into production, but there are times when specialized monitors are built into the testing tools and can be used instead. Whichever monitors are used should be gathering utilization data to feed into the capacity trend and timing data to serve as a baseline for system performance. The data should be gathered for all the test cases, and that data will serve as the basis for the utilization estimates.

Taking the data gathered from testing and the known characteristics of the system being developed, you should be able to estimate what the trend graph will look like. For example, consider a new telecommunication expense management system. This new system tracks office phones, cellular phones, fax lines, and voice mail boxes and makes sure that the appropriate departments are charged for these expenses. During requirements definition, the team gathered data on how many of each kind of telecommunication device need to be managed, how many people will use the new system, and how many months worth of historical data should be saved. During the definition phase, the team created test cases to ramp up each of these numbers and executed those tests to show how the system performs with various loads on it.

After all the testing is complete, you will have a load of data to use in your capacity estimates. Work with the project team to understand whether data will be entered over a period of time or migrated from one or more existing data stores. If the data will be entered over time, you can use that period to estimate a ramp-up in the utilization of the system as more devices and expenses are processed. If the data will all come in at once, you can assume that the utilization of the system will not ramp up, but will jump close to the expected capacity immediately.

Hopefully, during the requirements phase the project team also got some expected growth estimates. If desk phones are declining and cellphones are becoming more popular, use that information to project the anticipated system usage. Use any data you can get to make the initial capacity plan stronger.

Architecting for Capacity Growth

Of course, a capacity plan is much more than a trend line. The trend must be used to indicate when capacity will run out or when there will be a surplus. This prediction is used to formulate one or more recommendations that describe what to do when the prediction comes to pass. It is the project architect or system designer who is in the best position to help create these recommendations.

Most IT projects are designed to scale either vertically or horizontally. By vertically, we mean that additional resources such as memory, processors, or disk space are added to the existing configuration. This growth in resources enables the system to handle more users and transactions, and thus the capacity of the overall system is increased. When we say that a system scales horizontally, we mean that we can add more computers to the system and spread the work out over those additional resources rather than growing any specific computer to be larger. When designing a system for any IT project, the architect should specify whether the intention is to scale vertically or horizontally.

The benefits of vertical scaling are simplicity and cost. As long as the hardware has been purchased with growth in mind, it is generally fairly simple to add another memory module, processor card, or disk drive. In some cases you can even scale vertically without taking the system down. Even if the system needs to be out for this hardware to be installed, when brought back online most modern operating systems and applications immediately recognize the new hardware and take advantage of it. The result is a simple upgrade that can normally be done in a couple of hours without software changes. Adding extra resources to an existing computer also costs less than adding one or more complete computers.

The weakness of vertical scaling is that there are limits to the expansions you can do. Every computer has an upper bound of how much memory, disk, and CPU it can hold. If your initial growth projections are too low, you may purchase hardware that doesn't have as much scalability as you need. On the other hand, if the system doesn't grow as quickly as you expect, you will purchase a very expensive computer with lots of room for growth when all the system really needed was the smaller model that was less scalable.

The strength of horizontal scaling is that it adds all the resources you need at the same time. Instead of simply increasing memory and CPU, adding a second or third computer adds more power supplies, expansion slots, disk drives, network interfaces, and system boards. Although you might be able to add all of these to an existing system, odds are that you won't. By adding additional nodes, you spread the workload more widely, which adds capacity to the overall system and also provides you a higher degree of availability because no single hardware failure can cause the entire system to fail. Horizontal scaling adds redundancy and is often seen as a strategy that enables capacity scaling and fault tolerance at the same time.

The weaknesses of horizontal scaling are cost and complexity. The project becomes more complex from the beginning because having two or more computing resources generally means you have to add complexity at the network layer to ensure that the systems talk to each other as well as to their users. You normally add complexity at the software level as well because the application and middleware need to be aware that it is running on multiple nodes. Of course, this complexity comes at a cost because the additional nodes cost money, as does the additional labor to install multiple nodes and the multiple copies of software that you need to license on the nodes.

During the design phase of every IT project, your system architect should be aware of this distinction between horizontal scaling and vertical scaling and choose one basic approach or the other for the future of the system. Of course, a combination approach is also possible in which individual computers are grown within specified bounds, and additional nodes are added when those bounds are reached. Whichever approach is adopted should be documented within the system architecture and then reflected as part of the capacity plan for the overall system.

Engaging Capacity Management in the Project

The key message you should take away from this chapter is that the capacity management team should be engaged in any significant IT project that your organization undertakes. Without some kind of engagement and awareness from the capacity management team, the project ends up without an adequate capacity and performance test and without a capacity plan for the future. Those shortcomings quickly become problems for the capacity management team to address, so out of self-defense the capacity team should get engaged in each IT project.

The first point of engagement should be a review of the project requirements. As described earlier, this review should consist of a series of questions about "how many" and "how long." The capacity manager has more experience with situations that have resulted from a lack of capacity or poor planning around capacity and thus has a much better knowledge of whether the documented capacity and performance requirements are adequate. If the requirements aren't adequate, the capacity planner can help by asking leading questions for the project team to explore until the requirements are clear, complete, and measurable.

The second point of engagement is with the project architect. The capacity management team should review the defined architecture to see how it compares with existing systems and whether the proposed design meets the capacity and performance requirements that have been documented. Again, the capacity team has experience working with many combinations of hardware, software, and application code and can spot any weaknesses in design, because they have learned from experience what tends to work and what tends to fail. The capacity team most likely cannot comment on most of the architectural decisions, but they should certainly review those that will impact the capacity and performance of the system to be built.

The third point of engagement between the capacity management team and the project team happens during preparation of the test cases. The capacity manager should review those test cases that pertain to capacity and performance testing. Of specific interest is whether the proposed tests actually stress the system and verify that it is capable of meeting the projected capacity demands in production. Many teams try to skimp on capacity and performance testing because it is seen as just another hurdle before they can move their system into production. The capacity management team should insist on the importance of capacity testing, and should make sure the proposed test cases actually validate whether the system can meet all of its capacity goals.

Finally, capacity management should be engaged with the project at the point of testing. The capacity manager and the project architect should work together to study the results of the testing and craft the initial capacity plan for the new service, component, or application. This partnership ensures a smooth handoff to the capacity management team when the new system goes into production and the project team is ready to move on to other assignments.

Figure 14.2 summarizes the four engagement points for the capacity management team and describes the benefits of each.

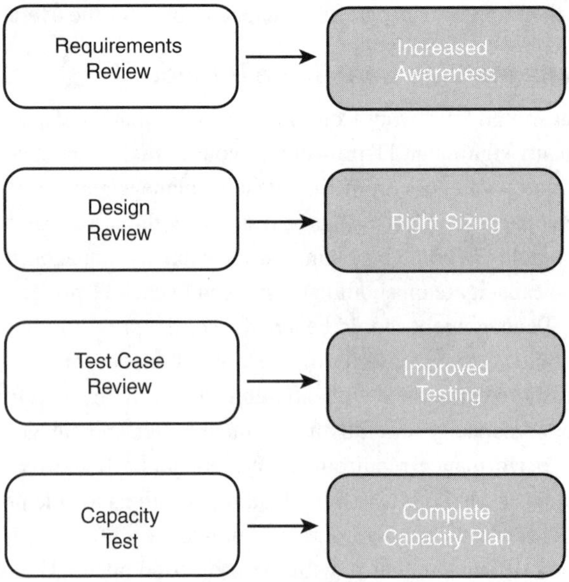

Figure 14.2 The capacity team is engaged with a project at four specific points.

Turning the Capacity Plan Over to Operations

I am often an idealist, and throughout this chapter I've been giving you the idealist's perspective on how capacity planning and project management should work together to provide the optimal transition from the end of an IT project to steady-state capacity management operations. Unfortunately, the real world isn't all that ideal. Your entire capacity management team may be just one person, and there is no way you have time to get engaged on every project that goes on. Or perhaps your project budgets are so tight that there is no way they can ever do effective capacity and performance testing as part of the project. Recognizing that as a capacity manager you will most likely need to deal with less than ideal turnover, this section describes some ways you can still help project teams get you the information you need in order to manage the capacity they have created.

When Capacity Management Has Been Engaged

At times the capacity management team can be engaged in an IT project but all the right deliverables are still not produced. Perhaps the requirements were incomplete and the capacity team didn't have an opportunity to improve them. Maybe the system architect didn't know how or didn't remember to define a growth rate for the system. Perhaps the testing was shortened and didn't include sufficient capacity and performance tests. I consider each of these potential scenarios here and describe how you can recover from them to still get capacity management of the new system under control.

Let's begin with requirements. If inadequate or incomplete requirements are discovered early enough in the project cycle, you can simply stop the project to create requirements. For example, if the capacity team is reviewing the system architecture and finds that there is no plan for how to scale out the system, the capacity manager might ask about what capacity requirements the architect was using. If it is found that there were no requirements, the capacity manager and the architect can work with the project team to define some capacity and performance requirements. The architect can then update the system design to take those new requirements into consideration, and the project is back on track and ready for the full engagement of the capacity management team from that point forward.

If the project team or the capacity team learns about missing requirements late in the cycle or after the project is finished, the best that can be done is to define those requirements and incorporate them into the subsequent capacity plan so that they are at least considered in the trend reporting and ongoing capacity plan that is managed in an ongoing way.

If the system design doesn't consider capacity growth because of lack of architect knowledge or lack of review by the capacity team, there are several things that can be done to recover. If it isn't too late, the design can be modified and the system built correctly from the start. If the system has already been built, the design can still be changed, but modifications may need to be done over one or more future releases rather than before the system goes into production. I have seen cases in which the lack of good requirements or the poor planning by the system architect actually caused the system to fail less than a month into production. At this point there was no choice but to change the design, purchase additional hardware and software, and rebuild in a way that would support the real production workload. Needless to say, this does not leave a good impression of the project team or the capacity management team!

A very common situation is that a project has inadequate or nonexistent capacity and performance testing. Many times the capacity team is welcome to sit in on requirement and design reviews because those processes are already going on, and there is no added project cost to inviting the capacity management team. But when it comes to defining and executing test cases specifically to see whether the capacity requirements are met, the project runs out of money. If this is your case, you should essentially consider the first month of production as the best capacity test you are likely to get. Be careful to note how many users, how many transactions, and all the rest of the "how many" details during this first month. Compare the numbers to those predicted or requested by the requirements and see how the system stacks up. Evaluate the system utilization frequently during the first month and see whether you can draw correlations between the users, system transactions, and other requirements and the CPU utilization, memory usage, and disk space that is actually used. Together you can use this information to build your performance and capacity profile of the system that you would have already had if a capacity and performance test had been conducted.

Using these techniques, the capacity team can catch up to the project and still build the essential capacity plan based on how much you are able to catch up. With some luck, the project team members will still be available to you so you can get the answers you need in order to build that plan.

When Capacity Management Was Not Engaged

Of course, if the capacity management team has not been involved at all in an IT project, you may need to build all the capacity management work products rather than simply catching up on a few of them. Perhaps the project team is aware of the implementation of capacity management for your organization and has been considering capacity throughout the life cycle of the project effort. Or maybe your organization isn't very aware of capacity management yet and you have to deal with a project that has had no sense that capacity planning is needed. Whichever case makes sense for you, I'm here to help.

If the project team has been at least somewhat aware of capacity issues during the project, you are likely to have an architect who has thought about the correct sizing. Those thoughts might or might not have been grounded in a set of requirements, but at least you have some flexibility and the ability to scale up or down because of the design. In this case you again want to use the first month or two of production operations as a way to determine whether the initial size of the system is correct. After you've established a baseline for utilization, work with the architect to determine the most likely growth characteristics and adjust the system if it seems that too much or too little capacity was specified. This might be difficult if the system uses dedicated hardware, but perhaps you can redesign things a bit to make over large dedicated hardware into part of a shared pool.

If the project team has been completely unaware of capacity issues throughout the entire project and you are left with a system that has no capacity requirements and has never been tested, then you are exactly where the rest of this book assumes you are—starting from scratch to implement capacity management. The capacity team needs to establish a baseline, create a capacity plan and manage the new system without help from the project team. You might get a few of these when your program is just getting underway, but if you do a good job of establishing and publicizing your capacity management program, the number of project teams that are completely unaware of capacity management issues should decline over time.

Essentials of Operational Turnover

Whether or not the capacity management team was involved with the project team, there are several essential elements of a good operational turnover. When a new system is turned over to the support teams, including the capacity management team, you must insist on having solid documentation. At a very minimum you should get the system requirements that were defined, the design that was created, and the results of any tests that were conducted. These project artifacts help you understand how thoroughly capacity management concerns were addressed during the project life cycle.

One good IT practice is to have a turnover meeting during which the operational teams can ask questions of the project team. If you have this opportunity, you should certainly ask about expected capacity needs and growth patterns. You should also ask whether members of the project team will help you create the initial capacity plan for the new system. If they are, it will make your job much easier.

Summary and Next Steps

Every IT organization experiences the tension between an operational team that is trying to keep the environment stable and one or more project teams that are trying to introduce beneficial changes to the environment. As a steady-state capacity manager, you should pursue the opportunity to work with as many project teams as you can because every project will either consume some of your existing capacity or introduce new capacity to the environment. In this chapter we looked at the many ways in which the capacity management team can and should interact with IT project teams.

We considered four key deliverables of every IT project and thought about how those deliverables can be influenced and used by the capacity management team. You learned how to influence project requirements, design test cases, and implement capacity testing to make the project team aware of the impact they have on capacity management.

We looked at the elements needed for a capacity plan and considered how that plan could be developed as an additional project deliverable. Understanding capacity trends and helping the architect choose a plan for future expansion not only enables the project team to build a stronger system but also helps the capacity management team build a solid capacity plan with a minimum of guesswork required.

In the final section of the chapter, we recognized that not every project has the benefit of working with the capacity management team, and we considered some strategies for dealing with projects that neglect capacity concerns. It is never too late to manage the capacity of an IT system, even if that system is already in production operations.

In the next chapter we conclude our look at the operational issues surrounding capacity management. We specifically consider how the capacity management program and process should interface with other ITIL-aligned processes. By focusing on the intersection points between the processes and tools, you can reach beyond the capacity management program to improve the operational effectiveness of all IT processes.

CHAPTER 15

Integrating Capacity Planning with IT Processes

Although capacity management by itself brings many benefits to your organization, capacity management integrated with a complete set of ITIL-based processes transforms your IT organization into a powerful business advantage. The core belief behind ITIL, especially in version 3, is that no process is complete until it is viewed as part of the complete life cycle of service management. This is especially true of capacity management because there are many linkages between the capacity management practices you've learned in this book and the other IT process areas. In this chapter we explore some of those linkages and provide a better understanding of how to place your capacity management program into the overall context of a transformed IT organization.

Integrating with Availability Management

Availability management is one of the forgotten processes in many ITIL implementations. Very frequently, organizations assume that if they manage incidents well and reduce the number of service outages, they will have availability completely under control. But availability management is much more than reducing outages. It is the art and science of making every IT service available when it needs to be without spending too much money by making the service available when it isn't needed.

If this description of availability management sounds familiar, it is because availability management is in many ways a complement to capacity management. Organizations that truly manage the availability of their services watch availability trends, create availability plans, and seek to enhance those plans through careful prediction of what is likely to happen in the future. In this section we more closely explore the integration of capacity management and availability management.

Process Linkage

The capacity management process is linked to the availability management process in two fundamental ways. If you are implementing capacity management in an organization that is already practicing availability management, you have an opportunity to create these links from the beginning. If you have not yet tackled availability management, you will at least want to think about how your capacity management program could be integrated with a future rollout of availability management.

The first linkage between capacity and availability is clear. Every time you add new capacity, you will have an effect on the availability of some system. For the best availability, you should add redundant capacity to create a highly available system. For example, if you are deploying a new business application that calls for a web server, you can choose to deploy a single web server that has enough capacity to handle the expected load. This would accomplish the goals of the capacity management team and would meet the needs of the application. On the other hand, you could implement two smaller web servers and a load balancer, which would provide the capacity needed by the project but with a much higher availability characteristic. This decision between providing individual capacity and providing redundant capacity occurs with almost every new system design.

The second process linkage between capacity management and availability management works through incident management. Every capacity shortage that occurs causes some sort of service disruption or incident. Those incidents decrease system availability. The process linkage is such that avoiding capacity shortages thus improves availability. During your deployment of the capacity management program, you can consider these two linkages between capacity and availability management to strengthen both process areas. Figure 15.1 shows the process links.

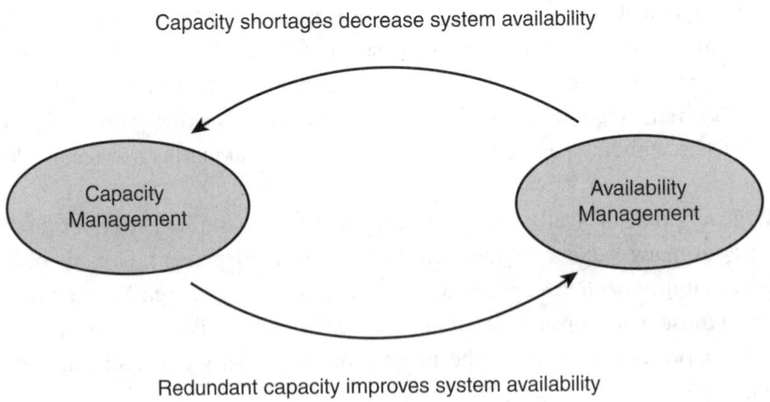

Figure 15.1 Capacity management can improve or decrease system availability.

Data Linkage

Like so many ITIL processes, capacity management links to availability management through the configuration management system. Both process disciplines depend on configuration items and relationships between configuration items to describe the components and IT services that they manage. Because these configuration items are given common identifiers by configuration management, both the capacity management service and the availability management process can relate to the same set of items.

When they do relate, it is to share information about utilization and availability. As you learned earlier in this book, each significant component and every IT service has its utilization tracked by capacity management. Similarly, each of them also has its availability tracked by availability management. Putting the two together provides a very complete view of the future for that component or service. For example, if the utilization is growing while availability is decreasing, you will most likely need to take action urgently. On the other hand, if availability is steady or even getting better for a growing component, action may not be as urgent. In addition, the capacity management process uses the CMDB dependencies to understand the impact of capacity-related incidents.

Another area where capacity data and availability data may overlap is in the plan. Each component or service has both a capacity and an availability plan, and often these should and do interact with one another. As described in the preceding section, the architect can often influence availability in the way that capacity is provided to a component or service. Because of this frequent interaction, many organizations prefer to create a combined capacity and availability plan for their key IT services and components. The single plan can then be managed jointly by the capacity and availability teams.

Benefits of Integration

I've already hinted at the major benefits of the integration between capacity management and availability management. By integrating these two process areas, you can provide a more complete prediction of the future of any component or IT service, and thus ensure that service continues to serve your organization without disruption. In addition, linking these two process areas can save you time and effort if you choose to create a single capacity and availability plan for a component or service. The single plan is easier to maintain and more informative than a capacity plan or availability plan alone can be. For smaller organizations, some of the capacity management roles can be combined with availability management roles, reducing the overall staff needed.

Integrating with Configuration Management

The linkages between capacity management and configuration management are very strong. I would almost say it is impossible to have an effective capacity management program without a good configuration management discipline. Conversely, if you already have an effective configuration management program, you are missing much of its power if you don't use it for capacity management. In this section we explore why this is so, and you should understand the benefits you'll get only if your capacity management program is linked with a strong configuration management program.

Process Linkage

The configuration management process is responsible for keeping track of configuration items and the relationships between them. This is a very simple, yet extremely powerful, concept in ITIL. Although I've been intentionally referring to "components" rather than configuration items, they are for all practical purposes the same thing. A configuration item is any discrete piece of the IT environment, including software programs, hardware components, service elements, and even less concrete items such as organizational units, business processes, and operational processes. The relationships between configuration items help to define the key constructs of IT. A rich set of relationships defined between a business application, two or three middleware packages, several servers, a local area network, and a block of storage might constitute what you would consider a single application system. By knowing how these are related, and how this application system is related to another, the configuration management system (CMS) can create a technical definition of an IT service.

This is exactly where capacity management comes into play. Without the relationships defined by configuration management, the capacity database would have to keep track of the various pieces of an IT service in its own way. But with the CMS in place, capacity management can simply leverage the information to deal with entire IT services. The complex logic used to understand the utilization of an IT service is based on having solid relationships defined by configuration management and stored in the CMS.

Capacity management is linked back to configuration management through change management. As capacity is increased or decreased to accommodate the project need, change records are entered and approved. As these changes are implemented in the environment, the capacity management system is updated to reflect the new reality caused by the increase or decrease in capacity. In this way the capacity management process changes the operating environment, and the CMS is updated to keep track. The reciprocal relationship between capacity management and configuration management is shown in Figure 15.2.

Data Linkage

As described in the preceding section, the capacity database is a key component of the configuration management system. It relies on the configuration item and configuration relationship records to help build definitions of IT systems, and then adds utilization data and capacity plans to the CMS. The configuration management system is essentially the sum of all service management data, and thus a key part of that system is the capacity data from the capacity management program. In essence, the capacity database relies on the configuration data to provide an indexing system for it.

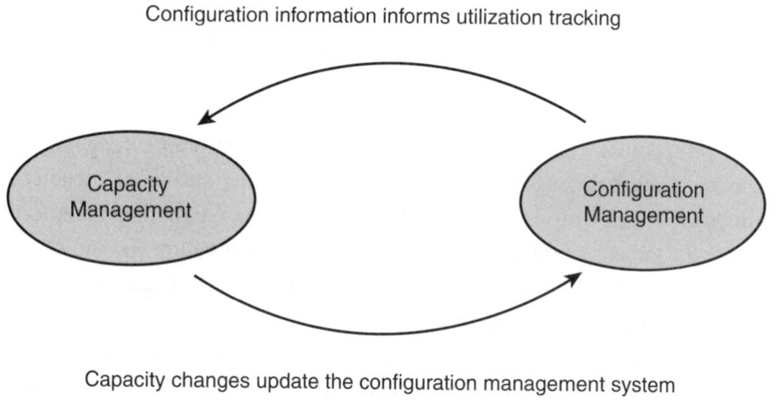
Configuration information informs utilization tracking
Capacity Management
Configuration Management
Capacity changes update the configuration management system

Figure 15.2 Capacity management both uses and updates configuration information.

One intersection point between configuration data and capacity data is your service-level agreements. Service-level agreements are the promises you make to the wider organization about how your IT services are delivered. When your capacity management program is mature, you will have service levels that promise both performance of systems and available capacity as systems grow. Those service levels should be based on configuration items and the dependencies between configuration items to allow you to measure the service you are providing and report accurately on the service levels you are achieving.

Benefits of Integration

Although it is possible to implement capacity management without linking it to configuration management, doing so can lead to extra complications and cost. Without configuration management linkage, the capacity management program needs to establish its own version of components and relationships to form IT services. Either you duplicate much of the central purpose of the configuration management process or you settle for managing the capacity of simple components only. Integrating capacity management with configuration management enables you to manage IT services and even business processes without suffering the overhead of maintaining information about the composition of services or processes.

Integrating with Change Management

Within the ITIL framework, change management is the process that ensures control over the production environment. Although the actual deployment is part of release management, permission to deploy anything new is granted only through change management. The goal of change management is to make informed decisions about proposed changes to the environment and permit only those changes for which the benefit is higher than their risk. This section explores the ways in which capacity management can be integrated with change management.

Process Linkage

From a process perspective, change management is a major supporter of capacity management. The capacity management process constantly evaluates whether sufficient capacity is deployed, and when it finds too much or too little capacity, it invokes change management to make adjustments. The capacity management discipline provides the justification for the change, but only change management can help the team understand the correct schedule and ensure that the capacity change gets the correct reviews and approvals.

Conversely, almost every change that is made to the IT environment has some impact on capacity, so capacity management can be very useful in helping change management fully understand the impacts of a proposed change. As an example, consider a request for change (RFC) that proposes to take down one server in a cluster. Although the cluster may be configured to allow continual operation even with the loss of this server, the capacity management team should be consulted to understand whether the remaining three servers have enough capacity to handle the load. Although the design point might have once ensured that each server kept at least 25% spare capacity, over time the utilization may have grown without a corresponding growth in capacity. Thus, the capacity management process can be used to indicate whether the change can really be successful or whether there is a risk of causing an outage due to limited capacity.

Figure 15.3 shows this relationship between the capacity management process and the change management process. You will see that both processes have value to offer one another, and thus integrating these two processes adds significant value to your ITIL implementation.

Change management adds or removes capacity

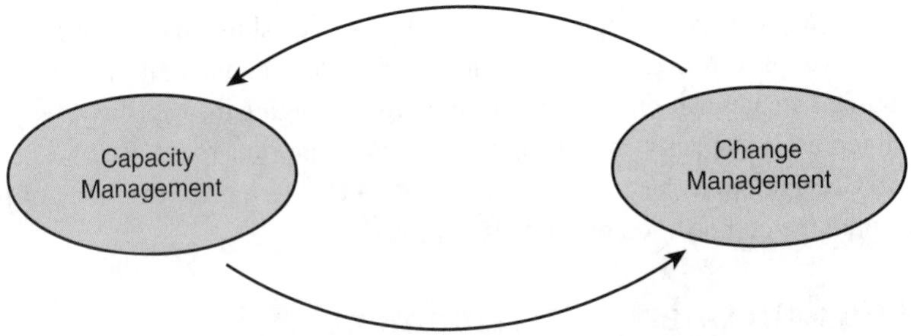

Capacity management defines the impact of a proposed change

Figure 15.3 Capacity management should be closely aligned with change management.

Data Linkage

The data linkage between capacity management and change management is less important than the process linkage. Most organizations don't tie change records back to specific capacity plans when adding or removing capacity. Instead, they link those change records to configuration items that are being changed, and thus they are indirectly linked to the capacity plans for those same configuration items. You will find that this approach is probably sufficient for most purposes.

Another potential link between capacity data and change records is that you could insert the latest capacity trend into a change record to support people trying to analyze the impact of the change. Although still not done frequently, this kind of integration provides much more value. Rather than each change reviewer having to go look up the latest trend graph for a component or service, you could use the technology available in the change management tool to either insert the graph as an attached file or insert a link to where the graph can be found on your local intranet. This enables reviewers to have more complete information and thus make a more informed decision about whether the change will be impacted by a lack of capacity.

Benefits of Integration

Integrating change management with capacity management is both necessary and helpful. It is very unlikely that your organization is implementing capacity management but doesn't have a change control process. Because change control is required in most organizations, you won't have a choice as to whether you invoke change control for capacity-related changes. Each addition or removal of capacity needs to be approved through the change control process, and thus the integration is necessary.

But integrating capacity management with change management is more than necessary. If you use the information provided by the capacity management process in making better change management decisions, you will find that the benefits are great. You can avoid implementing changes that immediately cause capacity shortages, and you can understand whether a change should impact your future capacity plans. This improved decision-making capability helps your IT organization see the future more clearly, and thus add much more value to the whole organization.

Integrating with Incident Management

The integration between capacity management and incident management is by far the most common, probably because it is the easiest to implement. Most IT organizations today have some process for responding to service disruptions or outages, and ITIL calls that process incident management. Of course, your process might or might not be aligned with the best practices described by the ITIL framework, but it almost certainly features someone taking calls from your IT consumers and registering those calls in some sort of trouble ticket system. Your trouble ticket system undoubtedly enables you to describe the problem in some way and then route it to someone who has the skills to do problem determination and resolution. Whether you call this process incident management or problem management, if you have those rudimentary steps you have enough to integrate with capacity management. This section describes that integration.

Process Linkage

From a process perspective, incident management deals with services that are disrupted or slowed down for any reason. The main goal of incident management is to minimize the duration of those disruptions when they do happen. Stated differently, incident management is about resolving incidents as quickly as possible. One of the essential elements of a healthy incident management process is the ability to classify or categorize incidents so you can quickly get the right team working on the issue. Clearly you wouldn't want the network support team working on a server hardware problem, or the storage management team working on an application software problem. So ITIL-aligned incident management seeks to record an incident and then categorize it as quickly as possible so that the right resolver group can get to work on the resolution.

This is exactly where incident management integrates with capacity management. One of the possible classifications of an incident is that a shortage of capacity could be causing the incident. These capacity-related incidents can be moved quickly to your capacity management team, which can consult the predefined capacity plan for the component or service experiencing the outage and quickly resolve the incident. This is one of the primary reasons for having those capacity plans documented and continually maintained.

Of course, it is even better if the capacity management team is using the trend data and real-time capacity monitors to spot potential incidents and take action before an incident occurs. Preventing future incidents is the domain of ITIL problem management, so capacity management has essentially the same interface to problem management as it does to incident management.

Conversely, there are some incidents that are not caused by lack of capacity, but can be resolved by finding excess capacity. Take, for example, an HP server performing as a web server for one of your key business applications. If the server experiences a hardware problem, you can sometimes resolve that problem if you have enough capacity elsewhere to host the web server either on spare hardware or as a virtual server in existing hardware that isn't overloaded. The capacity management team should be able to recommend where spare capacity can be found to restore service to the business application as quickly as possible. Figure 15.4 shows the relationship between capacity management and incident management.

Data Linkage

Incident data is easily linked to capacity data. The first thing you should do to integrate these two processes is add capacity incidents as a category to your incident management ticketing system. You might want to be even more granular and add both the incident classification and the failing configuration item to indicate which capacity pool is the cause of a capacity or performance incident. If you have already implemented ITIL configuration management, you are already capturing a failing configuration item for each incident record. In that case, simply indicating the incident classification as capacity related is sufficient because you can tell exactly which component or service is causing the capacity incident by looking at the failing configuration item as recorded in the ticket.

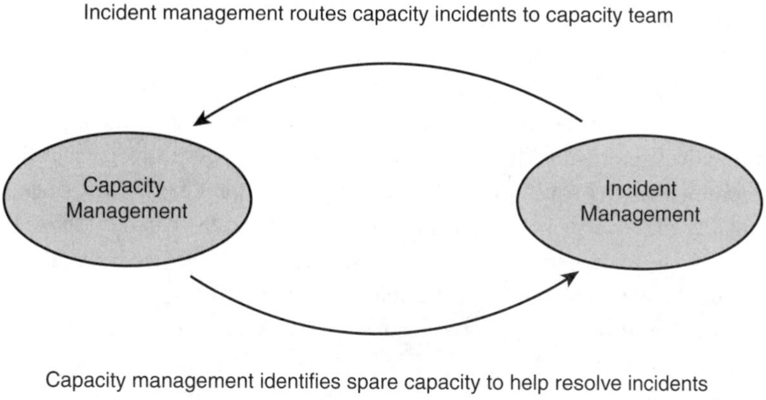
Incident management routes capacity incidents to capacity team
Capacity Management
Incident Management
Capacity management identifies spare capacity to help resolve incidents

Figure 15.4 Capacity management greatly helps the incident management process.

After you have begun tracking capacity-related incidents, you can generate extremely helpful reports. You can plot a capacity-related incident trend to find out whether your capacity management process is helping to reduce these incidents. As long as you have information about failing components or services, you can track which class of components or service causes the most capacity incidents and focus your improvement efforts in that area. For example, you might have great capacity management over your servers but continually have capacity incidents from your storage devices. This would indicate that you need a renewed focus on managing storage capacity more effectively. Tracking capacity incidents can be extremely useful in helping to improve your capacity management program.

You can also track capacity data in incident records. This is especially true of performance incidents in which one or more users report that a specific application or IT service is running slowly. You can use your performance monitoring tools and a trend graph over the previous day or few hours to indicate exactly where performance started to degrade. Using this capacity and performance data can help pinpoint the time when things went wrong, which can help you look in system logs or at other monitoring tools to more quickly isolate the source of an incident. In this way pulling capacity and performance data into the incident management process can be a big help.

Benefits of Integration

There are two clear benefits to integrating capacity management with incident management—fewer incidents and faster resolution of the incidents that do occur. Because the central purpose of capacity management is to ensure that you have adequate capacity when and where it is needed, you automatically reduce capacity-related incidents simply by implementing an effective capacity management process. But until you integrate that process with incident management by tracking capacity incidents specifically, you won't have data to substantiate the claim that capacity-related incidents are on the decrease. After you've linked incident management with capacity management by tracking those incidents, you begin to gather solid evidence of the effectiveness of your capacity program.

When incidents do occur, whether they are capacity incidents or any other kind, having your capacity management program integrated with the incident management process helps you resolve those incidents more quickly. If the incident is capacity related, you can resolve it by acting on the recommendations you'll find in the capacity plan for the failing component or service. That plan contains concrete steps that you can take to alleviate the capacity shortfall, and those plans do not have to be imagined in the heat of the moment while service is disrupted. If the incident is not capacity related, you might still be able to resolve it more quickly because the capacity management team can help to find spare capacity that can be brought to bear to replace a failing component. In either event, having capacity management as an integral part of your incident management process enables you to more quickly resolve the incidents that occur, making incident management more effective.

Integrating with Service Continuity Management

Service continuity management is the ITIL term that covers the area that many organizations call "disaster recovery." Of course, there is much more to ITIL-aligned service continuity management than simply recovering from disasters, but dealing with significant events that adversely affect multiple IT components and services is a large part of service continuity management. The goal of service continuity is to ensure that regardless of the circumstances you can continue to provide critical IT service to your organization. In this section we explore how integration between service continuity management and capacity management can help you be more effective in that goal.

Process Linkage

For many organizations, the route to ensuring continued service availability involves some scheme to have alternate capacity available for those applications and services that are considered critical to the business. One form of additional capacity is a traditional disaster recovery contract with an organization like Sungard or IBM's Business Continuity and Resiliency Services. With one of these contracts your organization determines in advance how much infrastructure would be required to recover your critical services, and the service provider agrees to make that much capacity available to you both during a testing cycle and in the event that an actual recovery becomes necessary. Clearly, you need to have a good handle on the capacity in use by your critical services, or your contract can become outdated and you risk not having enough capacity available should you really need to recover those services. Thus, capacity management is a critical element of creating and maintaining a disaster recovery contract.

Another possibility is that your organization may choose to provide its own disaster recovery capability by provisioning extra capacity. A popular choice is to provision development and test environments for your important applications and services in such a way that you could reuse the same equipment as production servers should you need to. The general plan in this scenario is that you have one data center with your production environment and then you have a second data center that has your preproduction environment. Using storage replication technology or simply shipping tapes between sites, you keep production data ready, and if anything happens to the production facilities you can restore those tapes to prepare the secondary data center to continue your production services. Clearly, you could accommodate the same capability by building your own disaster recovery site with idle equipment rather than development and test environments, but this is often too expensive to be a realistic solution.

In any scenario in which you want to recover critical business applications and IT services in another location, capacity information is essential. You need to understand how much storage is required, how much network bandwidth is needed, and how much computing power it takes to host the applications and services you want to recover. Without linking your recovery plan into current capacity management data, you will only be guessing at how much you need. If you guess too high, you waste money on your disaster recovery contract or in provisioning your alternative data center. If you guess too low, you cannot recover all the applications and services that you deemed critical. You can clearly see why linking capacity management to your service continuity efforts is extremely important. The relationship between these two disciplines is shown in Figure 15.5.

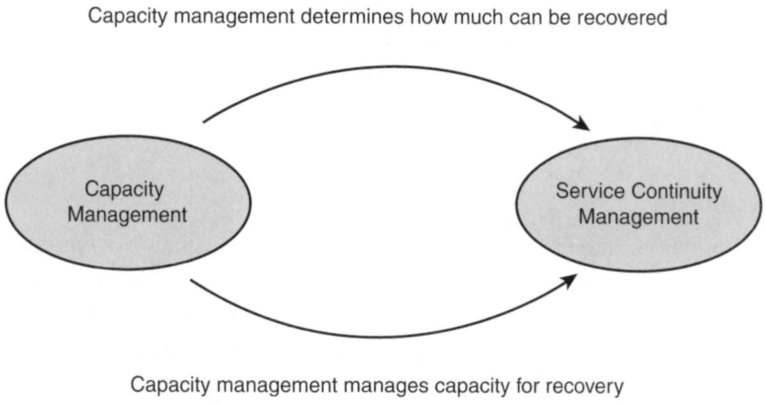
Capacity management determines how much can be recovered
Capacity Management
Service Continuity Management
Capacity management manages capacity for recovery

Figure 15.5 Service continuity management depends heavily on capacity management information.

Data Linkage

The key data element of service continuity management is a continuity plan for each significant IT service. This plan should be managed and updated much like a capacity plan. The service continuity plan should include data from capacity management to indicate the size of the environment to be recovered. Typically, this can be done by simply copying the latest information from the capacity utilization data into the updated service continuity plan. This update is typically manual and isn't necessarily handled by any automated tools.

Benefits of Integration

The benefits of integration between service continuity management and capacity management is very clear. As in other areas where capacity planning is critical, you can spend too much money in preparing for service continuity if you don't integrate your thinking with the information provided by the capacity management program. The other danger of creating continuity plans without adequate information from capacity management is that you can fail to provide enough capacity in the alternate data center as your business applications and IT services grow in your primary data center. Many organizations have allowed their business continuity or disaster recovery plans to get outdated because they failed to integrate effective capacity management with their continuity planning activities.

Integrating with Release and Deployment Management

Release and deployment management are concerned with adding or changing IT services in an organized and planned fashion. Each release consists of one or more IT components that are grouped together because they form a cohesive unit that makes architectural sense to be upgraded or installed as one piece. The process of release management involves determining which components will be released together, planning for the release, gathering requirements and coordinating the design and build of all components in the release, testing the components both individually and as an integrated release, and then deploying those components into the production environment. This section describes how this release management process can be integrated with capacity management.

Process Linkage

Many considerations go into planning a release. There are considerations of business needs and which functions of the release will meet those needs. Those considerations are called "functional requirements." In addition, the release manager must plan to meet the availability, reliability, and serviceability needs of the application along with understanding the performance and capacity that are needed by the release. Collectively, these are called the "nonfunctional requirements." As described in Chapter 14, "Capacity Management in a Project Context," the capacity management process plays an important role in helping to define the capacity and performance requirements, or at least in ensuring that those requirements are complete and testable. Thus, capacity management is linked to release management because it contributes to the release plan.

But capacity management is also linked to release testing. Before a new release can be deployed to production environments, it must be thoroughly tested to ensure that it meets all functional and nonfunctional requirements. Since some of those requirements involve capacity and performance, the capacity management process is integrated with release management to help perform or monitor those tests.

In both planning and testing capacity, management provides important information to the release management process, as depicted in Figure 15.6.

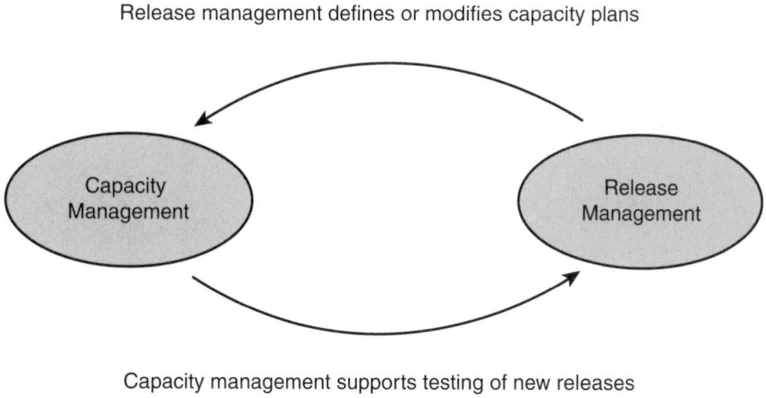
Release management defines or modifies capacity plans
Capacity Management
Release Management
Capacity management supports testing of new releases

Figure 15.6 Capacity should be taken into account in both planning and testing a release.

Benefits of Integration

Capacity management alone can help your IT organization go from chaotic to highly functional. When coupled with release management, capacity management can virtually eliminate the nasty surprises that often happen with new releases.

By establishing a capacity plan for each of your business applications, and then looking out for the plan during release planning, you can guarantee that your user does not see slowdowns or blockages when the new release goes live. Instead of chasing capacity problems after the system has gone into full production, you can shake them out during testing and find ways to eliminate them. Building this kind of foresight into your release plans makes your "go live" events much less eventful.

Chapter Summary

Hopefully, throughout this book you've learned how to deploy an outstanding capacity management program and mature that program by continuous improvement. The theme of this chapter is that you can bring even more benefit to your organization by implementing other processes within the ITIL Version 3 framework. In fact, the more processes you implement and the more tightly you integrate them, the more benefit your organization sees.

You learned about the integration between capacity management and six specific processes in the ITIL framework. There are many more processes, and each can and should integrate with capacity management. These integrations shouldn't be done simply because I say so or because your process engineers want to appear clever. Instead, they should be done because they provide significant business value to your organization and because they make your IT organization more effective at meeting the needs of the business. Over time, you'll find that each new process you implement and each additional step you take toward tighter integration pays huge benefits and typically funds the next process or integration. As your capacity management process matures, you'll find more ways to integrate it with the rest of your service management processes, and each one will bring greater value.

Index

H

I

J–K–L

M

N–O

T

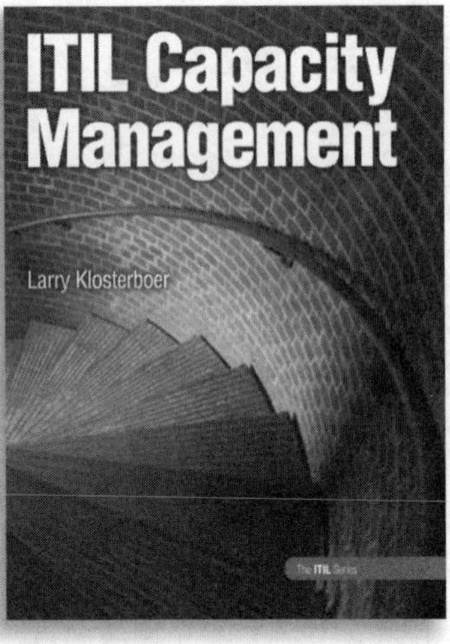
ITIL Capacity Management
Larry Klosterboer